Poetry for Life

A Practical Guide to Teaching Poetry in the Primary School

LINDA HALL

CASSELL

Cassell Educational Limited
Artillery House
Artillery Row
London SW1P 1RT
England

First published 1989

Phototypeset by Input Typesetting Ltd, London
This book has been printed and bound in Great Britain
by The Camelot Press Plc, Southampton

POETRY FOR LIFE

Literature

Contents

In the beginning of our childhood we are all 'versifiers' – it is only later that we begin to learn to speak in prose.

Kornei Chukovsky, From Two to Five, p. 64

Preface

This is a handbook for practising teachers and for student teachers. It is intended as a basic introduction and guide to the subject of poetry and poetry teaching in primary, middle, and lower secondary schools. It is for use by those on BEd and PGCE courses and also for those on in-service courses. Given the limitations of its length, it cannot be a definitive account of poetry teaching, but it tries to be as thorough as possible in its references and resources within the space allowed.

My aim has been to attempt to divest poetry of its fairy-godmother role in the primary/middle curriculum. By that I mean that if poetry appears at all in our schools, it is always in order to introduce or sponsor something else. We have all seen or even taught the lesson that 'uses' poetry to stimulate pupils' own creative writing or to illustrate a theme in an integrated scheme of work. This is what I mean by poetry as fairy godmother. What I wish to do in this book is to show *how* and *why* poetry should be read *for itself alone*. In other words, I shall suggest that it is not before time that poetry be seen as the Sleeping Beauty it really is and that it be restored to its rightful place, centre stage, so to speak.

One of the problems with a book of this kind is that the very mention of the word 'poetry' is enough to send shivers down many teachers' spines. This is because it is perceived by some as 'highbrow', 'difficult' and 'obscure', which is certainly forgivable if their last experience of poetry was to study something like *The Waste Land* for A Level. Among pupils, too, it seems that poetry generates more antipathy than maths, particularly among secondary boys. HMI reports, which are usually so moderate in their pronouncements, do not spare us the depressing facts, stating unequivocally that large numbers of pupils leave secondary school actively hostile to poetry, while most of the rest are simply indifferent to it. It seems that it is only a tiny minority who actually like it.

This book tries to show through a wide variety of examples just how misguided is the perception of poetry as 'highbrow', 'difficult' and 'obscure', certainly of the kind of poetry that one would read with children in the primary/middle years (5 to 13). I hope to make it plain how eminently accessible primary-level poetry actually is, even when, like *Beowulf*, it is over a thousand years old. Nothing in the primary/middle curriculum in fact offers more ready opportunity to excite pleasure and delight in its audience than poetry. No other subject could be easier, because it succeeds best when the teacher does least.

The book also suggests many ideas for successful poetry lessons which the specialist and the non-specialist alike will be able to employ, because the method is simple and straightforward. All that is essential is the willingness to begin. The poems and our pupils' enthusiasm will do the rest. As long as the poems are allowed to speak for themselves, teachers cannot go wrong.

Acknowledgements

The author and publisher wish to thank the following people who have kindly given permission for the reproduction of material that is their copyright. Every effort has been made to trace copyright holders. If we have inadvertently omitted to acknowledge anyone, we should be glad to hear from them so that their names may be included in future editions.

The literary trustees of Walter de la Mare and the Society of Authors as their representative for 'Five Eyes', 'The Fly', 'Snow', and 'Then' by Walter de la Mare. A. & C. Black (Publishers) Ltd for 'The Dustman' from *Speech Rhymes* by Clive Sansom; and for 'Ducky Daddles' from *A Book of Rhymes and Jingles* by W. Kingdom-Ward. Michael Joseph for 'A Dragonfly' and 'The Tide in the River' from *Silver Sand and Snow* by Eleanor Farjeon. Cadbury Ltd for 'The Ladybird' by Leoma Rushton, which appeared in *Cadbury's Third Book of Children's Poetry*. James Reeves, for 'Slowly' and 'Explorers', from *The Complete Poems for Children* by James Reeves, reprinted by permission of the James Reeves Estate. Wilma Horsbrugh and Methuen Children's Books for nine lines from 'The Train to Glasgow' and seven lines from 'Clinkerdump' by Wilma Horsbrugh. Ian Serraillier for eight lines from *Beowulf the Warrior*, by Ian Serraillier © 1954 Ian Serraillier. William Krasilovsky of Feinman & Krasilovsky, New York, NY, for four lines from 'The Shooting of Dan McGrew', by Robert Service from *Collected Verse of Robert Service*. Mrs Claudia Flanders for two stanzas from 'The Spider' by Michael Flanders and Donald Swann. Macmillan Ltd for 'Feather Game', 'Stitching Game', and 'Snow, Snow', by Mona Swann, from *Trippingly on the Tongue* by Mona Swann. Unwin Hyman for four lines from 'The Holiday Train', by Irene Thompson, from *Child Education*.

I would also like to thank the many children to whom I have taught poetry over the years and from whom I have learnt so much. I have an especial debt of gratitude to the pupils of the Holy Ghost School, Balham, for allowing me to quote so fully from their work for me. I am also grateful to the many students I taught on the BEd and PGCE courses during the ten years I was at Bulmershe College of Higher Education, with whom I discussed and debated the many pedagogical issues raised in the following pages. Nothing has helped me hone my arguments more than their dose of opposition.

I am most grateful to the Society of Authors for their generosity in making me an award from the Authors' Foundation to help me defray the cost of permission fees.

I must thank, too, the staff of my local library service in Battersea, at Northcote Road and at Lavender Hill, for their unfailing helpfulness in enabling me to track down the many books I sought. In particular I must mention Ferelith Hordern, Northcote's children's librarian, for her enthusiastic support.

Finally, I owe a very special debt of gratitude to my husband for the not inconsiderable task of typing the manuscript as well as being an uncomplaining sounding board for my ideas. He also gave unstintingly of his own time, sacrificing his own historical researches to entertain our 3-year-old son in parks and on commons all over south London as the book neared completion. It is to his continued support that the book owes its existence.

Linda Hall,
London,
October, 1988

Chapter 1

Why Teach Poetry?

THE STATUS OF POETRY IN THE CURRICULUM TODAY

It is clear from HMI surveys and from reports by other interested bodies that poetry has for some time been in a state of decline in our schools. Twenty years ago, *Half Our Future*, the report of the Central Advisory Council for Education, admitted that poetry was thought of as 'a minor amenity' even if, paradoxically, it was regarded at the same time as 'a major channel of experience' (Ministry of Education, 1963, p. 156).

In the 1970s, the Bullock Report recognized the value and importance of poetry but devoted only three pages to it out of six hundred. Within that brief space, it did, however, call attention to the fact that poetry appeared to be the least liked of all the forms of literature studied at secondary school and cited a survey conducted in 1972 of 1,000 O- and A-level candidates which found that only 170 said they would read any more poetry after leaving school. This evidence suggests that even when poetry is included in English schemes of work, it makes few converts. The responsibility for this failure was felt by the Bullock Committee to lie with the methods that schools employ when they embark on poetry teaching. I shall return to this important issue in Chapter 3.

More recently (1984), a Schools' Council publication from the 'Helping Individual Teachers Become More Effective' programme, jokingly entitled *Not Daffodils Again — Teaching Poetry 9–13*, also complained of a widespread neglect of poetry in our schools, tried like Bullock to provide reasons to account for that neglect and offered, through examples of schools' good practice, some helpful strategies for developing poetry appreciation in both primary and secondary schools.

In 1987, a DES booklet, *Teaching Poetry in the Secondary School — An HMI View*, cited (pp. 4–5) specialist one-day visits and reports of full inspections to bear witness that in many secondary schools

> there is very little poetry included regularly in the work in English . . . The evidence is that, in national terms, poetry is frequently neglected and poorly provided for; its treatment is inadequate and superficial. Many pupils spend much more time completing language exercises of little value than they do in reading, writing or talking about poetry. They are very much more likely to be given a course book for work in English than

they are to be given an anthology of poetry or the opportunity to read widely in the work of particular authors.

This is at the secondary level where one would expect poetry to have a discernible presence and even a high profile, if only for instrumental reasons. After all, poetry is, or used to be, a compulsory element of some O-level literature examinations. As a result, it wasn't included in English syllabuses solely in the two examinable years (four and five) but made an appearance lower down the secondary school, in the third, second, and sometimes even first years, in order to acclimatize pupils to its distinctive mode and the methods required to discuss it.

The new GCSE may well put a stop even to this limited appearance at the secondary level. As with the GCE it is possible to take two GCSEs in English, one being a purely literature paper. It is clear from correspondence in *The Times Educational Supplement* that schools are not obliged to enter their pupils for the English Literature GCSE, and that many teachers regard two GCSEs in English as too demanding and time-consuming for their pupils. If the old CSE is anything to go by, in which texts of fiction predominated, poetry will make a poor showing in the new, plain English GCSE. Of course, the enthusiast will see to it that poetry does maintain a presence in her schemes of work for the GCSE.* However, relying on the discretion and interest of the individual teacher is bound to be a hit-or-miss method of ensuring widespread provision.

POETRY'S CURRENT STATUS AT THE PRIMARY/MIDDLE SCHOOL LEVEL

At the primary/middle level, it appears there is similar cause for concern. Various HMI general-curriculum survey reports have also commented on the relative neglect of poetry in the primary/middle years. The Bullock Report (DES, 1975) found that the majority of primary pupils did not read any poetry voluntarily in school or out of it. Only three years later, the survey of *Primary Education in England* (DES, 1978) not surprisingly endorsed Bullock's findings. It noted that although poetry was read in nine out of ten classes to all three age groups (7, 9, and 11) as a stimulus for language work, it was read voluntarily by children in only about two-fifths of the 11-year-old classes. The First School Survey (DES, 1982b) report commented (p. 16) that 'although all the children listened frequently to stories, most had fewer opportunities to listen to poetry . . . In the majority of schools poetry was not treated as an important aspect of the curriculum and most children heard it irregularly'.

The *9–13 Middle Schools* survey (DES, 1983) reported (p. 52) that if poetry made an appearance in the classroom, it did so 'only as source material for comprehension exercises and for handwriting practice; for some children their only contact with poetry was through course books'. The survey found (p. 52) that the 'provision of poetry books was good in only 9 schools of the sample' (of 48 schools). It felt, too, that some teachers undervalued the benefits children derived from hearing good material read effectively. According to the *Education 8–12 in Combined and Middle*

---

*To avoid the cumbersome evenhandedness of 'his/her', 'he/she', etc, every time I refer to a pupil or a teacher, I have adopted the (albeit artificial) convention of assigning the female gender to all teachers and the male gender to all pupils/children and poets.

Schools survey (DES, 1985a), in only half of the schools visited was poetry teaching deemed satisfactory.

POETRY IS AN OPTIONAL EXTRA

It is true to say, therefore, that in many schools today poetry's status is as a mere optional extra, that is, if it appears at all. Its place is neatly summed up in the sort of comment that goes as follows: 'We'd include it if we could find time for it but only after the real work has been done'. *Teaching Poetry in the Secondary School: An HMI View* (DES, 1987, p. 5) recognizes that this is a prevailing point of view, reflected even in course-books for English which treat poetry as some lightweight afterthought, always left till last:

> The message children receive about poetry from its placing in most course books is clear enough: it comes a poor third behind the 'For written answers' section and 'Find out more about' demands. Teachers should not themselves reinforce that message by relegating poetry to the end of the day or the week or the term, when resistance is low and all the 'essential business' of English has been completed.

POETRY IS FOR EXAMINATIONS

It is clear, then, that by and large poetry is confined to the secondary curriculum where its inclusion is principally for the purpose of acclimatizing pupils to its particular mode of expression, in readiness for possible examination questions on it at 16 and later. But teaching for exam purposes, because of its emphasis on investigation and explanation, must to some degree ultimately distort the very nature of poetry for most pupils. This book is not concerned with that thorny problem. For those who have exam teaching in mind, it would surely be easier to do that job and to do it well if pupils already had a love of poetry and a propensity for reading widely in it developed in them during the earlier stages of their schooling. Breadth of reading in a variety of poets and across a range of poetic forms and styles can help to foster the more advanced business of analysis. Comparison makes it easier for pupils to detect common themes and to note differences in tone and mood. Through wide reading, in what the historians would call 'primary sources', pupils can learn to practise the art of criticism without resort to cribs, commentaries, or books of students' notes. For too long the study of poetry in the examinable years of secondary schooling has been excessively narrow, while understanding has been dependent not on a personal engagement with a poem but on authorities like teachers and critics.

REASONS FOR NEGLECT

Curricular Pressures

In some ways this state of neglect is understandable, given the myriad demands made on schools in recent years by the many new curricular initiatives and pressures. The supplanting of what so many regard as 'a minor amenity' must seem inevitable when room has to be found on an already full timetable or schedule for new learning areas like primary science, technology and computing. But if the new subject areas eat into the time allocated specifically for English work in the primary/middle years, it does not follow that it should be poetry reading rather than comprehension exercises that should be jettisoned. As I shall show later in this chapter and generally throughout the book, poetry reading develops many more skills than comprehension exercises involve. Moreover, it is a very convincing way of catching our pupils' interest in reading as a pleasurable activity. Above all, it fosters a desire to read *more*, which I am not aware of comprehension exercises ever doing.

Poetry Is Not Testable

Perhaps, too, teachers give poetry a wide berth because in a strictly materialistic and utilitarian era like our own it is harder than ever to justify something that is, and should be, as Raymond O'Malley (1969, p. 94) insists, 'a delight in itself', not a means to something else. It may well be, too, that poetry falls by the wayside partly because we cannot effectively assess and evaluate our pupils' responses to it. And it's death to poetry if we try. Janet Ede outlines the problem in her contribution to the Schools Council publication, *Not Daffodils Again — Teaching Poetry 9–13* (Calthrop and Ede, 1984, p. 91):

> In modern classrooms we are much beset by the neurosis of constantly evaluating the effectiveness of our teaching and at present teachers are in some ways more accountable than they have ever been — to heads, parents, education authorities, the DES and other groups in society. Sadly, being human, we seize on the concrete. What can we see has been accomplished? Yet that which we can easily measure is often relatively trivial in its power to explain the effects of teaching on the whole child. As human beings we are infinitely more complex than, for instance, the results of a maths test can reveal.

What do our pupils get out of a poetry lesson? In terms of hard facts and clear-cut skills, teachers obviously feel that this is a hard question to answer. The answers of the past, like 'awakening a love for the beautiful in thought and language' (*Handbook for Teachers*, HMSO, 1927, p. 81), like promoting 'personal and social development' (Raymond O'Malley, 1969, p. 94), like nourishing the imagination and the child's inner life, are too intangible for clear-cut assessment procedures.

As far as benchmark testing at the ages of 7 and 11 goes, I can't imagine any government, however crass, requiring pupil encounters with poetry to be subjected to such forms of evaluation. The most that could possibly be demanded would be that each 7- and 11-year-old should read a poem aloud expressively and with attention to its meaning. This is because at 7 and 11 pupils are far too young, thankfully, for the critical and analytical approach that marks the teaching of poetry at the secondary level.

Poetry Creates Unease

It is my feeling that another reason for poetry's neglect is unease. If poetry appears at all on the curriculum it so often seems to be a duty rather than a delight. Those primary/middle-school teachers who are not English specialists often perceive poetry as difficult and highbrow, more of a problem to be solved than a pleasure to be shared. This is hardly surprising if their experience of it has been to study, for A-level, difficult texts like T. S. Eliot's *The Waste Land* which need detailed exposition and explanation.

The essence of the teacher's problem is summed up by that nagging question of what should be *done* with poetry once we make room for it in our lessons. Herein lies the unease. Michael Benton highlights this concern in the very first article on poetry in 29 issues of the journal, *Children's Literature in Education*, incidentally indicating the enormity of the neglect that poetry suffers even among academics interested in children's literature. Inevitably what happens is that

> worry about rightness, both of a poem's meaning and of our teaching methods, predominates and the worry is conveyed to the children so that the classroom ambience of poetry becomes one of anxiety at a difficult problem with hidden rules rather than one of enjoyment of a well wrought object.
>
> (Benton, 1978, p. 111)

The statistics of the Assessment of Performance Unit's first report, *Language Performance in Schools: a secondary survey* (HMSO, 1982), suggest that pupils shared their teachers' sense of unease and that a high proportion regarded it with unconcealed hostility. Where 47 per cent of pupils indicated they read no poetry out of school, as many as 36 per cent professed to be utterly hostile to it. It is true that many will have spent their secondary years being exposed not only to the ambience of anxiety that Michael Benton describes but also to the kind of academic approach to poetry that is so alienating for the generality of pupils. By academic I mean a way of handling poetry in the classroom that is more suited to the cognitive areas of the curriculum, in which technical matters are given undue prominence and tend to replace the experience of the poem as a totality. Michael Benton (*ibid*. p. 111) calls it 'metaphor hunts and simile chases'. It is the whole analysing and dissecting business which is supposed to further appreciation but which usually stops it dead in its tracks. The choice of poetry and the method of handling it have been quite off-putting. *Teaching Poetry in the Secondary School: An HMI View* (DES, 1987, p. 5) makes it clear, however, that it is not yet a thing of the past: ' "In this year metaphor, simile, onomatopoeia, assonance, alliteration, synecdoche and oxymoron will be taught" — and in one school these were defined, copied out, learnt for tests, with not a single reference to a complete poem'.

Poetry may also evoke disquiet among many pupils because they sense that of all the subject areas incorporated into the curriculum it is the one that is the most personally exposing. It makes pupils vulnerable in a way that other subjects do not, or rarely, do. In more cognitive areas of the curriculum, getting the wrong answer can be shrugged off with the reassurance that one hadn't time to do the homework properly, or that one had missed the previous lesson. Not so poetry. Failure to respond to poetry shows one up as inadequate or deficient in sensibility, a failure of quite a different order. The Bullock Report put its finger on the problem:

> In a very real sense a pupil is himself being judged each time he responds in class to a piece of literature, particularly a poem. More is at stake than his knowledge of the text. Is the value judgement he forms the one the teacher finds acceptable? Is he betraying himself, he may well ask, as one who lacks discrimination? In no other area of classroom operations is there quite the same degree of vulnerability, with poetry the most exposing element of all.
>
> (DES, 1975, p. 132)

POETRY NEEDS THE PLEASURE PRINCIPLE

In the end, it is the way poetry is approached or 'taught' in the classroom that will determine whether or not our pupils feel secure in its presence. As we shall see in Chapter 3, the best way to ensure a sense of security is to foster an atmosphere in which the sharing of enjoyment and pleasure is paramount. At the primary/middle level this is certainly not hard to achieve, even though the general perception of serious poetry (and that really means poetry written for adults) is as something that requires much more effort from the reader than fiction. It *is* admittedly harder work, but only in that poetry is the most condensed form of language that we have, in which every word counts and, as a result, it has to be more closely attended to than prose. However, the kind of poetry we are likely to offer at the primary/middle-school level is not going to be of an excessively demanding nature.

In fact, I have written this book to de-mystify what is an eminently *easy* and happy subject area which should daunt no one, not even the non-specialist teacher. I write as an English graduate with a genuine love of poetry, yet I have come to the conclusion that for many years I was perhaps least fitted to teach it. The non-specialist is ideal for the job because she is not burdened with preconceptions that derive from studying poetry for a degree. It's the idea of *studying* poetry every time we introduce it to our pupils that we have to get away from. The rest of this book tries to demonstrate just how easy and feasible this proposition actually is.

POETRY DEVELOPS SKILLS

I hope it is quite clear from what I have said so far that the last thing I would want to adopt is an instrumentalist approach. I am aware, though, that it is imperative to allay the fears of many teachers who feel it is impossible, in today's climate, to justify to their headteachers, their parents, and even to themselves such a pleasurable subject as poetry on practical educational grounds. It is certainly true that many teachers feel insecure when confronted by the idea of a lesson, partly because the rest of the curriculum is based on the testable acquisition of 'skills and knowledge', neither of which seems to offer much purchase on poetry.

A CHECKLIST OF WHAT CHILDREN GAIN FROM POETRY

Despite the above reservations, poetry does exercise certain very basic skills and here lies our justification.

1. Poetry motivates *reading* by generating delight and even rapture.
2. *Listening*, too, is an essential skill which a poetry-reading lesson must inevitably foster.
3. Without its more advanced partner, *concentration*, nothing worth while in schooling is possible. Whether or not we include them in our objectives, listening, concentration and reading are automatically developed in a poetry lessson.
4. *Oral communication* is also often a prominent feature of a poetry lesson. This can mean quite simply pupils and teacher sharing their enjoyment of the poems

read in a lesson. At a more advanced level, it includes directed and controlled talk, related to a specific text or texts. *Bullock Revisited* (DES, 1982, p. 5) stresses the importance of these two major aspects of oracy — listening and talk:

> Most communication takes place in speech; and those who do not listen with attention and cannot speak with clarity, articulateness and confidence are at a disadvantage in almost every aspect of their personal, social and working lives . . . Improvement of education in the spoken word should be a a particular concern of schools.

Teaching poetry will certainly encourage children to read aloud with clarity and to talk with confidence, while it will also promote the ability to listen with attention. For this reason it is important that, when we conduct poetry lessons, we do urge the quiet and stillness of close attention from our classes. To put up with anything less, like whispering, making faces at one another, or even wandering about, is to deny our pupils the opportunity to develop these crucial skills and to disadvantage them in later life.

5. *Literal comprehension* or understanding is also exercised through a poetry lesson whether the teacher asks questions on the poem or not. Because we fail to test that understanding does not mean that it hasn't happened. For that reason, we should not need to ask lots of comprehension-type questions.

6. Even more *complex comprehension skills*, such as making inferences, are generated through poetry reading as children begin to grasp the implications of a poem as opposed to what is badly stated. Poetry is eminently suited to fostering this ability 'to read between the lines' because much of it works by hints, suggestion and allusion. In fact, poetry rarely uses language in a scientific way, that is, for its strictly denotative value. Its use of language is figurative, or symbolic, relying on the connotation of words. For example, the lily is not simply a flower of the genus *Lilium* but a symbol of purity (because of its whiteness), of beauty, and often of death.

Already we have six clear-cut skills to justify the presence of poetry in our English schemes of work. There are six more areas of benefit still to come, but it is clear even this far that poetry can be very useful (in a strictly instrumental way) without appearing to be so at all. In the form of nursery rhymes, for example, it gives the appearance of being light-hearted, even frivolous, and certainly enjoyable. Yet these rhymes frequently help small children to memorize numbers up to twenty — 'One, two, buckle my shoe' — or remember factual information — 'Thirty days hath September' — long before they start school.

7. As we shall see, later in this chapter, and in Chapter 5 on infants and the youngest juniors, poetry plays a crucial role in *promoting the language development* of all our pupils in a way that prose cannot. This is certainly a role that HMI wish to stress, as I shall make clear shortly.

8, 9, and 10. Because poetry has more than just what might be called technical features, and because it has in fact an emotional and imaginative and even spiritual dimension, it must inevitably work on that level as well. Poetry can play an important part in developing the *imagination*(8), in *nourishing the emotional life of our pupils* (9), and in *extending their experience and insight* (10). All who have ever pronounced on the subject agree that, at the profoundest level, poetry helps to make us more fully human, in part by inviting the recognition of common human experiences. Much depends, of course, on what choice of poems we make, but for Charles Causley (1966), children's poet and retired primary teacher, the English traditional ballads, for example, present us with the essentials of human experience: birth, youth, marriage, hate, love, infidelity and death. He himself has written many ballads in the traditional mould, telling powerful stories in a moving, memorable way.

11. Teachers are not in the business of simply turning children into automata of skills, although at the same time one would not wish to denigrate the importance of the acquisition of basic skills. What poetry does is to complete the education of what used to be called *the well-rounded person*. Even the much disliked DES discussion document, *English from 5 to 16* (DES, 1984), made room for aesthetic/imaginative experience in English, as well as a return to a knowledge of grammatical niceties. They are not mutually exclusive but complementary.

12. Finally, and most importantly perhaps, some of the most beautiful and profound literature in the language is in the form of poetry. Many of *the greatest minds and spirits of our culture* have committed themselves to this form and no other. Our pupils will ultimately have no access to this enormously enriching and inspiring source, if the habit of reading, and reading poetry, is not developed in them from an early age.

THE IMPORTANCE OF POETRY

As poetry is the least mechanical and least instrumental area of the primary-school curriculum, I was loath to suggest anything as mechanical as a checklist of skills. But that is what I have done in order to help those teachers who feel hard-pressed to justify the inclusion of poetry in their schemes of work. It could be argued, however, that there is little outlined here that could not apply equally to prose literature. What I want to do now, therefore, is to examine in greater detail some of the elements mentioned in the list to show why poetry is so important.

Despite the gloomy picture that HMI surveys and other reports paint of the current provision of poetry in schools, there is considerable room for hope. HMI itself is encouragingly positive in what it has to say about the value and importance of poetry. All the recent HMI documents referred to so far that deal at any length with poetry appear to hold it in very high esteem. It seems to me that this bodes well as far as poetry's presence in any national curriculum is concerned. It does not seem that poetry will be ignored, even though a great many more subjects than at present may well find their place on to a primary class's weekly timetable. Any English committee worth its salt should, like HMI, recognize the centrality of poetry to English. At the very least its members can make suggestions as to what sorts of verse should have been read by certain ages; for example, that by the age of 8 or 9 all primary pupils should have encountered some of the verse of Edward Lear and Lewis Carroll.

Poetry's Vital Role in Language Development

From the tenor of its recent documents, HMI is clearly in favour of a more prominent place for poetry in English work. In stressing why it is vitally important that children experience more poetry at school, reports tend to echo Matthew Arnold's definition of poetry as *a quality of language*. This is Bullock on poetry: 'language which consists of the best words in the best order, language used with the greatest inclusiveness and power' (DES, 1975, p. 135). This is Arnold himself — poetry is 'simply the most beautiful, impressive and widely effective mode of saying things' (*ibid.* p. 135).

More recently, the booklet, *Teaching Poetry in the Secondary School: An HMI View* (DES, 1987, p. 1), stresses the crucial role poetry plays in the language development of our pupils. Its introduction begins

> Poetry matters because it is a central example of the use human beings make of words to explore and understand . . . Poetry embodies delight in expression, stretched between thought, feeling and form. As we become aware of the 'true soundings' of poetry so we become aware of what we ourselves might do with language.

and concludes

> Poetry needs to be at the heart of work in English because of the quality of language at work on experience that it offers to us . . . It is the place of poetry in English teaching to help us to restore to pupils a sense of the exuberance and vitality in the acquisition of language and in the power and savour of words.
>
> (*Ibid.* p. 3)

A more central role for poetry in English teaching would ensure that its special linguistic and formal qualities exercised more influence on children, with the effect that their own language, in writing and in speech, would become more precise, more appropriate and more deliberated. The tendency to resort to clichés in our speech is all pervasive. These cannot quicken either the mind or the spirit, nor adequately communicate a person's thoughts or feelings. Cliché is dead language that is often resurrected, whereas the language of poetry is alive because it is accurate and precise. A simple example will illustrate this. The use of 'get' is widespread today in place of a variety of synonyms that would express our meaning more accurately. Yet the simple little nursery rhyme, 'Jack and Jill', is much more precise than we are in that it uses '*fetch* a pail of water' instead of today's ubiquitous 'get'. And what's more, Jill doesn't just 'fall over' or 'fall down', she 'came *tumbling* after'.

Because the language of poetry is highly compressed, it has to be more precise and accurate — more alive — if it is to leave any impression on us. Ted Hughes, the Poet Laureate, calls a poem (1967, p. 17) 'an assembly of living parts moved by a single spirit. The living parts are the words, the images, the rhythms. The spirit is the life which inhabits them when they all work together'. Every word, however simple and ordinary on its own, counts and contributes to the final effect. The language of poetry is alive, not just because individual words are precise, but also because its combinations of words are original and unexpected. The following verses are by the nineteenth-century American poet, Emily Dickinson. They are part of her description of a snake's sudden movement through the grass and her reaction to it. Not a word could be altered or moved without damage to her meaning and to the life in the words themselves.

The grass divides as with a comb,
A spotted shaft is seen;
And then it closes at your feet
And opens further on.

. . .

Several of Nature's people
I know, and they know me;
I feel for them a transport
Of cordiality;

But never met this fellow,
Attended or alone,
Without a tighter breathing
And zero at the bone.

What Brain Studies Reveal

Although *Teaching Poetry in the Secondary School: An HMI View* (DES, 1987) is concerned solely with poetry at the secondary level, what it has to say about language development is of even greater significance for the primary years, particularly in the light of what brain studies tell us about early childhood education. Between the ages of 5 and 10, children are especially impressionable. Parents and even experienced teachers marvel at the miracle of progress that children make during those few years in the infants, when the barriers to adult skills like literacy and numeracy are breached. Brain studies reveal that while the brain is at its *most* absorbent from birth to 4 years, and makes its most rapid gains in learning during that period, it is still very receptive and flexible throughout the whole primary-school phase. By the start of secondary schooling, however, the brain's growth is largely complete and it is already losing its marvellously 'adaptive plasticity' for speech, among other things (Brierley, 1987, p. 34).

Whatever side one takes in the great debate over nature versus nurture, it appears from the work done recently in brain studies that, while it is true to say that heredity largely determines individual mental capacities, there is still considerable room for environmental factors to exert an influence. 'Most of the cortex at birth is like a blank slate on which the lessons of experience will be written including those of language. The nature of the slate is, of course, determined by heredity' (Brierley, 1987, p. 17). A biologist and former staff inspector at the DES, John Brierley draws from this new area of inquiry its implications for educational practice. He suggests that much can be done in a child's early years to give heredity a helping hand —

the early and middle years of childhood are likely to be *foundational*, and not a mere layer of bricks, which will determine to varying degrees, depending upon later experience at home and school what kind of adult will emerge.

(Brierley, 1976, p. 71)

If this is so, then a stimulating early language environment is vital, both at school and at home. The promotion of language development (which begins, of course, in the pre-school period on the mother's knee) seems, also, to bear a crucial relationship to later success in school work. Teachers may feel that they can do little to rectify the linguistic deprivation some children may suffer in the pre-school years, but John

Brierley (1987, p. 29) makes it clear that the infant and junior phases can also make an enormous difference to final outcomes:

> The years from birth to puberty are a crucial time when the ability to learn is at *flood readiness*.

Evidence seems to show that even though intellectual capacity is stabilizing considerably towards the end of the primary school, many children can and do make great advances in mental growth in the later junior and early secondary years. School can help or hinder this progress. The more children are exposed to a rich linguistic resource like poetry, the better this will be for their own individual language acquisition and intellectual development. Ideally, this should begin with nursery rhymes in the pre-school period but it is certainly not too late to start in the infants and juniors. For this reason alone, it is of vital importance that primary as well as secondary pupils should read poetry on a regular basis.

The Role of Rhyme in Early Reading Success

Recent research into early reading difficulties among middle-class children and children of average and above-average intelligence seems also to offer evidence to support the need for a more thoroughgoing inclusion of poetry reading in the primary-school curriculum. This research consists of a major longitudinal study of more than 400 children. It was conducted by Peter Bryant and Lynette Bradley at the University of Oxford, and was published in *Children's Reading Problems* (Blackwell, 1985). In short, it indicates that experience of nursery rhymes in the pre-school period seems to play a crucial role in children's early reading success, by enabling them to recognize phonological patterns like alliteration and rhyme. Conversely, it found that weakness in phonological awareness at the age of 4–5 is a significant predictor of a child's later difficulties in learning to read or developing fluency. If this is so in the earliest stages of schooling, it must raise urgent questions as to the place of poetry reading in developing reading skills and fluency throughout the primary years. It seems to argue for a much more central and more frequent presence for poetry in primary/middle curricula.

At the first international conference of the British Dyslexia Association (see *The Times Educational Supplement* 7 April 1989), Dr Bradley reported that the Oxford research has made it 'possible to identify very early on children who are going to run into problems with reading and writing'. Dyslexia is usually regarded as difficult to diagnose until a child is at least 7 years old, but what is also important about the research is that it shows that appropriate teaching can bring about a marked improvement. By following the development of a group of children from before they embarked on learning to read, the team could predict from their low scores on rhyming ability which children were likely to encounter reading, writing and spelling problems. A selected group of such children were given a little extra help in making connections between letter patterns and sound patterns. This help amounted in total to only 7 hours over a period of two years, yet the children helped in this way made significant progress compared with the control group. It was clear, though, that 'phonic help on its own was not enough' (*Ibid*). In other words, continued reading of a wide range of rhyming poetry and verse is vital and, in the case of children with learning difficulties, must go hand in hand with appropriate teaching strategies.

Incidentally, the implications of this research appear to be borne out by test scores recorded in the primary survey (DES, 1978), which found (p. 96) that 'stories and poems were read to children in a higher proportion of the classes with above average NFER reading scores than in other classes'. The survey cannot, of course, tell us if it was a regular diet of poetry that produced better reading scores or if it was simply that abler readers were allowed contact with poetry. Taken with the research by Bryant and Bradley, however, these reading scores offer an interesting gloss on the issue.

Their research also raises questions about the kind of verse that we read to our pupils. The need to choose rhymed poetry is obviously vital, but it is true to say that when poetry makes an appearance in the primary classroom, more often than not it does so in the form of 'free verse', which is a non-rhyming form. This would not be such a problem if poetry reading were a more regular occurrence at the primary/middle level. At the present time, though, its appearance is so intermittent and fleeting that it cannot possibly help to promote the reading skills indicated in the research. The problem of 'free verse' is examined more closely in Chapters 2 and 9.

POETRY'S AESTHETIC VALUE

Poetry's importance does not stop at its capacity to enlarge young children's awareness of the rich potentialities of the English language and to promote their early reading success and later reading fluency, as vital as these functions are for language acquisition and development. This is because language and literacy do not exist in isolation. Language is inextricably bound up with experience, thought and feeling. Poetry may be different from prose in that it is language at its most concentrated and memorable, but like prose literature, it, too, is essentially engaged in trying to explore and understand human life and emotion, and to respond to the immensely varied world which human beings inhabit.

Poetry can also evoke an appreciation of beauty where it is least expected, and a recognition of the value of what is normally dismissed as insignificant in human and natural life. It helps us to see aspects of the world afresh and even to notice what we had hitherto missed. Such delicate disclosures represent a common thread in English poetry. Because poetry has this capacity to develop sensitivity, it has long been regarded as a major civilizing influence.

Feeling, which is poetry's life blood, rarely exists on its own in poetry. In the best poetry, feeling carries alive into the heart abstract ideas that are often concerned to impart universal truths. This is because poetry seeks for *meaning* in the experiences it recreates. This preoccupation with purpose and value in life gives poetry a moral and a spiritual dimension. In the present period of over-emphasis on the utilitarian and practical in our schools, poetry, above all other areas of the curriculum, can put its readers into contact with aspects of reality that touch us at the deepest levels of our being — as long, that is, as we do not spend all our time reading poetry of a comic nature. The First School Survey (DES, 1982b, p. 17) found that there was 'a tendency to rely overmuch on comic verse'. Such a tendency gives poetry's profound emotional and spiritual satisfactions little chance to find their way to our pupils' inmost selves.

It is true to say that poetry can play an important part in nourishing the imaginative life of our pupils and in stimulating their imaginations. In poems like John Clare's 'The Badger', we are encouraged to enter imaginatively into the last hours of a hunted animal. In Keats's 'Ode to Autumn' we are persuaded to 'see' with the poet's eyes (and other senses) that autumn is as beautiful in its own way as the more usually praised and anticipated season of spring. We respond emotionally and intellectually to the rich sensory experience that Keats recreates for us and inevitably assent to his point of view.

In *Poetry in the Making*, Ted Hughes (1967) locates the origins and growth of his own later interest in writing poetry in his early childhood passion for capturing animals. When he was about 15 he stopped these activities because he began to look at animals from their own point of view. His imagination at last became engaged on behalf of something outside himself. It is poetry's invaluable role in what might be described as 'the education of the feelings' that the contemporary poet, Vernon Scannell, stresses in *How to Enjoy Poetry* (1987, p. 26):

> Through the reading of authentic literature — and poetry is its highest form — we can experience modes of consciousness from which otherwise we would be totally debarred, and our sympathies, our tolerance, our understanding of life itself may be immeasurably enriched.

Poetry often tries to express what is largely inexpressible in the rational language of prose. This is possible because poetry is a different kind of utterance. It operates by using images and symbols, instead of the direct, discursive language of statement.

> A man of words and not of deeds,
> Is like a garden full of weeds.

This opening couplet of an anonymous English folk poem serves in a very simple way to show how poetry works. It employs a striking image of a garden choked by weeds to convey the poet's feelings about someone who fails to keep his promises. This image makes for greater emotional and imaginative force than if the idea behind the poet's words had been couched in discursive language, which would probably have been expressed in something like the following manner: 'Someone who breaks his promises is hateful'. The force of the image is also derived from its being compressed into two short lines that have a compulsive rhythm. The power resides in the picture that the image evokes, in the feelings that it expresses, and in the rhythm or sound transmitted through the verse form. All three elements work together as a unity to convey a powerful impression of anger and of hatred. These two lines alone seem to prove the truth of Benton and Fox's words in *Teaching Literature: Nine to Thirteen* (1987, p. 24) that 'To deprive children of poems is to deny them the society of clear, simple voices and a range of feeling for which there is no alternative'.

In the thousands of years that poetry has been in the making, it has been variously described. One of the best descriptions that I happen to like the most is that poetry is 'felt thought'. In other words, it gives expression to abstract meanings that we, the readers, are made to feel have been 'proved upon our pulses' (to use Keats's memorable phrase). As I have already suggested, this is achievable because poetry uses language in a way that is far removed from its use as normal statement. In poetry the sound that words make is as important as the images the words conjure up: 'The actual form of the words, their varied and subtle acoustic qualities, the very shape and sound of the poem have an importance inseparable from the poem itself' (Reeves, 1967, p. 37). The opening lines of Keats's 'Ode to Autumn', offer a good example of what James Reeves means:

> Season of mists and mellow fruitfulness,
>> Close bosom-friend of the maturing sun;
> Conspiring with him how to load and bless
>> With fruit the vines that round the thatch-eaves run;

These four lines are soft and languorous, thanks to the poet's use of long vowel sounds and the echoing sounds of the soft consonants 's', 'm' and 'f'. The languid richness of the auditory effect here and later in the poem is wholly calculated. It conveys the poet's meaning as much as the lush images of autumn's overflowing and almost everlasting bounty do. Sound, sense, rhythm and images all work together in a unity to appeal to our understanding through our senses as well as our intellects.

Reading a wide range of poetry on a regular basis can eventually foster in children a growing appreciation of each poem's formal, metrical and linguistic appropriateness. A good example of what I mean came in a lesson on Arthur Waley's translation of the Chinese poem about homecoming, which I read to a class of 11-year-old girls. It is a short, simple poem which begins:

> At fifteen I went with the army.
> At four score I came home.

It tells how stricken the old man is to find his house deserted and Nature reclaiming her own. It ends with the man making a meal from wild ingredients. But there is no one to share it with and this causes him immense sadness.

We were coming to the end of the period of 35 minutes on this poem, which had elicited some very sensitive and thoughtful responses when a girl unexpectedly asked why the poet had used such an unusual word in the last line:

> While tears fell and wetted my clothes.

Why hadn't the poet simply said 'wet', she wanted to know. This was something I had missed in my preparation of the poem at home, but the class had obviously become so deeply engaged in the process of thinking and feeling their way through the poem that it was not surprising that one at least should have become sensitively attuned to the change of usage. This change was obviously deliberate and the pupil was quite right to notice and question its use. Because we had been sharing our responses, a process in which my usual reaction to a question was to ask the class what they thought, they didn't wait for me to respond first. Indeed, before I had time to sort out my thoughts on the question, another pupil ventured to suggest that it conveyed how much crying the old man had done. His clothes were really wet, soaked, she insisted, which the word 'wet' could not convey half so well. It just didn't sound right, she thought. It was here that the girl's ability to articulate her insight faltered. This is where the teacher can come in, helping her pupils find the words they are at a loss for. I agreed that 'wet' with its light, quick sound would not have done the job as well. The rest of the class confirmed that 'wetted' was a heavier sound that was much more appropriate, given the old man's emotional state.

It is clear that in poetry every word, every sound of every word, is carefully chosen by the poet in order to make the experience live again in the reader's heart and mind. This brings appreciation back to the importance of language. Vernon Scannell (1987, p. 13) sums it up:

> Poetry then is first a matter of using language with the greatest possible precision, evocativeness and sonority in order to convey emotion through the presentation of things; it is sensuous, passionate and penetrating. For the poet, words are not simply ciphers whose sole function is to communicate abstract meanings; they are not static counters but living, changing things, each with its own colour, texture, weight and flavour.

AREAS OF LEARNING AND EXPERIENCE

Poetry seems to enjoy unqualified official support. It is clear from the many HMI surveys and reports of the last few years that there is a strong desire that poetry should appear regularly on the curriculum of all schools from 5 to 16. Perhaps one reason for this is because poetry can make such a comprehensive contribution to the 'areas of learning and experience' that HMI catalogues in its discussion document, *The Curriculum from 5 to 16: Curriculum Matters 2* (DES, 1985b). Of the nine areas which, it is suggested, should be embodied in the curriculum of all schools from 5 to 16 if pupils are to receive a rounded education, as many as five are involved in poetry. The nine 'areas of learning and experience' are as follows (the five involving poetry are in italics):

aesthetic/creative
human/social
linguistic/literary
mathematical
moral
physical
scientific
spiritual
technological

Schools are enjoined to make sure that 'however the work of the pupils is organised, each of the above areas of learning and experience is represented sufficiently for it to make its unique contribution' (*ibid.* p. 16) to pupils' development. We usually perceive these areas as mediated through particular subjects. For example, history reflects mainly the human and social area, though it will sometimes involve the moral area as well. As HMI recognizes, 'a single activity can contribute to several areas' simultaneously (*ibid.* p. 16). Nothing could be more true of poetry. As a result, it should not be difficult to justify a more prominent place for poetry in the curriculum generally, and in English in particular.

Enough has been said in this chapter on the first three areas to make further explanation superfluous. The suggestion of a spiritual dimension, however, does require comment. It does not, of course, apply to every poem that we are likely to read to our pupils, but poems don't have to be on specifically religious themes to possess this effect. It is helpful that HMI recognizes that much of the awareness of 'otherness' that we subsume under the meaning of the word 'spiritual' is likely to come from areas other than that of religious instruction. This is because the spiritual involves 'feelings and convictions about the significance of human life and the world as a whole which pupils may experience within themselves and meet at secondhand in their study of the works' of literature (*ibid*. p. 32).

> Sometimes it may be awe at the natural world or an aesthetic rather than an explicitly religious experience which induces this insight, or sense of disclosure. But whatever their source and significance, such moments of insight are perhaps an indication that there is a side of human nature and experience which can be only partially explained in rational or intellectual terms.
>
> (*Ibid*.)

Literature generally and poetry in particular is a crucial witness to the element of mystery in human experience across the centuries and throughout the world. Like religion, the greatest poetry 'reflects upon those aspects of human life and the natural world which raise questions of ultimate meaning and purpose' (*ibid*. p.33).

In that poetry presents pupils with the views and feelings of others and requires them to be taken into account as on a par with their own, it can play a role in the moral area of learning and experience. However, a word of warning. It would be wrong to see poetry as an 'area of learning' and indeed there is a real danger inherent in this formulation. For, in Elizabeth Cook's excellent phrase (1976, p. x), poetry (like myth, her own subject) is 'a *mode* of apprehension, not an area of apprehension'. It doesn't of itself assist in the development of knowledge, concepts and attitudes. Instead, it embodies a way of thinking and feeling. This is because poetry appeals essentially to the sensibilities of our pupils, and it speaks of that which has been half-sensed but can't perhaps ever be fully articulated.

There is evidence from the recent surveys that though poetry is not an area of learning, schools have a tendency to treat it as such. It is subjected to such mechanistic approaches as being used for comprehension exercises and quarried for the amount of learning it will yield of those technical features that make poetry so effective a means of communication. At a time when most subjects are being forced to find a practical element — as the influence of TVEI percolates down into ever younger age groups — poetry above all can offer a respite from the mechanistic and the utilitarian. It speaks to children not about the world of work but about the universal and more enduring features of their lives and the world about them: about people, animals, and the natural environment. And it does so in ways that enable them to recognize beauty and truth and significance — all those intangible and elusive aspects of life for which no amount of practical work can substitute.

POETRY'S ADVANTAGES OVER PROSE

It is not my wish to attempt to diminish the value of imaginative *prose* literature for children, for there are so many children's novels, like *Tom's Midnight Garden*, without which the world would be a poorer place. It is clear, though, that all the authorities quoted so far on the subject seem to agree that poetry can play a more important role in enriching the personal language store of our pupils than prose can. Benton and Fox (1987, p. 24) state it quite bluntly: 'A child's awareness of what language is and does will become deeper and more subtle through poetry than through any other sort of language use'. This is largely because of the *memorableness* of the emphatic rhymes and rhythms that poetry employs. Just as we easily remember such jingles as 'Thirty days hath September' because of its insistent rhythm and simple rhyme scheme, so rhythm, rhyme and metre enable us to retain the more hard-won language of real poetry. Although it is more than twenty years since I studied Shakespeare at A Level, I can still recall without prompting the stirring words of Cleopatra's vision (V. ii, lls. 82–90) of her now dead Antony, words that I was not made to learn. The rhythm as well as the incredible picture of a superhuman figure imprinted the words on my memory:

> His legs bestrid the ocean: his rear'd arm
> Crested the world: . . . For his bounty,
> There was no winter in't; an autumn 'twas
> That grew the more by reaping: his delights
> Were dolphin-like; they showed his back above
> The element they lived in.

Through rhythm and metre (this extract has no rhyme, being in 'blank verse'), unfamiliar words hook themselves into our memories much more readily than reading them in prose would.

Children have in any case a natural affinity for rhyme and rhythm as the work of the Opies and Kornei Chukovsky has shown. Children's street and playground jingles, like much of the pre-school child's language, are caught up in their love of the *music* and ritual of sound. Meaning is actually immaterial. In his great book, *From Two to Five* (1971), Chukovsky cites numerous cases of pre-school children chanting interminably nonsense rhymes they had just accidentally made up themselves on the spur of the moment. Which of us knew what 'eeny, meeny, miney, mo' meant when we chanted it all those years ago? Such ignorance does not bother young children if the sounds themselves and their rhythms are the perfect accompaniment to their games. It is through such *aural* pleasures that we first catch the interest of our pupils. What T. S. Eliot called 'the auditory imagination' (1933, p. 111) is very strong in the earliest stages of schooling as in the pre-school years. With younger and less able pupils (of all ages) poetry's principal appeal is to the ear.

There is also the fact (mentioned several times already in this chapter) that, as Leonard Clark (1966), children's poet, ex-teacher and retired HMI, points out, language is seen at its best and strongest in poetry. In other words, it is more powerful and deliberated in poetry than in prose thanks to the compactness of the form.

It is also true that poetry can do anything that fiction can do, only poetry does it better because it does it in a smaller compass and shorter space of time, which is a great advantage to bear in mind for those of our pupils without the stamina to plough through a whole novel, however short. Poems can paint pictures, describe people (like Ted Hughes's *Meet My Folks*), create moods, evoke our excitement or tingle our spines, move us to laughter or to tears. The repetition of refrains and choruses, as in ballads, invite more active group participation. Indeed, repetitive word patterns have a compelling quality. One usually finds pupils of about 8 joining in with Edward Lear's 'The Jumblies' or Lewis Carroll's 'The Lobster Quadrille', whether one asks them to or not.

But best of all, perhaps, poems can tell stories. As every primary teacher knows, the fascination of story is universal among young children. Poems that can tell stories have a very special appeal as Benton and Fox (1987, p. 29) suggest:

> The sense of narrative may be no more than the natural propensity to link pictures into sequences, the ordering of experiences to represent them to ourselves coherently. Yet the enthralling power of story in poetry can go beyond this. Stories in verse hold children in a double spell: the enchantment of the fiction and the form.

When the eternal fascination of story is compressed into a memorable verse form, conveyed in compelling rhythms and uttered in language that is both evocative and highly concentrated, then something magical is at work. It is not hard to find such powerful material. English poetry is particularly rich in narrative poems, especially in the traditional literature of ballad that comes down to us directly from the oral inheritance. Modern poets for children, like Charles Causley, are keeping up the tradition with an equal vigour and vividness.

SUMMARY

It seems that where poetry can truly come into its own without the distorting impact of exams — that is, in the primary/middle years — it is mostly conspicuous by its absence. It is for this reason that I have written this book; to help teachers take the plunge into poetry which is a huge reservoir of marvellous material at the moment largely untapped. The next chapter tries to indicate something of the incredible range of poetry just waiting to be discovered for the delight of our pupils.

The surveys and reports stress that hitherto poetry has mainly been the preserve of examination candidates. If it does appear on the primary/middle curriculum, it is rarely 'taught' in the particular ways you will find recommended in this book. But before we come to that, the one point this chapter tries to make clear is that it is essential for poetry reading to start much earlier than it is embarked upon at present. As the evidence examined in this chapter suggests, it needs to begin as early as possible, certainly with the youngest juniors and even, if possible, in the infants where most of what teachers will do will be to build on the nursery-rhyme tradition children will have learnt at home in the pre-school period. Nothing could be simpler or more enjoyable.

If we do not start poetry at the primary/middle level, we appear to reserve it for those pupils considered older and brighter and thereby create a 'hidden curriculum' which suggests that poetry is not accessible until pupils have reached advanced years or exalted standards. Because of the enormous range of poetry in English, this certainly need not be the case. A student on teaching practice impressed a class of 13-year-old, fairly unruly and reluctant boys when she entrusted them with some First World War poetry, material that some of them knew older siblings studied for A Level. Her faith in them also worked wonders for her classroom control. It is not so much *what* we present as *how* we present it and handle it in the classroom that distinguishes one age or ability level from another. Chapter 3 looks more closely at this issue.

English poetry is too rich and too varied to be limited to a few scholars. There is something in English poetry for everyone because there is so much of it. Of all European literatures, it is the genius of English literature to excel in poetry, and yet for most of our teaching it appears that we ignore this vast resource. We have 1,200 years of poetry to choose from and even the indisputably great poets, like Shakespeare, offer much that is actually accessible to children. They are not just for adults and sixth formers.

Perhaps I should say that by English poets I mean those writing their poetry in English, whether they themselves are English, Australian, American or African. I even include in this poetry translated into English, but only when it has been done so by a poet of talent, for one of the definitions of poetry is that it is something that cannot be translated without loss. However, there are scholars and poets of genuine ability, such as Arthur Waley, who specialized in translating ancient Chinese poetry into English, and Edward Fitzgerald, whose hauntingly romantic version of the Persian classic, *The Rubáiyát of Omar Khayyám*, bewitched me at the age of 14.

In the last analysis, teachers are entrusted with one of the most noble and awe-inspiring jobs there is. It may not seem so in the day-to-day exigencies of our work, but the ultimate and hidden goal of everything we do in school is surely to inculcate in our pupils a love of learning that we hope will last them for life. The enjoyment and pleasure that poetry *reading* generates is certainly a powerful motive force in that pursuit of reading for its own sake that is the first step on the long road to self-fulfilment.

Chapter 2

What to Read

Once we have been persuaded of the vital need to include poetry reading in our English or 'language' schemes of work *on a regular basis*, the next question is what, specifically, do we select from the vast pool of English poetry to read to primary/middle school children? And, equally important, where do we go for sources of information about what is available? It has already been mentioned that English literature offers as much as 1,200 years of material, most of them packed with poetry. From that tremendous store there is something for all our pupils, of whatever age or ability, however fluent or reluctant a reader. It is such a rich reserve that there is certainly enough to keep teachers going for as long and as often as they wish. Poetry reading can be organized in a variety of ways, as there are no hard-and-fast rules, but whatever arrangement one settles for — for example, reading one poem every day or having a session of 30–40 minutes every week — we are not likely to run out of material even though in both cases we shall probably have read nearly 200 poems by the end of one school year.

SOURCES OF INFORMATION

To help teachers to develop some idea of the range of material that is available, the following two guides are invaluable. They offer useful starting points and will also stand teachers in good stead as they get into their stride:

1. Kaye Webb — *I Like This Poem* (Puffin, Harmondsworth, 1977).
2. Jill Bennett and Aidan Chambers — *Poetry for Children — a Signal Bookguide* (Thimble Press, Stroud, 1984).

It is worth while taking a closer look at each one in turn in order to discover just what helpful pointers they provide for busy teachers. They will certainly help to put a stop to that time-consuming business of scanning library shelves when one is not quite sure what one is looking for.

I Like This Poem — Kaye Webb

Kaye Webb's collection offers an all too brief but illuminating guide to poems that were popular among children from 6 to 15 who were also members of the Puffin Club. The poems are arranged by age, starting with those chosen by the youngest children.

It is a unique collection of poems in that, to my knowledge, it is the only one chosen for children *by* children. As an added bonus for teachers, it includes the children's own personal and often telling comments on the poems they chose to recommend. These comments enable us to reach conclusions as to the particular features of poetry in general that makes it attractive to its child readers. Significantly, these conclusions bear out the emphasis in Chapter 1 of this book on the quality of language and the importance of strongly marked rhythm and rhyme.

The collection as a whole is a salutary reminder of the divergences in response between adult and child readers of the same poem, a factor we as teachers have to bear in mind. The collection certainly dismayed some adults, like Aidan Chambers, because of the largely traditional nature of the children's choices. But Kaye Webb does well to remind us that where anthologies chosen by adults are almost always imaginative and stimulating, they often tend also to be limited by the adults' sense of what is over-familiar to them. In other words, adults forget that to young children the old favourites have not become trite because they have not yet been discovered. They are still fresh and new. The collection certainly bears witness to how enthusiastically children can respond to their choices, however tarnished by time those choices might seem to adults.

Of the nearly 1,000 recommendations from which the representative selection of 115 poems was finally made, the most popular poets were R. L. Stevenson, Walter de la Mare, A. A. Milne, and Spike Milligan. However, Kaye Webb limits each of those to no more than three or four appearances. There is room, therefore, for the expected and the unexpected from Shakespeare, Keats and Browning as well as from modern poets writing specifically for children, like Roy Fuller, Michael Rosen and James Reeves.

It is clear that the younger children found 'funny words' and 'good rhythms' appealing and liked especially poems about animals (cats, dogs, frogs, mice) and the weather. The 9- and 10-year-olds were still susceptible to jokes, rhyme and 'nice rhythm', but were also interested in more exotic animals and in people, places and 'a spot of action' (p. 6). For the 11- and 12-year-olds, hidden meanings, feelings and beautiful phrases were most important. What was most noteworthy was how little 'literary critical' terminology intruded. The responses seemed to be genuinely personal and were expressed in truly individual, unscholastic terms. The following examples are typical of the range of comments in the collection:

1. Six-year-old Marie chose 'The Witches' Spells' from *Macbeth* because 'The rhyming words sound like the cooking gaining energy' (p. 9).
2. Ten-year-old Suzanne found Robert Frost's 'Stopping by Woods on a Snowy Evening' most appealing because the repetition of the last two lines 'gives the poem a sense of ghostliness and vastness' (p. 67).
3. Thirteen-year-old Ceinwen loved Alfred Noyes's 'The Highwayman' because 'the rhythm is like the beating of horses' hooves and gives the poem a lovely

atmosphere . . . the poem is written in a very sensitive way. I often cry after reading it. The tension is built up very well' (p. 150).

4. Finally, 14-year-old Teresa's favourite was Shakespeare's 'Fear no more the heat of the sun' because

> it is so exhilarating. It sweeps me along in the splendid, stormy words, then there is the quiet, peaceful lagoon of the last 2 lines of each verse. It is a wonderful poem, as hard, proud and fierce as a rock in a storm' (p. 154).

I make no apologies for spending so long and looking so closely at this slim, little volume. It is rarely that the recipients of all our efforts have an opportunity to show what the reading of poetry can mean to them. We would do well to pay heed to the factors of rhythm, rhyme and language that promote such intense pleasure among children as recorded here.

Poetry for Children — Jill Bennett and Aidan Chambers

As an annotated guide to 125 books of poetry at present in print, in hardback or paperback, most of them by modern poets writing for children, this little booklet presents the other side of the coin from *I Like This Poem*. It will certainly extend our ideas of what is available within the rich vein of poetry written specifically for children and help us when it comes to ordering class and school library copies.

Of its two compilers, Jill Bennett has extensive experience as a teacher of very young children while Aidan Chambers is a children's author and lecturer on children's books. The booklet is divided into two sections, the first part being devoted to books suitable for ages up to 8. This section includes illustrated collections of nursery rhymes and traditional verse, nonsense and humour, picture-book poetry, and younger anthologies. Despite its modern emphasis, the booklet still finds room for such old favourites as Robert Louis Stevenson and A. A. Milne (see entries 43 and 63, and also 49), who never seem to be out of print however dated some adults may find them. It is pleasing to note that the Victorian bestseller *A Visit from St Nicholas* by the American writer, Clement C. Moore, has been re-issued in an illustrated edition as *The Night before Christmas*. Once heard, its galloping anapaestic rhythm fixes the lines permanently in the memory bank:

> 'Twas the night before Christmas when all through the house
> Not a creature was stirring, not even a mouse.

The second part of the booklet lists poetry for 9–14-year-olds and includes single-poet collections as well as general anthologies and humorous/comic verse. It also tries to repair the recent neglect of the wealth of narrative verse in the language by devoting a subsection to ten books of narrative verse from a wide range of sources. Chambers also describes in detail two versions of Coleridge's *The Rime of the Ancient Mariner* — one illustrated by the Victorian, Gustave Doré, the other by the modern Mervyn Peake. He also has some very helpful comments about the value of reading *The Ancient Mariner* ('a hinge poem in the English language' (p. 31)) to 12-year-olds as a touchstone of their poetic experience:

> If twelve year olds can't manage to live with *The Mariner* in one reading then we know there's a lot of work to be done yet before they can be happily set loose on their own.

We may have to go back to Rosen and the popular ballads and to call in McGough again; they'll need to hear *Figgie Hobbin* (probably they haven't if they can't take *The Mariner*).

(pp. 31–2).

As with *I Like This Poem, Poetry for Children* is an invaluable source of interesting and attractive material that will long stand us in good stead. Teachers would do well to have their own personal copies: At about £1.50 and £1.95 respectively, at the time of writing, they represent a very reasonable investment.

1,200 YEARS TO CHOOSE FROM

The poetry we shall want to read in the classroom falls into two separate categories:

1. There is first the whole of English poetry and verse as written and conceived with adults in mind, from AD 700 to the present day. This means Anglo-Saxon and medieval poetry as well as Shakespeare, John Clare, Thomas Hardy and so on. In other words, the work of both major and minor poets, much of which, surprising as it may seem, is actually accessible to primary/middle pupils.
2. Secondly, there is poetry and verse written specifically for children, of which there is a very rich seam within English poetry as a whole. One thinks immediately of Lewis Carroll and Edward Lear. This grouping also includes verse that was once adult fare though it is now deemed suitable only for very young children. I mean, of course, nursery rhymes. Although it has a history of over 400 years, poetry for children as we understand the phenomenon today belongs to the last 120 years or so — that is, ever since Edward Lear and Lewis Carroll introduced the idea of fun and merriment into children's verse. Until then, levity was an alien element. For anyone wanting to pursue the historical dimension, *Written for Children* (Chaps. 1, 11, 15, and 24) by John Rowe Townsend (Penguin, Harmondsworth, 1983) and *The Oxford Book of Children's Verse*, chosen and edited by Iona and Peter Opie (OUP, 1973), are indispensable guides.

   It is this category which will lay the foundations in the early primary years for our pupils' later literary experience and development. As Aidan Chambers suggests above, pupils will not be able to manage poetic experiences like reading *The Ancient Mariner* — a poem written for adults — unless this second category has been adequately explored first.

These two categories are not, nor are they meant to be, mutually exclusive. Many poets like Robert Browning, Christina Rossetti, T. S. Eliot, Sylvia Plath and Ted Hughes have deliberately written for both adults and children. Others, such as Blake and de la Mare, seem to be able to speak to adults and children alike in the same poem. Some like John Clare, Thomas Hardy and S. T. Coleridge, have unintentionally written individual poems that are accessible to the junior/middle pupil, even if the bulk of their work is addressed to adults.

Fortunately, anthologies for children usually include something from both these areas even if they are weighted in favour of children's verse. It is important not to forget nor ignore the adult area altogether, as it is more likely to be there that we shall find the material that will strike a deeper chord in our pupils or evoke in them a sense of mystery and wonder. Poetry and verse written specifically for children tends, by and large, to be humorous. Even intensely serious poets for adults have written the most surprisingly lighthearted and jolly verses for children. Eliot's *Practical Cats*, Sylvia Plath's *The Bed Book* and Ted Hughes's *Meet My Folks* are three noteworthy examples.

As the first school survey (DES, 1982b) revealed, it is tempting for teachers to stick with humorous verse, especially as it is always an instant success. However, children do need to be exposed to a range of poetry so that it doesn't come to assume only one acceptable face — the lightweight and funny. They need to realize that enjoyment does not just mean laughter, but can also involve quieter, more heartfelt and thoughtful responses. Fortunately, some children's poets like Rossetti, de la Mare, Farjeon and, more recently, Charles Causley in *Figgie Hobbin* (Puffin, Harmondsworth, 1983) are a great help here. Their poetry can take children to deeper levels of thought and feeling than they are likely to meet in the ubiquitous nonsense verse. They also give expression to that childlike apprehension of the magical, especially within the ordinary features of everyday life. Christina Rossetti's 'The Flint' is a typical, if severely simple, example of what they have to offer:

> An emerald is as green as grass;
>   A ruby red as blood;
> A sapphire shines as blue as heaven;
>   A flint lies in the mud.
>
> A diamond is a brilliant stone,
>   To catch the world's desire;
> An opal holds a fiery spark;
>   But a flint holds fire.

De la Mare's 'Mrs Earth' is similar both in its richness of suggestion and in its smplicity of expression and form. Both are accessible to 6–7-year-olds as well as to older children in the juniors. I have known rather withdrawn and quiet 9-year-old girls take great pleasure in 'Mrs Earth' and volunteer to learn it by heart.

POETRY FOR INFANTS

Nursery Rhymes

Reading poetry has a natural place in the infant-school phase even if pupils have not yet mastered the actual reading process. This is not as contradictory as it sounds. The kind of poetry we choose to read to them will be what most of them know extensively already. Pupils will, therefore, have the chance to join in with the reading from memory. Few children come to school without having heard and learnt some nursery rhymes, finger plays and action rhymes, either at home or in the play-group or nursery school. But if learning such traditional rhymes at home is on the wane, as Jill Bennett suggests it is (1984, p. 2), then exposure to them in the infant school is even more vitally important:

> Undoubtedly the oral tradition was stronger years ago; in my experience many parents today know no more than a handful of nursery rhymes, so books of them are more important than ever.

Chukovsky, the pioneer researcher into pre-school children's language development, firmly believed that the prime role of the kindergarten or nursery phase was to promote the hearing, learning and reciting of nursery rhymes. This is because they put children in touch with a wide range of vocabulary and sentence structures at the early and most formative phase of their linguistic and intellectual development. I shall examine this issue more closely in Chapter 7.

Today these rhymes are to be found in a wide range of attractively illustrated editions which teachers ought to share regularly with their classes. Hearing them and looking at the often delicate or humorous illustrations is a great spur to motivating in the very young child the desire to conquer the first 'R'. Indeed, many children in the past actually learned to read by following the printed versions of nursery rhymes they already knew by heart. The Opies (1977, p. 9) suggest this is still perfectly feasible:

> Few books are more attractive to a small child who wants to learn to read than a nursery rhyme book. He already knows a number of rhymes or parts of them and he can gain confidence by pretending to read what he already knows. The illustrations guide him to the subject matter, and when he has to guess a word the rhyme and rhythm are sometimes a powerful assistance.

At this stage we should not scorn the over-familiar — in fact, the more familiar the better. After all, the greatest compliment a child can pay to a book is to ask that we 'read it again'. Repetition, therefore, is vitally important, connecting pleasure with print and promoting the recognition of phonic relationships, as we saw in Chapter 1.

The Signal Bookguide, *Poetry for Children*, is a great help here as it describes twenty-odd collections of nursery verse and traditional rhymes from which we can choose to stock our class library shelves. The best investment is to select collections with a good number of rhymes in them. Raymond Briggs's *Mother Goose Treasury* (Puffin, Harmondsworth, 1983) has more than 400 rhymes, all illustrated. My own favourite collection is *The Mother Goose Book* (Beaver, London, 1982), compiled and illustrated by Alice and Martin Provensen. This is probably because my 3-year-old has enjoyed it so much for so long. I find, too, that I never tire of its delicate watercolour illustrations and, with over 150 rhymes, it is excellent value for money. For the multi-cultural classroom there is Rosemary Stones and Andrew Mann's *Mother Goose Comes to Cable Street* (Puffin, Harmondsworth, 1980) in which the detailed illustrations reflect life in London's East End with its ethnically diverse working-class population. The most extensive collection — 800 rhymes — remains *The Oxford Nursery Rhyme Book* (OUP, 1967) compiled by Iona and Peter Opie.

I shall have more to say about nursery rhymes in Chapter 7. It is an important topic, for all the authorities who have ever written about poetry for children agree on this one fact — that nursery rhymes constitute the best start as far as language and imaginative experiences go. Like other traditional verse that also belongs to the oral tradition, they are possessed of a 'rhythmic vitality', as James Reeves so aptly termed it (1958, p. 7). They are also vigorous and direct. And they are never mawkish or sentimental, a trap that verse written with children in mind can easily fall into. This no doubt has to do with the fact that most of the 'Mother Goose' melodies were originally intended for adult consumption. Why they lost their adult appeal and found what now seems their rightful place in the nursery phase we may never know.

Many of them are the fragments of ancient songs, the cries of street vendors

('Muffin Man', 'Old Chairs to Mend'), riddles, prayers, the remnants of old rituals, and the political squibs of their day. It is probable that once the topicality of verses of a political nature had faded, they must have seemed both obscure and childish — especially given that at a time when monarchs exercised absolute power, the expression of adverse political comments had to be oblique in order that their propagators might avoid imprisonment or worse. 'Mary, Mary, Quite Contrary' is today a pretty, seemingly pastoral-type nursery rhyme with some amusingly odd, if not surreal, little touches. It seems originally to have been a squib about 'Bloody' Mary Tudor, who tried to put the clock back (hence her contrariness) by restoring Protestant England to Catholicism (hence 'silver bells' which are rung during the Mass and 'cockle shells', symbols of pilgrimage). 'I Had a Little Nut Tree' seems to be an English comment on the sixteenth-century super-power, Spain, and its envy of Portuguese dominance in the lucrative spice trade. A Spanish and a Portuguese boy in my class of 9-year-olds last year were thrilled to think this might be so. Not that I wish to suggest that one would attempt to 'explain' nursery rhymes to pupils in the infants. Explanation (which is not always possible anyway) is superfluous at this level where the music and ritual of sound is everything. Those wishing to pursue meanings further should consult the Opies' *Dictionary of Nursery Rhymes* (OUP, 1962).

It is not hard to deduce why such adult rhymes have survived among children. Joan Cass (1967, p. 42) recognizes the persistence of children in memorizing what they love the sound of. Nursery rhymes

> are steeped in the vigour, vitality and humanity of ordinary folk, built up on simple human experience. One can imagine children listening to them, absorbing, even if not understanding them, and demanding their constant repetition, so making them a part of their everyday lives, remembered for ever.

Nursery rhymes, then, are the foundation of our work at the nursery/infant level. After starting with the familiar ones, we should begin to extend our pupils' experience by reading ones that are unfamiliar, and by venturing out into the wider world of traditional verse from the oral inheritance. I have in mind folksongs like 'John Cook's Mare' and 'The Fox Went Out on a Chilly Night'. These have the benefit of simple refrains that invite participation by the class while the teacher reads the more taxing verses.

We are lucky that our store of nursery rhymes has been added to, in the last century and this, by two very accomplished poets. Christina Rossetti's collection of nursery verses is called *Sing Song*, some of which are included in *Doves and Pomegranates*, a mini-anthology of her poetry in the Bodley Head series (London, 1969) for young readers. Her poems are noted for their simplicity, musical qualities and gentleness. They invariably encourage us to think about creatures more lowly and vulnerable than we. Try 'Hurt No Living Thing', 'The Caterpillar', 'Horses', 'The Sound of the Wind', and 'The Ferryman'.

Eleanor Farjeon wrote an enormous amount of poetry, spanning the whole primary age range, including *Nursery Rhymes of London Town* (Duckworth, London, 1973). She also has a delightful series of character sketches of children by name — Peter who is a little nervous of being sucked with the water through the plughole in the bath, and Fred who is a collector of lots of little creatures — which can be found in *The Children's Bells* (OUP, 1976).

Action Songs and Speech Rhymes

Also essential for the infant classroom is *This Little Puffin* (Puffin, Harmondsworth, 1985) compiled by Elizabeth Matterson, which is a very extensive anthology of finger plays and nursery games. Even if 5-year-olds have outgrown 'This Little Piggy', they still delight in action songs like

> I'm a little teapot, short and stout;
> Here's my handle, here's my spout;
> When it's teatime hear me shout,
> Tip me up and pour me out.

At the nursery and infant level children love to accompany verses like this with appropriate actions as they recite. Action songs are enormous fun. They also promote body control and word/action co-ordination. But primarily they are a marvellous source of active participation, strong rhythm and rhyme, and thorough-going enjoyment. Fortunately for us, traditional verse especially displays this delight in words and action that infants love, so that the desire to join in can frequently be met, either by mime or simply by reciting memorized lines. A good number of particularly useful examples for this purpose is to be found in Chapter 3 of James Reeves's excellent handbook, *Teaching Poetry* (Heinemann, London, 1958). I particularly like his comments on the poem about King Arthur and the bag pudding, which he read to 7-year-olds.

A similarly useful form of participatory verse are speech rhymes. I shall have more to say about these in Chapter 4, when I discuss choral speaking. Suffice it to say here that they do not pretend to be poetry, because they have been written for a specific purpose of exercising certain speech situations. Speech rhymes are meant, with practice, to promote greater clarity of diction. They are not, therefore, primarily intended to be fun. Yet fun they are. Children derive great enjoyment from them, possibly because some come close to the tongue-twisters of traditional verse. And they are all very short. James Reeves recommends that a poetry lesson with 5–7-year-olds should always start with a speech rhyme or two. After all, they take no more than a few minutes to read or speak. Clive Sansom, who is also an accomplished children's poet, has produced several collections of these useful little rhymes: *Speech Rhymes* (A. & C. Black, London, 1974), *Counting Rhymes* (A & C. Black, London, 1974), and *Acting Rhymes* (A. & C. Black, London, 1975). Ruth Sansom's *Rhythm Rhymes* (A. & C. Black, London, 1964) is also helpful for this purpose.

Picture Poetry Books

Collections of nursery rhymes are almost always illustrated boldly in colour. As the Opies point out, this enables a child to associate a favourite rhyme with a particular picture and to find it and 're-read' it with ease. Such is not the case, however, with poetry for children beyond the nursery-rhyme stage. Some anthologies sport black-and-white woodcuts or line drawings but 'illustration' is intermittent and not a prominent feature. Twenty years ago, Joan Cass (1967, p. 49) was lamenting the lack of picture poetry books for young children:

> We all know how quickly a child learns a short tale by heart, and we often imagine a

child can read when, in actual fact, he is — with the help of the pictures — recalling the written words that go with them because he has heard them so often. How much easier poetry is to remember with its rhythm, beat and the sound and pattern of its word arrangement. Books of this kind, picture poetry books, would provide young children with a background of known verse that would last them all their lives.

Today, matters have improved a little, especially in the provision of original poetry books for pre-school children. It is not so true, unfortunately, of verse produced for older children, particularly those in the juniors. Anthologies continue to offer no more than line drawings or minimal decoration. However, the last decade has witnessed a mini-publishing boom in the appearance of picture poetry books that often consist of one long(ish) narrative poem which is accompanied by original and colourful illustrations in a variety of representational styles. The pictures complement the text and are in no way inferior to it. Some first-rate artists have been employed for the purpose.

What is more, pre-school picture poetry books like Janet and Allan Ahlberg's *Peepo* (Puffin, Harmondsworth, 1983) and *Each Peach, Pear, Plum* (Kestrel, London, 1978) last well into the infant phase of schooling. Indeed, it may well be that they are better appreciated at 5–7 than at 2–3. *Each Peach, Pear, Plum* is a most attractive book with its simple predictable 'I Spy' couplets requiring recognition in each picture of a largely hidden *but fresh* figure from the world of fairy story and nursery rhyme, who then becomes the main character in the following picture — ingenious but satisfying. The interplay of pictures and words is here closer than is usual in illustrated books, and the words lead the reader out to traditional verse and stories.

Peepo is equally rich and riveting. The illustrations reflect a working-class, Second World War setting which is in itself unusual in picture-books for children. The verses recount the baby's day, partially glimpsed at first through the peepholes cut in the pages, later fully revealed as we turn the pages, look at the pictures and read further verses. The peephole device encourages a closer look at the detail in the pictures than would otherwise be the case. We are gradually led into total involvement with a warm and caring family.

Pat Hutchins's *The Wind Blew* (Puffin, Harmondsworth, 1978) is another simple picture poetry book that is suitable for both pre-school and infant children. Not only do the pictures lay clues for us to anticipate what is to come next, but also its language is wonderfully precise. Hutchins employs such accurate and vivid verbs as 'snatched', 'tossed', 'plucked' and 'whirled'.

Peter Spier seems to have specialized in the illustration of traditional verse, like folksong, nursery rhymes, sea shanties and American work-song. His appeal spans an enormous age range because the material he illustrates is not limited to pre-school or infant phases. My child first came across *London Bridge Is Falling Down* at the age of two and loved the incredibly detailed drawings which are also full of dramatic incident. Infants and young juniors also find him an enjoyable and stimulating read. Look out for *Hurrah, We're Outward Bound* (World's Work, Tadworth, 1969), a collection of sea shanties and folksongs, *The Erie Canal* (World's Work, Tadworth, 1971), an American work-song, and *The Fox Went Out on a Chilly Night* (Puffin, Harmondsworth, 1981), a folksong. James Reeves (1958, pp. 38–40) suggests how to divide this last poem up between different speakers once the class has heard it several times and memorized it.

Because traditional verse was originally sung not spoken, Spier's books always include the musical score in their final pages. It is a good idea in the infants to try to bring words and music back together. If the teacher herself can't play the guitar or piano, then the music specialist might help. Failing that, a taped recording would help to re-integrate music and song. Burl Ives has recorded many traditional pieces for children. However, this won't be possible with all traditional verse as many tunes have been lost.

One of the most infectiously lively and amusing picture poetry books is Sylvia Plath's *The Bed Book* (Faber & Faber, London, 1976). It is illustrated in Quentin Blake's usual spidery line drawings, which seem to complement the bizarre text perfectly. Again, this is a book that spans a wide age range — even top juniors will enjoy reading it on their own for some light relief and zany ideas.

Recently, a small part of the long nineteenth-century American poem, *The Song of Hiawatha*, has been re-issued as *Hiawatha's Childhood* (Puffin, Harmondsworth, 1986) and illustrated with fabulously rich and jewelled pictures by Errol le Cain. Neither the incantatory rhythms of the text nor the gorgeous illustrations are to be missed. This is a poem whose lack of rhyme is more than made up for by its insistent rhythm. Interestingly, it was selected by one of the few boys who sent their favourites to the Puffin Club for inclusion in *I Like This Poem*.

We should not forget the Bible as a source of both dramatic story and poetic language (at least in the Authorized Version). It has certainly inspired some good modern narrative poems which although accessible in the infants because of their dramatic happenings, are more suited perhaps to junior-age pupils. Roger McGough's *Noah's Ark* (Dinosaur, London, 1986) includes much facetious word-play, while George Macbeth's *Daniel* (Lutterworth Press, Cambridge, 1986), illustrated in an impressively stylized fashion by Pauline Baynes, is dramatic but rather long.

The Giant Jam Sandwich (Cape, London, 1972), by John Vernon Lloyd, is a colourful and amusing poem, just the right length, tempo and subject-matter for 5–7-year-olds. The Dr Seuss books also mix humour and verse with their simple illustrations to make a very light but appealing combination. Try *The Cat in the Hat* (Collins, London, 1958) and *The Foot Book* (Collins, London, 1969), my own son's favourite at 2. Look out for books by Theo le Sieg, who is also Dr Seuss. For beginning and early reading practice, these books are easy, fun and helpful because the auditory effect of the rhymes prompts the recognition of only half-remembered words.

We must not forget A. A. Milne's *When We Were Very Young* and *Now We Are Six* (Methuen, London, 1924 and 1927 — and still in print), collections with something for all children between 2 and 8. No poem is without an illustration in an appropriate but simple line drawing by E. H. Shepard. These are the infant collections *par excellence*. Even their size has been given careful consideration. They are small, slim books and therefore easy to handle for a small child. So many books of poetry are dauntingly large and thick. There is more to their appeal, of course, than this not-unimportant point. However dated they may seem to many adults with their references to nanny and nurse (employees) and the nursery room, they still touch unerringly on what it is to be a child. Anyone who has ever had a child will recognize the essential truthfulness of 'The Engineer', 'Journey's End', and 'Come Out with Me' from *Now We Are Six*, and 'Rice Pudding', 'Halfway Down' and 'Sand between the Toes' from *When We Were Very Young*. Not only does Milne possess the child's-eye view (capturing the 2-year-old perfectly in 'Hoppity'), he is also an extremely accomplished versifier. Shepard's drawings are discreet and modest, yet they supply a perfectly modulated accompaniment to the verse. Anything bolder would detract from the quiet intimacy of these delicious poems.

Picture-books are an accepted and everyday feature of the infant phase because they make the process of learning to read more palatable and attractive. Picture poetry books, like the ones examined here, will not, therefore, seem out of place, as they can certainly serve the same function. But once the reading hurdle has been overcome, picture-books whether of stories or verse seem largely to disappear. Unalloyed print becomes the order of the day. This is a pity as even older children need a varied diet. A light snack from time to time can be just as healthy as a set meal.

Picture poetry books for junior children are much harder to find. This is not to say that quite a few of the books mentioned already will not be enjoyed by pupils up to the very end of the primary phase: they will. The humorous ones like *Noah's Ark* and *The Giant Jam Sandwich*, and the long ones, like *Daniel*, will give pleasure to all abilities at 11 and even 12. We shouldn't scorn a quick dip into a picture poetry book for older juniors. It may be just as valuable as a more prolonged engagement with an unillustrated poem. It will at the very least be keeping the association of print and pleasure to the forefront in the reader's mind.

Other picture poetry books to look out for are as follows:

Verna Aardema — *Bringing the Rain to Kapiti Plain* (Macmillan, London, 1981), an African 'House That Jack Built' repeater rhyme.
Quentin Blake — *Mister Magnolia* (Cape, London, 1980).
Lewis Carroll — *Jabberwocky and Other Poems* (Faber & Faber, London, 1968), with pictures by Gerald Rose.
Lewis Carroll — *The Walrus and the Carpenter* (Warne, London, 1974), illustrated by Tony Catteneo.
T. S. Eliot — *Growltiger's Last Stand* (and other poems) (Faber & Faber, London, 1986), from *Old Possum's Book of Practical Cats*, with pictures by Errol le Cain.
Edward Lear — *The Owl and the Pussy Cat* (Piccolo, London, 1982), illustrated by Gwen Fulton.
Alfred Noyes — *The Highwayman* (OUP, 1981) illustrated by Charles Keeping.
Michael Rosen and Quentin Blake — *You Can't Catch Me* (Deutsch, London, 1981).
Dr Seuss — *Green Eggs and Ham* (Collins, London, 1962).
R. L. Stevenson — *A Child's Garden of Verses* (Gollancz, London, 1985) illustrated by Michael Foreman.

Poems about School and its Work

At the earliest stage while children are still getting used to school and all its ways, why not employ verse to make the process fun? Both Eleanor Farjeon and James Reeves have written a large number of little poems about the world of school and its work. In *The Children's Bells* (OUP, 1976) Eleanor Farjeon has a section, 'The School Child's Alphabet', containing 26 poems that are both amusing and appropriate. 'Books', which expresses the magic and friendship that reading can give, should be a must. Also good fun are 'India Rubber', 'Knowledge', 'Rules' and 'Yawning'. 'Jabbering' and 'Questions' are my favourites and rival Allan Ahlberg's best in *Please Mrs Butler* (Kestrel, London, 1983).

James Reeves's collection, *Ragged Robin* (see his *Complete Poems for Children*, Heinemann, London, 1973), contains a poem on each of the 26 letters of the alphabet. 'J is for Jargon' is a really lively and clever piece enumerating all the nouns beginning with 'J' in the dictionary — or so it seems. It is for older pupils because it is rather overpacked with difficult words like 'jacinth' and 'jamboree'. However, Eleanor Farjeon has another section in *The Children's Bells*, entitled 'An Alphabet of Magic', which includes a much more accessible piece for infants on the letter 'J' — 'J is for Jinn' (or 'Genii'). Read it after or before telling the story of Aladdin and his magic lamp.

SOME COMMON SUBJECTS

Poetry can be 'about' almost anything, as I hope is already apparent from the examples quoted so far. There are no restrictions on its subject-matter. In fact, the poems referred to in the course of this book range in subject from dustmen to drowning, trains to treachery, ghosts to grief. There are poems for nearly every occasion if only we know where to find them. What we need to do in our own time is to read as widely as possible within the two categories mentioned earlier. Only then can we build up an extensive repertoire of the poems and verse we have enjoyed reading. That is where we start — with ourselves. And it could not be more enjoyable.

The more we read the more we are likely to notice that poets return again and again to certain common subjects. Like small children, they never seem to lose interest in the physical world around us and in all its living and growing things. Nature in all its diversity, sunny or threatening, immense or minute, is a recurring topic. Within this enormously wide area some subjects, like the eternal fascination of the animal kingdom — fish, flesh and fowl — span the whole infant to sixth-form age range. The following few examples reveal the amazing variety and richness within what appears to be a well-worked field.

De la Mare's 'Five Eyes' (see the next chapter for the text) about three lively, rat-hunting mill cats is suitable for infants and younger juniors. Its matching of its own rhythms with the cats' stealthy or sudden movements is a marvellous introduction to the art of poetry. The old folksong, 'The Fox Went Out on a Chilly Night', makes for a dramatic experience in which the class can join in with the refrain. 'A Frog He Would A-Wooing Go', a creature with a different mission, invites similar partici-pation. Also for infants is 'The Grey Goose Is Dead', which is easy to memorize and join in because of its extensive use of repetition. It is sometimes called 'Go, Tell Aunt Rhodi'.

For older pupils there is Laurie Lee's strutting but doomed 'Cock Pheasant' (the embodiment of heedless vanity) which I have taught to top-middle pupils as well as for O Level. Ted Hughes's monstrous 'Pike' is calculated to chill the spine of maturer readers with its brooding malevolence; while his 'Thought Fox' for 11-year-olds and over is a vivid evocation of creating a poem and describing a living creature, one that ironically Hughes never succeeded in keeping alive during the animal-catching days of his boyhood. William Blake's 'Tiger' is one of those rare poems that can be read, enjoyed and pondered by all pupils from top juniors to sixth formers. Older pupils will see that it questions the nature of God, while younger ones will be impressed by the vivid *picture* of a tiger that it evokes:

> Tiger, tiger, burning bright
> In the forests of the night.

We must never forget that poems appeal on different levels at different ages. But only a few are linguistically accessible to both sixth formers and primary-school pupils.

Incidentally, another poem that spans the full age range is 'The Wraggle Taggle Gipsies', whose ballad form one can examine in detail with sixth formers as well as discuss the balanced opposition of material versus spiritual satisfactions that the poem rehearses. For 9–11-year-olds it is an interesting *story* presented in a lively and insistent rhythm about an unhappy lady. One may or may not attempt to elicit why the lady was so unhappy when the gipsies arrived at her castle gate. It depends on how much discussion you aim to promote on each poem. There is usually one child in a class of thirty or so who knows about the medieval practice of arranged marriages and will help you open up that aspect of the poem if you wish to do so. But be prepared! In my experience, 9-year-old boys decidedly bubble with indignation on behalf of the male in such an arrangement!

To return to animal poems, James Reeves has written an enormous amount of verse for junior-age pupils. Among his many books are several devoted to animals, especially to imaginary creatures like *Prefabulous Animiles*, which juniors thoroughly enjoy. E. V. Rieu's 'The Shark and the Flying Fish' which I remember reading for speech practice in the first year at secondary school, is a humorous variant on the spider and the fly and another homily on vanity. T. S. Eliot's *Old Possum's Book of Practical Cats*, recently made more famous by the musical *Cats*, offers much enjoyment, too, although linguistically and syntactically it is more demanding than much junior-age material. Follow up with the verbal playfulness of Michael Flanders's 'The Gnu' ('the gnicest work of gnature in the zoo') either for pupils who know how to spell 'nice' and 'nature' and 'gnash' and so can recognize the jokiness, or just after teaching the spelling convention of the silent 'g'.

Lear's 'The Owl and the Pussy Cat' and Carroll's 'The Lobster Quadrille' are rhythmically compelling for 7–8-year-olds who will join in the refrains whether requested to do so or not. Eleanor Farjeon's 'Cats Sleep Anywhere' and 'Cat, Scat' are fast moving and good fun for infants and younger juniors. 'The Spider in the Bath', also by Michael Flanders, will evoke many a spinal shiver and much reminiscence (talk) for 8, 9 and 10-year-olds. John Clare's 'The Pettichap's Nest' is for older or abler readers for it demands a degree of concentration because of its length and the presence of some unfamiliar and even archaic words. However, it will certainly stretch and move good 11-year-olds (top juniors in the summer term just before they graduate to secondary school, perhaps) or upper-middle-school pupils, and provoke a sensitive response to the tiniest and most vulnerable creatures in nature. It has to be read with all the surprise and wonder than one can muster, because it seems that Clare, the countryman, didn't himself know where such a small and shy bird built its nest till the incident described in the poem. And its nest is in such a dangerous place that it is amazing the little thing survives unharmed. Read it especially for the sheer beauty and delicacy of the description Clare gives of the interior of the bird's nest:

> 'Tis lined with feathers warm as silken stole,
> Softer than seats of down for painless ease,
> And full of eggs scarce bigger even than peas!
> Here's one most delicate, with spots as small
> As dust and of a faint and pinky red.

Chesterton's 'The Donkey' is for slightly older pupils, being full of grotesque analogies though written in a simple metrical form and moving in its suggestion that an ugly outcast creature can also have a moment of glory. On the other hand, the Rev. Barham's 'The Jackdaw of Rheims' offers an amusing story for junior children who have a reasonable degree of concentration. The range of poems on this subject alone is enormous, partly because it has been a favourite one with poets. Although I have referred to twenty examples here, I am aware of having barely opened up this huge field.

As the Bullock Report suggests, poetry is not something children are likely to discover for themselves unless perhaps their parents read Kingsley Amis's column in the *Daily Mirror*. One must applaud his attempt to revive a general interest in a wide range of good verse and poetry. To judge from a brief but moving extract from the BBC TV 'Bookmark' programme, he has succeeded admirably. Two working-class men in their allotment shed talked feelingly about their love of poetry and one of them showed us the several albums into which his collection of Amis's weekly choice had swelled.

It is up to us as teachers to take the initiative and introduce our pupils to poetry and good verse. I feel sure that we shall succeed as well as Amis has done. As the Bullock Report reminds us (DES, 1975, p. 126),

> Various studies have revealed that teacher influence on a child's choice of book is considerable . . . Another important conclusion is that for the child who is not an habitual reader the simple fact of which book is where will often determine what he reads. These two factors — teacher influence and book provision — hold the key to an improvement in reading standards in the junior/secondary years.

In case we have forgotten, this should remind us that we can exercise a tremendous influence on children, especially at the primary level. So let us open up this wonderful new territory for our pupils and we will certainly find them wanting to explore further for themselves. After my very first lesson with 9-year-olds, five children went off to borrow books of humorous verse from the school library. After all, it is much easier to read a poem than a novel, even a short and undemanding piece of fiction. Poems are so much shorter and suit so well those children who have not much reading stamina or still find the business of reading arduous. Anything that comes in short bursts (like jokes and poems) is especially useful for the weaker reader. Even a long narrative poem like *The Pied Piper of Hamelin* is easier to read than a short story because the rhythm and rhyme help to sustain interest and propel the story along more rapidly and memorably, even if inversion and archaic expressions offer the odd stumbling block. Children would just skip these and read on if they were reading on their own. However, these should be no problem when the teacher is reading to the class, as practice beforehand can iron out such creases.

THE ORAL TRADITION

It is natural to feel constrained in our choice of suitable material for pupils within an age range as wide as 5–13 by the fact that such children are unsophisticated in their tastes, and because they are at the beginning of their personal, as well as their literary, development. This constraint does not actually prevent us from going back into earlier reaches of that 1,200 year time-span when we read nursery rhymes to our pre-school and infant-school children. Many of them have their origins in the Middle Ages. It should not, therefore, deter us from reading other early, traditional poetry to our older pupils. Surprising as it may seem, the further back we go in time, the more accessible the poetry becomes for junior/middle children to savour and enjoy. This is because in the early stages of our (and every other) civilization, poetry did not go in for any great intellectual or linguistic complexity. The poet was addressing an uneducated audience among whom illiteracy was the rule, not the exception. Poetry would be composed and delivered orally (and probably sung) to a group, not read by a solitary individual as today. Indeed, it would not be written down till many centuries later.

The oral nature of early poetry affects its composition and rules out the kind of psychological detail that we have come to expect from our modern experience of novel reading. The close analysis of the well-springs of motive, the exploration of the recesses of the human mind and soul, are not what interests the Anglo-Saxon and medieval poet — vigorous action, concrete details, the highlights of a good story are. This is true even of much later oral compositions, such as nineteenth-century work-songs like 'The American Railway'. As a result, such poetry is eminently accessible to primary-age pupils. Elizabeth Cook (1976, p. 7) notes that pupils are equally bewitched by a good yarn as long as the characters are simply defined:

> At about nine or ten they are beginning to be interested in character, but in a very straightforward and moral way; they see people as marked by one particular attribute, cleverness, or kindness, or strictness, or being a good shot, and they mind whether things are right or wrong. They are especially sensitive to the heroic virtue of justice and they are beginning to notice why people are tempted to be unjust.

The poetry of the oral tradition, whether it is Homer, *Beowulf* or the medieval ballads, offers children a mirror image of this stage in their interests. The two — the children and the literature — could not be more perfectly matched.

Our main consideration, then, becomes the length of a poem and the time it is likely to take to read to, say, 9–10-year-olds. A not too hasty reading of it at home beforehand will give a rough idea of how long it takes. Then whether we divide the reading into two or more sessions will depend upon our knowledge of our pupils' powers of concentrated listening. This is where versions for children are a great help because they engage in some judicious cutting to make these stories even more readily accessible to a young audience.

Fortunately for us today, the poetry of the oral tradition, which was originally composed and transmitted by word of mouth and survived for centuries in that way alone, has now been committed to print. For many hundreds of years, it was the only 'literature' that the ordinary people, our unlettered ancestors, had access to. Indeed, they ensured its survival. Other kinds of poetry may have been aristocratic or bourgeois in origin and inspiration, but the oral tradition lies at the root of the common people's heritage. Sadly, apart from nursery rhymes which still seem to maintain a presence in the pre-school and infant phases, the oral tradition is largely neglected in our schools today. Raymond O'Malley, like Charles Causley more recently, has stressed the importance of reading poetry from the oral tradition at every level of education:

> The value of folk poetry to the teacher is that it cuts across or spans all the usual classifications. It stretches from nursery rhymes to 'The Unquiet Grave', from infant school to the university, and *at every stage it is vital, passionate and impersonal*.
>
> (O'Malley, 1969, p. 87)

In addition to nursery rhymes, the oral tradition includes Anglo-Saxon poetry, the ballads and folksongs that had their origin in the Middle Ages, sea shanties and work-songs. I now propose to look in more detail at a few of the more outstandingly accessible poems within two of these different strands.

Anglo-Saxon and Medieval Poetry

I have already suggested that if we read about 200 poems every year through the primary years, we will still not run out of material, because we are dealing with such a rich resource. However, it will mean reading some Anglo-Saxon and medieval poetry in modern translation. Some teachers can be purists about this, but when translations are as vigorous as Kevin Crossley-Holland's *Beowulf* (*c*. 700) or Ian Serraillier's *Beowulf the Warrior*, as masterly as Nevill Coghill's version of Chaucer's *The Canterbury Tales* (*c*. 1390) and as lively as Serraillier's *The Challenge of the Green Knight* (*c*. 1375) we need not be purists. These three long, narrative poems (in the case of Chaucer's masterpiece a collection of narrative poems) were not, of course, composed originally for children. It is true to say, though, that their vivid descriptions, strange occurrences, and their themes of loyalty and courage put to the test are just what appeal to the primary-age child.

While the heroic story of the legendary Beowulf defending his community against monsters appeals in its verse translation to 9–10-year-olds, other more elegiac Anglo-Saxon poems can be enjoyed by top-middle-school pupils. The emotional realities of 'The Wanderer' (*c*. 950) and 'The Seafarer' (*c*. 950) certainly strike a chord with teenagers. The sense of desolation and loneliness they record, faced with the loss of the world they knew and within which they had their own secure place, seems to mirror with uncanny accuracy the effect of those unsettling changes from childhood to puberty. As alien as these two poems may seem, I have never known them fail to fascinate 13–14-year-olds.

Although Anglo-Saxon and medieval poems do not immediately strike teachers as eminently suitable reading matter for modern children, to ignore such poems is to neglect a marvellous source of story in verse, that potent combination which as we saw in Chapter 1, holds children in a very special 'double spell' (Benton and Fox, 1987, p. 29). Elizabeth Cook (1976, p. 93) confirms that 'nine year olds are usually clutching their desks' during the nightmare sequence of Beowulf's descent to the underwater lair of Grendel's mother when Serraillier's verse re-telling of *Beowulf* is read aloud.

We should not allow the venerable age of such poems to deter us from reading them. Highly respected children's writers like Serrailler and Crossley-Holland have recognized the thematic and emotional accessibility of these ancient poems for the young and seen fit to render them into modern English while trying to retain something of their unique linguistic and formal qualities. They have done teachers a great service in making such stirring poems available for, paradoxically, given that these are translations, they offer a very memorable experience of language. Chukovsky tells us how the heroic language of legendary stories in prose or verse considerably influenced his own 7-year-old son's expressiveness.

Age is, in any case, of little consideration. Children and adults still derive immense satisfaction from the story of the Fall of Troy, which is over 3,000 years old. What is vitally important is that children should occasionally experience a wider range of poetic language, and not simply be exposed continuously to the modern idiom. The heavily alliterated Anglo-Saxon style will be quite new and arresting:

> the lonely land
> Where dwell the dark spirits, by paths of peril,
> By cloud-haunted hills where wolves go hunting,
>
> . . .
>
> The dark wave swallowed him, downward he sank.
> Many a savage monster fastened upon him
> With cruel tusk and talon ripped and slashed
> His mailcoat while Grendel's mother, tyrant queen
> Of that dismal realm, laughed in her lurking place
> Deep at the bottom of the lake.
>
> (Ian Serraillier, *Beowulf the Warrior*, OUP, 1954)

Repetition (of letters here where alliteration is concerned) is always most satisfying to children. It appeals to their sense of ritual. When this is combined with a very dramatic story of a man matched against monsters, then its power is enormous. And it influences children's own language. You will have noticed it affected mine!

Sir Gawain and the Green Knight is one of the most linguistically distinctive poems in the language. As a story it has everything that appeals to 9–13-year-olds — 'forests and enchantments drear', a quest, a testing time, a monstrous green man who can challenge a knight even when his head has been chopped off and after he has stooped from his horse to retrieve it. There is also the chivalrous world of King Arthur's court. But the poem is long and so minutely and beautifully told it should not suffer drastic cutting and simplification for younger pupils. Elizabeth Cook recommends waiting till pupils are 11 or 12, when Serraillier's version of it can be read to one's class. By then children are more ready for the moral delicacy of the story as well as for its long elaborate descriptions of Gawain's temptations by the lady.

A reading of *Beowulf* when the class is 9–11 will be a good preparation for the mythical elements in *Sir Gawain*, while a foretaste of its moral concern with the difficulty of keeping one's word is provided by *The Pied Piper*, which is best read and discussed when pupils are 9–10-years-old. *Sir Gawain* may be harder to appreciate if these helpful foundations have not been laid, but it is certainly not impossible.

There is a tendency among some teachers to shy away from language that is unusual or 'old-fashioned', as it is often termed, because it is thought to be linguistically beyond their pupils. This is shortsighted in two ways. First, it condemns children to hearing nothing but their own modern, or limited, idiom; and secondly, it underestimates primary pupils' willingness to learn, which is never greater than in the primary years. The truth is that where a strange or even archaic language accompanies a gripping story it never fails to impress as long as it is mediated through an expressive reading by the teacher — as we shall see in the ballads.

The Ballads

The English and Scottish ballads, some of which were composed in the medieval period, are yet another source of that magical weaving of story-telling in the form of poetry. They are largely neglected in the primary/middle classroom as well as at the secondary level. Yet these are just the places where their appeal could be the greatest. They are instantly accessible because, belonging as they do to the oral tradition, they all display the same simplicity of style and form which they combine with some of the most powerful human passions, like love, death, betrayal and jealousy. No other poetry is more direct and vigorous. It is surely ironic that poetry that was proletarian in origin and was enjoyed by the common people for centuries should today be the preserve of scholars.

The mnemonic features the ballads employ, such as simple rhymes, incremental repetitions, choruses, refrains, use of dialogue, and internal rhyme, are all extremely popular with primary-age children. Such features are certainly to be found in the work of their favourite twentieth-century poets, like A. A. Milne.

The ballads vary so widely in subject-matter that no two ballad lessons need be alike. There is a whole series of ballads about the great English folk hero, Robin Hood. The long version of the death of Robin Hood takes all of 25 minutes to read aloud. There are ballads about historic battles ('The Hunting of the Cheviot', 'The Battle of Otterburn'), about royal treachery against some local hero ('Johnnie Armstrong'). The supernatural is a favourite topic. There are ballads about ghostly visitations from the dead who have been disturbed by a mother's or lover's excessive mourning ('The Wife of Usher's Well', 'The Unquiet Grave'), about men bewitched by supernatural agents ('Thomas Rhymer', 'Tam Lin'), and women outwitting such agents ('Lady Isabel and the Elf Knight', 'Tam Lin'). There are tragic stories of love and jealousy like 'The Two Sisters of Binnorie' and 'Lord Thomas and Fair Annet', and even some humorous ballads, such as 'Get Up and Bar the Door', and 'The Cooper o' Fife'.

Many variants of the same ballad are found within the British Isles. While some of them are exclusively English or Scottish, many of them are part of the common European stock of story as variants are scattered all over Europe from Scandinavia to Calabria. There are some motifs, like the wife who is such a harridan even the devil cannot stand her, that can be traced back to very early Indian sources.

Because of their length — 'Robin Hood and the Monk' is all of 90 verses long! — many are suitable only for top-middle-school pupils, that is, 12–13-year-olds. But there are some such as 'The Wraggle Taggle Gipsies', 'The Wife of Usher's Well', 'King John and the Abbot of Canterbury' and 'Sir Patrick Spens', that are perfectly accessible to top juniors. Where the tunes are known, as with 'The Wraggle Taggle Gipsies', it is well worth singing them as well as reading them.

As the stories are full of action and told in an immediate and dramatic way through dialogue that rapidly advances the action, they invite more than just a straightforward reading aloud. They cry out for dramatic 'saying' or even a little acting or mime. For a fuller examination of 'saying' and 'doing' poetry, see Chapter 4.

This section ends with 'The Wraggle Taggle Gipsies', which illustrates very well just how outstandingly accessible folk poetry is. The language couldn't be more straightforward and the action is crystal clear — an unhappy lady makes a momentous decision and runs away. We are not told why; the fact of her rejection of her present life and all its comforts is enough. We can, of course, deduce her reasons from the details that the poem provides, particularly from what her husband doesn't say to persuade her to return!

The Wraggle Taggle Gipsies

Three gipsies stood at the castle gate, a   9
They sang so high, they sang so low; b   8
The lady sate in her chamber late, a   9
Her heart it melted away as snow. b   9

They sang so sweet, they sang so shrill,
That fast her tears began to flow.
And she laid down her silken gown,
Her golden rings, and all her show.

She's taken off her high-heeled shoes
All made of the Spanish leather, O.
She would in the street with her bare, bare feet,
All out in the wind and weather, O.

'O, saddle me my milk-white steed,
And go and fetch my pony, O!
That I may ride and seek my bride,
Who is gone with the wraggle taggle gipsies, O!'

O he rode high and he rode low,
He rode through wood and copses too,
Until he came to an open field,
And there he espied his lady, O!

'What makes you leave your house and land?
Your golden treasures to forgo?
What makes you leave your new-wedded lord,
To follow the wraggle taggle gipsies, O!'

'What care I for my house and my land?
What care I for my treasure, O?
What care I for my new-wedded lord —
I'm off with the wraggle taggle gipsies, O!'

'Last night you slept on a goose-feather bed,
With the sheet turned down so bravely, O!
But tonight you will sleep in a cold open field,
Along with the wraggle taggle gipsies, O!'

'What care I for a goose-feather bed,
With the sheet turned down so bravely, O?
For tonight I shall sleep in a cold open field,
Along with the wraggle taggle gipsies, O!'

TRADITIONAL VERSUS MODERN

It is true to say that recent years have witnessed in schools a declining interest in reading from the whole range of English poetry in favour of concentrating on what has been produced since the Second World War. It is impossible to say if this is the cause or merely the effect of the large number of anthologies of contemporary poetry produced for schools in the last two decades. Whatever the reason, it is unfortunate as it ties our hands by drastically reducing the amount of material available to us and our pupils. It also denies children access to the common culture of these shores which was once enjoyed by educated and uneducated alike. Even the illiterate in the past had access to the aesthetic, emotional and linguistic pleasures of the old ballads, folksongs, sea shanties, etc. because of the oral nature of their transmission. The ballads had general oral currency (having been learnt by heart) till at least the early nineteenth century, by which time most had been written down, although Francis Child's definitive version of them did not appear in print until the late nineteenth century. The traditional folksongs of England were not given the permanence of print until the turn of this century, when Cecil Sharp collected them together after transcribing the songs of country people. Robert Burns had done the same for Scottish folksongs more than a century earlier.

Children themselves are, of course, the prime transmitters of some of the oldest songs and chants in our culture, as the Opies' work reveals. Incomprehensible rhymes that accompany street and playground games may well connect them and us in an unbroken line with the ancient British dwellers in this land. 'Eeny, meeny, miny, mo' is thought to preserve the numbers of the ancient Britons' language. It is ties like these that enrich life for all of us, yet education in its recent headlong pursuit of modernity and relevance is helping to sever our links with our past.

As will be clear from my examples so far, I want to redress the imbalance of recent years by showing how accessible older poems are, especially those from the oral tradition. It is not my wish to ignore contemporary poetry but I do want to suggest that in denying a place for poetry that ante-dates the First World War we reject a vast source of rich, meaty material which has tremendous imaginative powers and speaks directly to the primary child. Even the Bullock Report, which made a point of stressing the usefulness of contemporary poetry for secondary pupils, did not expect older poetry to suffer as a result:

> We have placed some emphasis on contemporary poetry, but it is not to imply that we recommend it at the expense of older poetry. It is simply that much of the work of this half century, and perhaps particularly the last two decades of it . . . is fresh to many teachers themselves and some feel able to read it to their pupils with the pleasure of a new discovery. Poetry of this century and earlier centuries can be read side by side, to the mutual illumination of both.
>
> (DES, 1975, p. 137)

The last twenty years' neglect of older poetry should mean that it too can now be read 'with the pleasure of a new discovery'.

It is possible to be parochial in time as well as place. Just as it is undesirable that pupils be narrowly fixated in their education on one small area, such as the town or village where they live, so too is it a mistake to concentrate on poetry or literature produced only recently.

Shakespeare

One poet whose potential is enormous for enriching our pupils' imaginative lives and their store of language is Shakespeare, the greatest poet and dramatist in English. Because he is such a revered figure and wrote nothing specifically for children, his presence tends to be felt in schools only by examination candidates. This is such a pity.

It is not unusual to come across teachers, especially at the secondary level, who are convinced that any poetry (or even prose) prior to the present century is likely to fail instantly because it is linguistically and conceptually beyond their pupils. This amounts, of course, to a grave under-estimation of children's openness to experience and readiness to learn. I found that in an EPA primary school in Inner London, where children's parents spoke 23 different languages between them, Shakespeare was enjoyed as much as modern poets writing specifically for young children, like Milligan, Reeves and Rosen. And what is more, what enthused my 8–10-year-olds was the densely packed metaphorical poetry of *Macbeth*. It is possible to choose easier poetry from Shakespeare! Where we go wrong is to assume that every word must be fully understood, every nuance grasped and internalized. What to expect from a reading is something I shall deal with in Chapter 3.

Because Shakespeare wrote full-length plays we tend to think in terms of 'all or nothing'. But just as we listen to operatic arias divorced from their immediate context, so it is perfectly feasible to take a short extract (speech, short scene or part of a scene) from one of Shakespeare's plays and to read it to one's class. It is a good idea, of course, to introduce the extract by setting the scene or even by telling the story up to the point when it occurs, so that it can be given a context in our pupils' minds. Once our reading is done, pupils will rightly want their chance to read, too.

The witches' spells from *Macbeth* and their conversations round the cauldron go down particularly well with 8–10-years-old, especially at Hallowe'en. The text of these spells is in Chapter 9, together with an account of how I taught them and the response they generated.

Even *King Lear*, which is considered the greatest of Shakespeare's plays, is accessible in part to primary/middle pupils. This is because underlying the play, and particularly prominent in the opening scene, is the familiar folk-tale motif of the Cinderella story. Sibling rivalry is, after all, well within the experience of most children. Two evil sisters compete with their good sister for their father's kingdom. The few lines where the good sister refuses to make gushing claims about her affection for her father has the true ring of folk tale about it in its simplicity, brevity and disastrous consequences. It offers marvellous opportunities for discussion with top juniors and middle-school pupils.

Success with extracts from Shakespeare depends very largely on our own commitment to a wide range of poetry and to a policy of restraint in our teaching method. In other words, we must refrain from trying to push our mature understanding of the speech in question on to our pupils. Explaining every word and metaphor is actually counterproductive — only tedium can result. At this stage in their literary development, all our pupils need is a taste of Shakespeare, not an indigestible meal.

I am convinced that it is possible to read practically anything from Shakespeare to our pupils as long as we ourselves love it and know it thoroughly. We can then read it expressively and set the scene adequately. That is all that should be needed at this early stage. I myself have found that 13-year-olds can cope with sections of *Richard III*, *The Merchant of Venice*, and *Henry V*, as well as with parts of *Macbeth* and *King Lear*.

As an introduction to Shakespeare's language, the songs from the plays are easier to prepare because they stand alone and therefore involve no scene setting or prior telling of the story or plot. They are also more likely to be found in anthologies than are speeches or extracts of scenes. They are short, light, lyrical and vary enormously in subject:

'When icicles hang by the wall' (from *Love's Labour's Lost*, V, ii) is a series of little pictures of rural life in winter (for pupils of 9 and over).

'Blow, blow, thou winter wind' (from *As You Like It*, II, vii) is about ingratitude and the feeling of being ill-used (for pupils of 11 and over).

'Full fathom five thy father lies' (from *The Tempest*, I, ii) paints a picture of a drowned man being changed by his watery grave (for top juniors).

'Now the hungry lion roars' (from *A Midsummer Night's Dream*, V, i) is about the fearsome middle of the night when witches ride and graves open and release their spirits (for 9 and over).

'You spotted snakes with double tongue' (also from *The Dream*, II, ii) is a spell to keep nasty creatures away from the fairy queen (for 8 and over).

Relevance

It was in the late 1960s and in the 1970s that the teaching of literature at both primary and secondary levels came under the influence of a narrow materialism. This was principally concerned with rejecting all that was old and traditional on the basis that it was 'irrelevant' to modern children. The notion of relevance, which still holds sway, is a difficult one to address because it is so ill-defined and vague. But, as Elizabeth Cook points out (1976, p. ix), reading literature in school has certainly suffered from the 'absolute value given to an increasingly narrow concept of relevance' and reality. For example, it brought about the widespread demise a couple of decades ago of the fantasy tradition, especially the myths of Greece and Rome, and the legends and folk tales of Northern Europe.

But relevance also seemed to mean that we ought not to read nature poetry to urban children because it was not part of their experience of life. This is, of course, a very silly argument as the people who go fell-walking in the Lake District and hike through England's 'green and pleasant land', staying overnight in youth hostels, are not usually country folk. Relevance tends in fact to be interpreted merely in terms of socio-economic background or the material details of a child's life. In other words, what children read at school or have read to them should reflect the world they perceive with their senses at the present time. This might have something to be said for it if it were true that we are all so standardized that we perceive the same in the world around us. Fortunately, human beings are not made to such limited specifications. Some of us may, in a minor way, resemble William Blake, poet and engraver, who could walk down the Strand and see not a major thoroughfare of late eighteenth-century London but a field full of angels. Notions of relevance assume that our minds are focused interminably on the here and now, which they are not.

Nor, by the same token, do we all respond to any one text in an identical way. It is clear that what one person (or child) finds important in any piece of literature will not necessarily be duplicated by another. Modern theories of reader-response, which I shall look at again in Chapter 9, suggest that a text can generate as many meanings as there are readers. If reading itself is a creative process with the personality and interests of the reader, his past experiences and present mood all coming into play to make meanings, then relevance becomes a superfluous consideration. For example, while Wordsworth's 'Daffodils' might well affect one child with the beauty and sprightliness of the spring scene, another might respond to the feeling that memory has the power to sustain us when life is less than rich and fulfilling. Indeed, this poem might well stand as an examplar of the range of responses that poetry can generate. Teachers have been known to reject it on the grounds that nature poems are 'irrelevant' to inner-city children. In only one sense is it a nature poem, a poem about one aspect of nature — a scene of particular vividness and life, in which daffodils' 'dancing' are matched by the waves on the lake. It is also about joy, an unselfish love of things outside oneself, unprompted by possession or use. It embodies in fact, the kind of spontaneous delight in living things that young children are so engagingly full of.

The meanings do not stop there, however. The poem is also about how we sustain that sense of childlike joy in the beauty of our world when we are cut off from the sources that feed those inner wells. The 'inward eye' of the imagination or memory is the mechanism open to all of us to keep alive and fresh the joy we once felt and the scenes we once saw. I am sure that critics more expert than myself may well find other themes and meanings in this short poem. My point is not to show how many meanings we ought to attempt to elucidate, but just how varied the responses of our pupils are likely to be.

Moreover, just because most children do not live in the constant sight of nature, it is a strange snobbery to assume they have no sensibility to which natural beauty can appeal. In fact, relevance under-estimates children in that it suggests that they cannot respond to anything unless it reproduces the external trappings of the environment they inhabit. It ignores the young child's openness to new experience and readiness to learn. In the case of working-class pupils, their environment has tended to be stereotyped as one of unrelieved gloom. To be relevant to them, literature has had to address sociological 'issues', usually problems considered topical and urgent.

An environment of unrelieved gloom may well be what many children are forced to grow up in, although how far they themselves between the ages of 5 and 13 would assent to this view of their world is, of course, another matter. Whatever the case, it seems an oddly perverse attitude to their education to perpetuate their deprivation by confronting them with only what they know. Such children surely need reason to hope, and reminders that this environment need not be so and is not so elsewhere.

There is a difference between being encouraged to feel and to think (which is what good poetry can do) and being constantly bombarded with problems that present-day adults have failed to solve. It simply isn't fair to impose an adult's sense of powerlessness on young children, to depress and harrow them before they arrive at adulthood when such problems will have to be tackled. It is trite but none the less true to say that great poetry makes us think about the everlasting questions of life — love, God, beauty, joy, death — but in a way that is exhilarating, even if sometimes sad, but never depressing nor destructive of value. In Laurie Lee's 'Field of Autumn', a poem for top-middle-school pupils, the contemplation of the imminence of Nature's decay is both breathtakingly beautiful and deeply sad at the same time.

If we gave modern children, whether middle class or working class, deprived or affluent, only what they know from direct experience, they would have a very meagre diet. We would never read them folk tales, fairy stories, historical novels, or stories about far-away places. Children of all backgrounds need their horizons widened, and this applies especially to children whose environment might be described as 'deprived'.

What these materialist notions of relevance miss entirely are the psychological and spiritual dimensions of literature — its very life blood. In other words, they miss those intangible, universal aspects that mean that the Greek myths of Phaeton or Icarus can still speak to us of recognizable emotional realities after three millenia. It is this enduring emotional correspondence that the Bullock Report stresses in rejecting 'relevance':

> We have heard the case for 'relevance' carried to the point of excluding fantasy or any stories with settings or characters unfamiliar to the pupils from their firsthand experience. We do not accept this view. Though we consider it important that much of a child's reading matter should offer contact at many points with the life he knows, we believe true relevance lies in the way a piece of fiction engages with the reader's emotional concerns.
>
> (DES, 1975, p. 129)

Clearly, all literature is embedded within a given society and must of necessity reflect that society's ways and means, but the greatest literature can and does rise above its immediate context as well, by being concerned with questions that are essentially and universally human. As Robert Frost, the twentieth-century American poet, said, 'A living poem is one that stays alive because it is rooted in mortal things and deathless emotions'. There is impressive evidence of our common humanity in the literature of Confucian China, ancient Greece and Anglo-Saxon England. What is conceptually and emotionally accessible to our pupils is a better guide for selecting material than the misleading and limiting modernity of 'relevance'. At the very least it would allow a wider range of poetry into our classrooms.

WHERE TO START?

One of the difficulties in embarking on something new is not knowing where to start. In the case of reading poetry, much depends on whether one's pupils have read any poetry before and, more importantly, what their attitude to it tends to be. I have found most primary children are quite open-minded and willing and eager to try anything new. However, the older they grow (especially in the secondary and upper-middle years) the more fixed in their views they are likely to become. The vexed question of reluctant older readers is considered in Chapter 8.

We cannot go wrong if we remember that for the very young and the less able of all ages, poetry's earliest and principal appeal is to the ear. It is through such aural pleasure that we will catch the interest of our pupils. The poetry we choose for regular reading sessions should, therefore, display rhythm, rhyme and metre. The use of repetition is very satisfying to young children. Repeating a pattern of words or a sound sequence has a magical and ritualistic quality about it. It is like weaving a spell. The predictable element also makes for a feeling of security as the poem moves back from the unknown to the familiar. It is in traditional poetic forms that the musical features of poetry are most readily and compellingly found. This must rule out poems in 'free verse' (a non-rhyming form) as a regular component of our poetry lessons at the primary level and for inexperienced readers of poetry in middle and secondary schools.

'Free verse' has no metrical regularity and as a result lacks the memorableness of rhymed and metrically regular poetry and verse. It is, after all, the memorableness of the metrical form which enables the condensed and well-chosen language of poetry to enrich our awareness of the enormous potential of English. If poetry is to promote our pupils' language development, 'free verse' must wait until pupils are sophisticated and experienced poetry readers. However, even then we must make our choice carefully for, as Vernon Scannell insists (1987, p. 50), most 'free verse' is merely 'inferior prose'. Ted Hughes's *Season Songs* (Faber, London, 1976) and *Moonbells and Other Poems* (The Bodley Head, London, 1986) provide a high standard of what to expect from 'free verse' (for a fuller account, see Chapter 9). It is the poet's fascination with the sheer magic of words and his pleasure in the shape and pattern conferred by metre and rhyme that is shared by all young and not-so-young readers of poetry. The quality of this linguistic and metrical experience must be our prime concern in selecting material for our pupils.

The vast range of poetry accessible to junior/middle pupils, some indication of which I have tried to give in this chapter, can be divided into three separate strands — humorous verse, narrative poems and poetry distinguished by the lyrical impulse.

Humour

For inexperienced pupils, whether young or older, we cannot fail if we start with verse of a humorous turn. Luckily, there is an enormously varied amount to choose from. Nonsense verse, in particular, has a long history and is well represented in contemporary 'urchin verse' by Michael Rosen, Roger McGough and especially Spike Milligan. *You Tell Me* (Kestrel, London, 1979) by McGough and Rosen is a typical collection. Try 'The Fight of the Year', in which the coming of spring, a traditional poetic topic, is presented in a surprising format — as a 'Sportsnight Special' boxing match. 'The Lesson' conjures up the sort of revenge teachers occasionally dream of, while 'Down behind the Dustbin' has that genuine touch of wackiness that is worthy of Lear himself. For sheer lunacy, however, one has to go to Milligan's *Silly Verse for Kids* (Dobson, London, 1975). The greatest exponents of nonsense verse, however, remain the Victorians, Edward Lear and Lewis Carroll, because no modern comic poet has been able to match their inventive word-play, their command of the skill of versification and their imaginative richness (for some appreciative words about Lewis Carroll, see Benton and Fox, 1987, pp. 81–2).

Lear's real work was as a scientific illustrator of birds and animals. Like Lewis Carroll, he wrote poetry for children as a relaxation and to entertain some children he knew. The limericks, which are his most well-known verses, he accompanied with humorous drawings. These are suitable for 6- and 7-year-olds. The less well-known 'Nonsense Botany', also illustrated by himself, is a gem for 11- and 12-year-olds. The invented words of 'The Pobble Who Has No Toes' and 'The Quangle Wangle's Hat' (for 7- and 8-year-olds) are great fun and link up with Carroll's portmanteau words in 'Jabberwocky' (for 11-year-olds and over). 'The Jumblies', who 'went to sea in a sieve', hark back to nursery rhymes like 'Simple Simon'.

It would be a pity to forget less anthologized examples of Carroll's poetry, particularly such pieces from *Sylvie and Bruno* as 'The Mad Gardener's Song':

> He thought he saw an Elephant
> That practised on a fife:
> He looked again, and found it was
> A letter from his wife.
> 'At length I realise,' he said,
> 'The bitterness of Life!'

These particular poems exhibit that love of the surreal so typical of the middle-school phase.

A command of variety and precision in the use of the language cannot be better fostered than by W. S. Gilbert, who produced some of the greatest comic verse in English. It is certainly unsurpassed for audacious rhymes, distinctive rhythms (even without Sullivan's delightful music), and sheer technical virtuosity. His scintillating way with words makes him a must in the middle-school classroom. For a taste of his expertise, here is a simple example from *The Mikado*. It will be necessary, of course, to explain briefly the context of the piece, which is that the Mikado had ordered that if a man was caught winking at or flirting with a woman, he was to be arrested and executed. (It *is* a comedy!) It had also been decreed that when a man was executed, his wife suffered the same fate, which explains Yum-Yum's reluctance to marry Nankipoo, whom she loves:

> *Yum-Yum*   Here's a how-de-do!
> If I marry you
> When your time has come to perish
> Then the maiden whom you cherish
> Must be slaughtered, too!
> Here's a how-de-do!
>
> *Nankipoo*:   Here's a pretty mess!
> In a month, or less,
> I must die without a wedding.
> Let the bitter tears I'm shedding
> Witness my distress.
> Here's a pretty mess!
>
> *Ko-Ko*:   Here's a state of things!
> To her life she clings!
> Matrimonial devotion
> Doesn't seem to suit her notion —
> Burial it brings!
> Here's a state of things!

Note the variety and precision of the language here, 'perish' standing in for the more normal 'die', 'cherish' instead of the obvious 'love', 'slaughtered' in place of 'killed', and 'witness for 'show', among others. Such precision can help to hone our pupils' perceptions of the tremendous range of opportunities within the language. For top-middle pupils, 'I've Got a Little List' and 'My Object All Sublime', also from *The Mikado*, are great fun and will encourage pupils to devise their own suitable lists of, and punishments for, their pet hates. 'The Nightmare Song' from *Iolanthe* has something of the quality of a tongue-twister, but its enjoyable difficulty lies in the excessive length of its lines, requiring dextrous breathing and voice control. Good readers among 10–12-year-olds love to take up the challenge. 'The Ruler of the Queen's Navee', from *HMS Pinafore*, is a witty account of how one well-known figure at the time Gilbert was writing had risen by unexpected stages to occupy the top naval post.

More recently, the verse of Michael Flanders, in partnership with Donald Swann, has followed in Gilbert's footsteps. He is an equally accomplished and witty versifier, often dealing in topics well within the experience of middle-school pupils, like the technicalities of hi-fi in 'A Song of Reproduction' (for 13-year-olds and older) or finding creepy-crawlies in the bath, as in 'The Spider'

> I have fought a grizzly bear,
> Tracked a cobra to its lair,
> Killed a crocodile who dared to cross my path;
> But the thing I really dread
> When I've just got out of bed
> Is to find that there's a spider in the bath.
>
> I've no fear of wasps or bees,
> Mosquitoes only tease.
> I rather like a cricket on the hearth;
> But my blood runs cold to meet
> In pyjamas and bare feet
> With a great big hairy spider in the bath.
>
> (5 more verses)

Now that 'The Hippopotamus' features on tapes for pre-school children, it should not be long before it becomes a firm favourite with infants and young juniors, despite the presence of such unusual words as 'inamorata' — sweetheart (see *The Songs of Michael Flanders and Donald Swann*, Elm Tree Books, London, 1977).

Hilaire Belloc's *Cautionary Tales* and *A Bad Child's Book of Beasts* (combined in one volume and illustrated by Nicholas Bentley, Duckworth, London, 1977) are witty send-ups of the sort of moralizing poetry produced for children in the eighteenth and early nineteenth centuries. Even then, some poets mocked that tendency: the irony of Thomas Gray's 'On the Death of a Favourite Cat Drowned in a Bowl of Goldfish' is for 13–14-year-olds.

Ogden Nash is another versifier for children who enjoys playing with language, offering 'elderly poems for youngerly readers' in *Parents Keep Out* (Dent, London, 1962). Charles Causley, too, turns logical expression inside out in such poems as ' "Quack!" said the Billy Goat', from *Figgie Hobbin* (Puffin, Harmondsworth, 1983). E. V. Rieu's humour is of a generally quieter kind, although he, too, can provide a boisterous piece as in 'Sir Smashum Uppe', about a disastrous visit from a clumsy fellow. It needs a good dramatic reading. He is well represented in Eleanor Graham's *A Puffin Quartet of Poets* (Puffin, Harmondsworth, 1967). James Reeves's witty creation in *Prefabulous Animiles* (Heinemann, London, 1976) of a series of creatures whose names, habits and habitats he had invented is enjoyed by children from 8 to 11, but I personally prefer the lighter touch he displays in poems like 'Mr Tom Narrow' and 'Mr Kartoffel', wild, outlandish types who prefigure Ted Hughes's *Meet My Folks* (Puffin, Harmondsworth, 1977). Allan Ahlberg's funny–sad pieces on school life, *Please Mrs Butler* (Kestrel, London, 1983), are deservedly popular.

Narrative Verse

Narrative poems, like the ballads mentioned earlier, extend our pupils' range by enabling them to enter into the larger world of more serious poetry without any feeling of disappointment after a diet of comic fare. Hearing stories is still a potent source of pleasure for primary pupils. Stories in verse are even more valuable, as I suggested earlier. Fortunately, many primary teachers still regard promoting stories as an essential feature of their work and so give over the last half hour of the afternoon to reading one aloud. It takes much less time to read a long narrative poem to a class than a short, easy-to-read piece of fiction like Betsy Byars's *The 18th Emergency*. It can also satisfy interest more rapidly and so prevent that interest flagging, especially for the younger and less able children. Poetry is so often forgotten or ignored as a vehicle for stories, many of them more intensely enjoyed because of their rhythm, rhyme, alliteration, etc., than they can be in prose. The jostling closeness of rhyming words in Browning's *The Pied Piper of Hamelin*

> And the muttering grew to a grumbling;
> And the grumbling grew to a mighty rumbling;
> And out of the houses the rats came tumbling!

eases the length and makes it seem short by comparison with prose:

> And even spoiled the women's chats
> By drowning their speaking
> With shrieking and squeaking
> In fifty different sharps and flats

and enables the poem to move along at a cracking pace.

Even a poem the length of *The Rime of the Ancient Mariner* (which takes all of 40 minutes to read aloud without abridgements) moves more quickly from incident to incident, thanks to its simple ballad form. However long they are, narrative poems — especially ballads — present us with a story and an experience just sufficiently developed and not over-encrusted with detail that our minds can muse over and ponder long after the books have been put away.

Other rhythmically compelling narrative poems include the following:

'The Inchcape Rock' — Robert Southey (10+).

'The River of Stars, a Tale of Niagara Falls' — Alfred Noyes (12+), a tragic story of Red Indians to be found in *Narrative Verse*, selected and edited by S. C. Paterson (Longman, London, 1967).

'The Tail of the Trinosaur' — Charles Causley (9+).

'The Hero of the Match' — Neil Adams (9+), in *Passport to Poetry*, Book 4, by E. L. Black and D. S. Davies (Cassell, London, 1980).

A great many well-known poets have been inspired by the anonymous oral tradition to write their own narrative poems in the ballad form and style. These later imitations are known as literary ballads. Coleridge's *The Ancient Mariner*, which has already been mentioned, is undeniably the greatest literary ballad in the language. No pupil should leave school without having heard it read aloud at some point in his school life. Only its length need concern us at this stage as we shall not be reading it to elucidate its many complexities, but simply to experience its story and its imaginative power. The crucial question we have to answer is: Can my pupils sit still and listen for the full 40 minutes it takes to read the poem aloud from start to finish without cutting? Abridgements are not advised because nothing can be left out without damage to the story's resonance. Pupils need, therefore, to be 12 or 13 before we embark on this poem, although I do know some teachers who had had it read to them as top juniors. However, 11-years-olds do need adequate powers of concentration. There is perhaps a danger in rushing into the poem too early because its themes are more accessible to children as they undergo the great journey into adulthood. Sin and guilt, suffering and how we can redeem the evil we do, often inadvertently, are not such urgently felt issues in the junior-age child.

Other literary ballads that are effective in the classroom are as follows:

'Ballad' — W. H. Auden (12+) to be found in *Narrative Verse* selected by S. C. Paterson (Longman, London, 1967).

'Lord Lovelace' — Charles Causley (10+) in *Figgin Hobbin* (Puffin, Harmondsworth, 1983).

'Two Red Roses Across the Moon' — William Morris (13+).

'Lock the Door Lariston' — James Hogg (11+). These two are to be found in J. F. Danby's *Approach to Poetry* (Heinemann, London, 1967) with helpful comments and divisions for speakers.

'The Eve of St Agnes' — John Keats (13+).

'La Belle Dame Sans Merci' — John Keats (14+).

Other examples may be gleaned from the Signal Bookguide, *Poetry for Children* (Thimble Press, Stroud, 1984), which has a section devoted to editions of narrative poems. Further examples are included in Chapter 8.

Lyrical Poetry

Lyrical poetry celebrates that light and quick, though sometimes sad, spirit of song out of which the very first poetry grew. Its musical qualities are often accompanied by an evocation of the more evanescent features of life. Since the time of Blake and Wordsworth, lyrical poets have been inspired to recover the child's innocence of vision and recapture its spontaneous delight in the ordinary things that surround us, especially in the natural world. These features have all been well caught in the work of those later lyrical poets, like Christina Rossetti, R. L. Stevenson, Walter de la Mare and Eleanor Farjeon, who have written specifically for children. Their poetry is often shorter and simpler in form and diction than narrative or humorous verse and is therefore more easily accessible to our younger and less able pupils.

Christina Rossetti's verse for children, which was mentioned in the section on infants, is always as clear as crystal, but sometimes within her extreme, formal simplicity is embedded an unsuspected depth. Unobtrusively, she alerts us to the value of the unvalued, as in 'The Flint', and elevates the ordinary in the same way that a young child's sense of wonder is expressed over things adults ignore. Try 'What is Pink?', 'Winter Rain', 'The Sound of the Wind', and 'The Wind'. The first verse of 'Summer' displays her delicate talent well:

> Winter is cold-hearted,
> Spring is yea-and-nay,

> Autumn is a weather-cock
> Blown every way.
> Summer days for me
> When every leaf is on the tree;

Robert Louis Stevenson's *A Child's Garden of Verses* recreates the poet's own experiences and feelings as a child. The child's-eye view is joined by the infant's voice, for these poems are written in the first person. The simple clarity and directness that this requires can be hard to achieve without toppling over into the sentimental, the banal or the downright twee. Stevenson avoids these dangers by keeping a lightly ironic distance, as a man, from the child he was. He has a firm grip on his memories, doesn't idealize and never indulges in self-pity for which he would have had some justification given that he spent much of his childhood ill in bed. Modern children find much in common with his playtime activities and momentary perceptions, as in 'A Good Play', when his imagination transforms a bundle of old chairs into a ship, and in 'The Wind' when he asks

> O you that are so strong and cold,
> O blower, are you young or old?
> Are you a beast of field and tree
> Or just a stronger child than me?

I have found that 7- and 8-year-olds enjoy discussing the youth or age of the wind. In its tenderness and simplicity, *A Child's Garden of Verses* is a perfect collection for the infant and early junior years.

It is Walter de la Mare who is rightly regarded as the finest of the lyrical poets writing for children. He combines a childlike freshness of perception with a musical ear that is second to none. His technical mastery of a wide variety of metrical forms matches the enormous range of his subject-matter. 'Snow', quoted in full in Chapter 3, displays his powers of delicate observation and exquisite verbal precision, while 'Off the Ground' is unalloyed and idiotic fun. Perhaps because his poetry so often gets right down to the worm's-eye view, depicting the world as experienced by the lowliest of its creatures (see 'Old Shellover', 'The Fly', and 'Sooep'), his topics really speak to young children in terms they can recognize. 'Alas, Alack' even allows a fish in a frying pan to speak up for itself! As short and apparently slight as these poems appear, they strike such a chord in 9-year-olds that many volunteer to learn them by heart. 'The Song of the Mad Prince', however, with its symbolic density, is for older secondaries to ponder and top middles just to taste. *Secret Laughter* (Puffin, Harmondsworth, 1972) is a good selection of his verse for the young, but see also his *Collected Rhymes and Verses* (Faber & Faber, London, 1970) for a much more thorough-going anthology.

Eleanor Farjeon deserves to be better known by teachers than she is. For one thing, her work spans the whole infant to middle-school age range. For another, her verse is always tuneful. She said once that her verse came to her as tunes singing themselves in her head. Humour is a forte of hers, but she can also capture with the minimum of detail and of effort a serious mood or an evocation of beauty and delight. Her musical range is immense. Compare the nursery-rhyme inspired 'Tailor' and its jaunty repetition with the haunting cadences of 'It was long ago'. Also compare the rollicking jollity of 'Wheelbarrow' with the noise and speed of 'Cat, Scat', and all of them with perhaps her single greatest poem, 'Mrs Malone', a must for 11–12-year-olds.

More recently, James Reeves and Charles Causley have made their own considerable contributions to children's poetry. While Reeves's poetry is best enjoyed by the younger juniors (7–9), Causley's profounder emotional appeal is for 10–13-year-olds. 'Slowly', 'The Snail' and 'Explorers' show Reeves at his observant best, while 'Spells' and 'J is for Jargon' are two pieces that positively skip with joy. Some of Causley's poems, such as 'Candlemas', 'My Mother Saw a Dancing Bear' and 'Miller's End' (all in *Figgie Hobbin*) have the power to weave a haunting magic for adult and child readers alike.

Other lyric poets for children who are worth looking at are to be found in the Chatto series of *Poets for the Young*, whose general editor is Leonard Clark:

An English Year, Clive Sansom, 1975. See 'The Poem I'd Like to Write' (about Wordsworth's 'The Daffodils'), 'October', 'Winter Morning' (like Hughes's 'Thought Fox') and 'Snowflakes'.
Secret as Toads, Leonard Clark, 1972.
The Apple Raid, and Other Poems, Vernon Scannell, 1974.
Young and Old, R. S. Thomas, 1972.

It is in lyrical poetry that we will find the richest nourishment for our pupils' burgeoning sensibilities. By all means use humour to catch our pupils' interest in reading poetry, but introduce lyrical poetry early on in order to refine and extend that growing interest. As Benton and Fox suggest (1987, p. 84), lyrical poetry offers a quality rarely found in humorous verse: 'a sense of mystery, a ghost of some strong emotion . . . which, while it may not be understood, will be felt through the language and rhythms of the poem'.

SUMMARY

The primary survey suggests that in recent years there has been a general tendency among teachers and student teachers to under-estimate the abilities and interests of our young pupils. As far as poetry is concerned, the effect of this under-estimation has been to restrict children to a limited diet of often inferior material on the basis that it is more at their linguistic and mental level. It could be argued that the more backward or poor in their command of English, the more lacking in imagination they are, the better the material such children need in order to enable them to improve. To reserve the better poetry for the abler and older, or middle-class pupils, is nothing less than élitist. English literature deserves to be enjoyed by more than just a university-educated few, or the members of a small élite social class. It is the birthright of all English-speaking people and certainly has something for everyone. The 1987 DES booklet, *Teaching Poetry in the Secondary School: An HMI View* suggests (p. 33) that the experience of poetry 'should not be a matter of chance but of entitlement' for all children.

How far a wider range of poetry will succeed with our pupils will depend very largely on what we teachers do with it in the classroom. Teaching method, which the next chapter examines in detail, is the key either to converting our pupils to poetry reading as a lasting, worthwhile activity, or to alienating them for good.

Chapter 3

How to Read Poetry

A love of poetry can only grow in an atmosphere in which poetry is associated with pleasure and delight, so that its readers can feel at ease with it. Thanks to the teaching methods that have been employed to introduce poetry to our pupils in the recent past, this has not been the case. The Bullock Report indicated that it was teaching method that was responsible for the dislike so many pupils felt towards poetry: 'It is clear that this antipathy rests substantially in the *method* of teaching it; and the comprehension approach is by no means confined to the examination years' (DES, 1975, p. 136). Despite Bullock's strictures, this method dies hard, for the more recent DES document *Teaching Poetry in the Secondary School: An HMI View* (1987) reiterates Bullock's criticisms. It is clear that teachers continue to employ a cluster of strategies, all of them linked to an overall analytical purpose. Our aim, it seems, is to promote 'understanding' which we test by detailed questioning. We imply that the text is 'a repository of answers to which the teacher holds the key' (DES, 1975, p. 132). In our urgency to decipher 'meaning' and to highlight technical features we lose sight of appreciation. Indeed, we confound appreciation with comprehension. We leave children no time or space to engage personally with a poem before probing their responses and 'plunging them into talking and writing' (DES, 1987, p.6).

WE NEED A LESS THREATENING METHOD

It is surely time that we tried to present poetry in a less threatening way. A gentler, more informal approach is needed. To cultivate in our primary/middle pupils an interest in reading poetry both in and out of school requires in fact the simplest of methods. We need do no more than read lots of poetry to our pupils on a regular basis. Let the poems speak for themselves. At the primary and early secondary level, the less talk and the more reading we do the better. In the early stages of schooling most poems will not need any investigation or 'help' other than an expressive reading by the teacher. The problem is that most of us cannot refrain from forcing our lessons to produce something tangible, like writing, and in this lies a real danger. We should not forget that a pupil's 'work' in a poetry lesson is largely individual and internal. There are creative responses that go on within the pupil's heart and mind that we cannot see in operation nor quantify in outward signs or by expressive activities. We tend to assume that our pupils are incapable of response unless we engage in careful prompting and probing. However, poetry reading is a quiet, inward activity which can set up a resonance that lives long after the lesson has finished.

As teachers we must learn to trust poems to work their magic unaided. Words-worth's dictum, 'We murder to dissect', is especially true in the primary and early secondary years (5–13). We simply wring poetry dry of its magic, its aura, its mystery, if we open it up too thoroughly too soon. All we need to do is to read poems expressively with love and understanding. The poems will do the rest themselves in their own way and in their own time. I think now that my most successful poetry lesson was of Laurie Lee's 'Field of Autumn', a most achingly beautiful tribute to the season's richness while recognizing the imminence of its decay. I read it feelingly and, as I finished, an audible 'Ah', like a quick gasp of pleasure and appreciation, or an awed intake of breath, came from my class of 13–14-year-olds in unison. That very second the bell rang for the end of the lesson, and I fumed and fretted for hours afterwards that the bell had cut short a marvellous opportunity for questioning. I'd failed, I thought, to exploit their pleasure. Much later, however, I became convinced that I had left their enjoyment intact and that they were more likely to re-read Laurie Lee and that poem as a result than if I'd discussed it to death. It is a matter of tact and knowing when to stop.

It seems to me that our 'work' for a poetry lesson is to sift material, to select accessible and suitable poems for the linguistic and emotional maturity levels of our pupils, and to know the poems so well that we can read them with such expression and feeling that questioning becomes unnecessary.

TIME FOR POETRY

Finding time for poetry is vitally important, of course. If its benefits are as profound as the evidence in Chapter 1 suggests, then we ought not to marginalize it by leaving it to the odd occasion when all 'the real work' has been done. We must treat it seriously by allotting it a regular slot. To replace the usual afternoon prose story-reading now and then with a narrative poem would not come amiss but it is not enough. To read one poem per day to one's class, as Benton and Fox (1987, p. 84) suggest, is much better and takes no more than a few minutes to accomplish. How-ever, given that poems frequently generate an interest that emanates in talk, some-thing that it would be a pity to cut short, it is better still to allocate a regular slot (or even two) of at least, say, 30 minutes per week to reading poetry to and with one's class and to stick to that. The danger is to feel it is not all that important and can therefore be easily jettisoned when time is needed for extra help in other subject areas such as maths.

The easiest way to accommodate poetry within the curriculum is to fit a regular poetry reading session into one's overall weekly English or language allocation. This is surely feasible when what I am suggesting need last no more than 40 minutes with top juniors, 30 minutes with 7-year-olds, and 20 minutes with infants. If it isn't allotted a regular and specific slot, experience shows that it won't get done at all.

Because of the many diverse areas now competing for a teacher's time and attention, and that will no doubt be enshrined in the national curriculum, there may well be less incentive to include poetry in one's regular English or language lesson plans. Under such pressure it is easy to feel that if you used a poem to promote a piece of 'creative writing' or in a theme or project, then that covers the poetry reading for the week. It most certainly does not. The DES booklet, *Teaching Poetry in the Secondary School: An HMI View* (1987), insists (p. 6) that 'approaches to poetry in the classroom must be at least as clearly structured and provided for as other aspects of English if they are to impart a sense of pleasure and direction'. This means 'regular reading and listening to whole poems read aloud' (*ibid*. p. 21).

Once we set aside a regular weekly slot of, say, 30 minutes or more, then we are faced with the vexing question of how we use all that time. Spending a whole 30 or 40 minutes on only one poem can rapidly lead to boredom and inevitably opens the poems up to being 'used' to promote some end other than the enjoyable experience of reading poetry. James Reeves advises us in his very helpful handbook, *Teaching Poetry* (Heinemann, London, 1958), not to spend too long on any one poem. He suggests that the length of time spent reading (and perhaps talking about) a poem should not exceed 1½ times the age of the class. Therefore, 'a teacher should not expect a class of seven year olds to be interested in the same poem for more than ten minutes or so' (*ibid*. p. 13). That time includes our first reading to the class, possibly a second silent reading by each individual child, and a final reading by teacher or volunteer.

This may seem an excessively tight rule of thumb. It can and will sometimes be broken. I remember spending all of 35 minutes on the Chinese poem about homecoming with a class of 11-year-olds. However, Reeves is right to remind us that if we wish to promote pleasurable anticipation whenever we embark on a poetry lesson, we should never spend too long on any one poem and that we should actually stop when interest is at its most intense rather than waiting for it to flag. After all, the cardinal rule is that we can always return to re-read a poem at a later date. For my own part, I always make sure that I have about half a dozen shortish poems ready at hand for a lesson of 30 minutes duration with junior pupils of whatever age. Of course, such a rule of thumb will be broken when reading a long narrative poem to the class, which may take all of the time available.

INTRODUCTIONS

As I mentioned earlier, Wordsworth's dictum, 'We murder to dissect', is especially true of analysis and discussion in the early stages of reading poetry. At the primary level and with less able and younger children in the secondary school, very little analysis of poetry (i.e. what it means and how it works) will be necessary. A simple introduction will suffice, something along the lines of the following 'Now we're going to read a poem about a man who buys a castle that comes complete with its own, very active ghost' ('Colonel Fazackerley' by Charles Causley).

It may well be necessary to give a brief account of the story line in your own words so as to whet your pupils' appetite and equally importantly to give them something to go on. Commitment and interest are greater if they know broadly what is to happen and have only to look for details. This is especially true for the least able pupils and younger children, particularly when we are reading a challenging poem to them. In fact, the more demanding the poem we choose to read, the more this need for an introduction applies. But for very slight and easy poems and verses like Milligan's 'Teeth', all that is needed is: 'This next poem is about the unlikely subject of teeth, as we'll see'.

But it is important to bear in mind that it isn't the subject-matter that can make a poem demanding or difficult. It's more likely to be the actual length of the poem and also the length of its individual lines as well as the degree of complexity of its vocabulary and syntax (the number of polysyllabic, Latinate words and sentences with subordinate clauses). For example, T. S. Eliot's 'Skimbleshanks; the Railway Cat' from *Old Possum's Book of Practical Cats* is a demanding poem for 8-year-olds because it is both long in itself (66 lines) and employs long lines and complex sentences. However, these difficulties are actually disguised by the compelling rhythmical nature of the poem. Like R. L. Stevenson before him in 'From a Railway Carriage', T. S. Eliot captures the motion of a steam train most memorably. For the reasons given above, comments as brief as those for Milligan's 'Teeth' would be inappropriate. Something fuller and more helpful is needed like the following: 'This next poem is about a cat that lives and works on the Midnight Mail Train. He seems to think that it is *he* who runs the train and looks after the passengers and that the train just can't go without him, as we'll see'. It is appropriate and helpful to encourage anticipation and generate excitement by reminding the class of a similar poem read in a previous lesson, like R. L. Stevenson's 'From a Railway Carriage' or W. H. Auden's 'Night Mail', especially if it was one that was thoroughly enjoyed.

Sometimes it is also helpful to heighten our pupils' awareness by first drawing on their own personal experience as in: 'I'm sure you've all seen or even handled an earthworm at some time or other. Do you remember how it felt? How did you feel when you touched it?' (Allow for experiences to be shared.) 'Well, this next poem is about just how very *clever* an earthworm actually is because it's deaf and blind, you know, and yet it's still able to find its way about underground'. ('Earthworm', by Leonard Clark). You may also wish to call your pupils' attention to the unusual shape of this 'concrete' poem before you start to read.

EXPLANATIONS/DISCUSSIONS

As I have already stressed, excessive talk or explanation on the part of the teacher is not to be recommended. English specialist teachers always want to milk a poem of all it's got, in order to lead pupils to the kind of understanding they have reached of it themselves, after years of re-reading and even, perhaps, of studying it for A Level or at university. They seem to aim at conveying a definitive reading. I know this to be the case as I myself have taught in just this way! But this approach to a poem destroys its magic and must dissipate most pupils' urge to return to re-read it, because it has already been fully wrung out by 'the meddling intellect' (Wordsworth) of the teacher. It is perhaps dangerous for children to be required to intellectualize too soon their response to a poem, especially to a really good or great one. This is not to denigrate the challenge to the intellect which most aspects of the English curriculum area must offer, but poetry is different. After all, it is not a cognitive discipline, but appeals to the emotions and nourishes the imagination. In the junior and middle years particularly, it requires a less rigorous and more sensitive handling. We should avoid the trap of assuming that a uniform approach applies across all the aspects within one subject area.

Leonard Clark, ex-teacher, HMI and writer of poetry for infant and junior children put it very neatly when he wrote in an article for Thomas Blackburn's *Presenting Poetry: A Handbook for English Teachers* (Methuen, London, 1966) that 'young children can apprehend truth and beauty better than they can comprehend them' (p. 54). This is because poetry's principal appeal for them is to the imagination and the senses. To require a child to articulate the golden glow deep down inside or the sudden sense of recognition that a poem may have given him or her is ultimately destructive. To adapt Wordsworth, there are thoughts that do often lie too deep for words as well as tears, and this applies to all people of all ages, not just to immature children.

Teacher discussion or explanation of a poem can often spoil a child's own personal response or private dream. Who knows just what pictures and feelings a poem may have evoked for a child? And who are we to pin such delicate butterflies down? L. A. G. Strong pinpointed the problem more than forty years ago.

> Explanations and annotations do not matter. A child's misconception may be of much greater value to him than the explanation which destroys it. I have heard more than once a heartfelt cry, 'oh, sir, *please* don't explain it!' which showed that imagination had been bruised already by the smashing of a cherished mental picture. Only a pedant will, in such instances, value accuracy above the magic which some word or phrase is exercising on a young imagination.
>
> (da Sola Pinto, 1946, pp. 11–12)

To try to treat poetry as some knowledge-based aspect of the curriculum, like history, is to undermine wherein lies its appeal for children. No wonder that at the secondary level the love of poetry quickly dies, because it is at secondary school that teachers feel the need to teach simile, metaphor, alliteration, etc., and to analyse in depth just what it is the poet is saying. Yet poetry is one of the few subject areas that deals with intangibles. When it is read expressively by a teacher and is successfully getting through to its listeners, it works in ways that cannot really be assessed or quantified. This is because, if it does anything, poetry nourishes the *inner* life of feeling and of the imagination. In other words, it is 'proved upon our pulses' as Keats said. It gives beauty and joy freely. Thankfully, there is no way of testing or measuring such effects.

It seems to me that the emotional force of a poem conveyed by the beauty of its expression, by its rhythm, its rhyme, its techniques and meaning must be allowed to work on the reader (or listeners) unaided. We teachers must learn to trust poems and not paraphrase them line by line in our own inadequate words. Nothing is gained by this and much is lost. The poem itself disappears under a welter of verbiage and what the individual child was beginning to internalize and make his own is shown to be the common, reducible property of all.

It is possible, of course, to look at what a poem 'means' and how it works, but not as a regular thing and much later on in children's schooling, certainly not at the primary school. It is not appropriate, either, in the first two years of secondary school and even later for less able pupils unless, that is, the children actually ask to explore such things. What few teachers seem to realize is that poetry can be safely left to win its audience by its own power and does not need our interventionist or instrumentalist policies. Teaching for exam purposes is another thing, of course, and will require some analysis. However, if we are to win our pupils over to reading poetry for life, much more reading of poetry and much less explanation and/or analysis of individual poems is required.

ISSUE-BASED DISCUSSION .

It also follows that we should beware of using poems or a poem to promote discussion on some sociologically relevant 'issue', like introducing 'The Wraggle Taggle Gipsies' to debate the pros and cons of gipsy sites today. For one thing, this is not what the poem is about, though such an argument would not have stopped the sociologically minded English teachers of the 1970s. Not only is it not about gipsy sites, it is not even about gipsies *per se*, despite its title. It is a poem that balances the attractions of the materially good life against a recognition of the need for spiritual satisfactions. This is not to say that one would hope or expect to elicit this sort of understanding from any pupils lower than sixth formers. The issue-based approach distorts and limits the appeal of poetry — confining its meanings to teachers' perceptions of a poem's significance.

REMINISCENCE

Reading poems does sometimes prompt spontaneous reminiscence, which we should not discourage. I once witnessed John Clare's 'The Pettichap's Nest' evoke feeling comments from 11-year-old boys about finding eggs and young fledglings that had fallen out of their nests. Such personal remarks are legitimate because they reveal pupils responding sensitively to the emotional content of the poem and sharing those feelings. They are still *with* the poem, so to speak, still thinking and feeling within its imaginative ambit.

This is an important consideration because there is a tendency in primary education today, obsessed as it is with 'doing', to be forever leading the lesson far away from its starting point. The habit is to use a poem merely as a springboard to promote talk, however inconsequential, and to link up with art, drama, dance, or craftwork. Yet, as Clive Sansom rightly points out, 'drawing or acting may externalize something which is better left to the *imagination*' (1978, p. 120). It is all a matter of tact. It is quite feasible and proper that occasionally one's poetry lesson should involve drama or art but not as a regular occurrence. It is important to recognize which poems genuinely submit themselves to drama (ones with refrains, choruses and dialogue), or have a strong visual quality or merely lend themselves to a shared and feeling response. Some, of course, are best left to silence.

LISTENING

Poetry reading is essentially about *listening* (and its requisite stillness), not about doing. It is such a simple thing really. Children listen to a poet's words — the expression of his or her heart and soul — through the medium of a teacher's voice.

Such an approach, despite its simplicity, can never be predictable or boring because poets vary so much one from another. Listening is a crucial skill, as suggested earlier. If we need reminding, *Bullock Revisited* (DES, 1982a, p. 5) stressed its importance: 'Those who do not listen with attention . . . are at a disadvantage in almost every aspect of their personal, social and working lives'.

EXTENDING READING

What this book offers is a plan of attack for primary and middle-school teachers who are not English specialists but who would love to teach poetry if only they had some guidelines. The point I have been trying to make in this chapter is that the simpler and easier the approach the better. Our aim in devising poetry lessons for 5–13-year-olds is to attract them to go off to read more for themselves. The Bullock Report insisted 'whatever else a pupil takes away from his experience of literature, he should have learnt to see it as *a source of pleasure* and something that *will continue as part of his life*' (DES, 1975, p. 137, emphasis added).

It is my contention that poetry above all other areas in the curriculum can create and foster that sheer enjoyment in reading that brings about children's addiction to it as a pastime. The Report went on even more pointedly (*ibid*. p. 132): 'the main emphasis in teaching literature should be on extending the range of reading. True discernment can only come from a breadth of experience. Learning how to appreciate with enthusiasm is more important than to reject'. Secondary teachers would do well to reconsider their own practice in the light of this last quotation: I know I spent much more time developing critical skills in my pupils than broadening the range of their experience of poetry.

FACTUAL INFORMATION

Our aim in teaching poetry can have nothing to do with what could be called extrinsic factors. For example, the three delightful poems for young junior children, 'Boating' (James Reeves), 'Clinkerdump' (Wilma Horsbrugh), and 'John Cook's Mare' (anon.), cannot be read to convey 'factual information about different modes of transport', as a student once suggested. The point of introducing all pupils, of whatever age, to poetry has to do with its ability not to convey factual information but to express vividly and skilfully various experiences, feelings and scenes. It is the quality of the expression — the sheer beauty of the language, the wittiness of the phrasing, the liveliness of the rhythm — that give pleasure or move us to laughter or to tears. It is the experience of language well used that is crucial and without which our pupils' own language will not progress very far.

In the introduction to his anthology, *Come Hither* (Constable, London, 1953, pp. xxix-xxx), Walter de la Mare points out how unimportant *facts* are and how vital is the word order, the form and the shape of a poem:

> I tried one day to alter the words of one or two of the simple and easy poems; or to put the words in a different order. And I found by so doing that you not only altered the sound of the poem, but that even the slightest alteration in the sound a little changed the sense. Either you lost something of the tune or runningness; or the words did not

clash right; or you blurred the picture the words gave you; or some half-hidden meaning vanished away. I don't mean that every poem is perfect; but only that when I changed them it was almost always very much for the worse.

> Old King Cole was a merry old soul
> And a merry old soul was he;
> He called for his pipe,
> And he called for his bowl,
> And he called for his fiddlers three . . .

Now, suppose, instead of these lines of the rhyme you put —

> Old King Cole was a jolly old man,
> The jolliest old man alive;
> He called for his cup, and he called for his pipe
> And he called for his fiddlers five.

By so doing you have actually added two extra fiddlers; and yet somehow you have taken away some of the old three's music. Or you may put —

"Cole the First was now a monarch advanced in age and of convivial temperament. On any festive occasion he would bid his retainers bring him his goblet and smoking materials and would command his musicians to entertain him on their violins. Which they did."

Well, all the *facts* are there and many more words but scarcely a trace of *my* old King Cole, and not a single tweedle-eedle of the fiddling. Would anyone trouble to learn that by heart?

Quite!

PARAPHRASE

In the same way, paraphrase — putting a poem into a teacher's own words — destroys utterly the shape, the form and the effect of the original poem. It is a grave mistake and a real disservice to the poet in fact to attempt to paraphrase a poem, even if you feel it is conceptually or linguistically or syntactically difficult. It is true to say that the linguistic form and metrical shape the poet chooses by which to express his or her thoughts or feelings are an essential part of what he or she has to say, so that paraphrase, however worthily meant, is utterly destructive. This is where 'leave well alone' and 'let the poem speak for itself' are the very best advice. If the poem strikes you as too difficult for some reason, then don't read it.

STIMULUS AND ILLUSTRATION

Despite the considerable evidence in Chapter 1 to show how widespread is the neglect of poetry in our pupils' education, it does not follow that it is universally absent from our schools. The Bullock Report suggested that 44 per cent of 9-year-olds spent up to (and no more than) 30 minutes per week on poetry (DES, 1975, p. 388). What Bullock failed to indicate was the *context* in which this poetry reading occurred. It is important to know if it was introduced to pupils simply on the basis of its own intrinsic pleasures (and its experience of words well used) or if its presence was dictated by the need to use it as a means to an end. My guess is that it was probably present briefly in the classrooms Bullock observed in order to provide a stimulus for children's own writing of poetry, or an illustration in verse form of a theme in project work or integrated studies. For this has been the status accorded poetry when it appears in school — to be a mere means to an end rather than an end in itself.

It is surprising that the modern concern with creativity has led to the kind of teaching of poetry that would warm the heart of Mr Gradgrind himself. For poetry is generally incorporated into lessons only to serve a strictly utilitarian purpose. It is rarely read for its own sake, as something of value in its own right. The intrinsic worth of a poem that is 'used' as stimulus or illustration is inevitably missed. In the attempt to goad children into their own creativity, the poet's own creative efforts and our pupils' pleasure in his achievement go for nought. To 'use' poetry for such purposes fails to allow pupils the opportunity to 'stand and stare' in admiration and wonder at a poem, to savour its language, to ponder its thoughts and immerse themselves in its emotion.

The Pavlovian 'stimulus and response' model of teaching poetry that lies behind the usual read-talk-write-your-own format has become inflexible. It also fails to take into account the special nature of poetry, which can provoke quite unexpected reactions. For example, one of the many possible responses after hearing a poem read aloud is *silence*. Our teaching strategies do not normally allow for this. That children do not attempt to articulate a response may well be a tribute to the depths to which the poem has touched them. It need not be lack of interest nor a failure of understanding, even though that understanding may be only hesitant and intuitive. So often we as teachers break the delicate butterfly of a child's apprehension of a poem on the rack of our commitment to lay bare the meanings that we perceive in it. De la Mare reminds us in his very interesting introduction to his anthology *Come Hither* (1953, p. xxxiii) that one of the pleasures of reading is that 'you may make any picture out of the words that you can or will; and a poem may have as many different meanings as there are different minds' to read it.

Poems are such many-faceted artefacts and a child's first engagement with them is such a private affair, even when mediated by a teacher's reading, that the teaching strategies we adopt should be sufficiently sensitive and flexible to allow our pupils to retain their own perceptions intact. This must mean a recognition that it is not a necessary outcome of reading poetry that children should venture to write their own. This is particularly so in the primary and middle years when interest in reading is still at the burgeoning stage. HMI suggest this is so even at the secondary level: 'the outcome of poetry teaching need not be writing at all and many poems can be read just for themselves, as an experience of the moment whose echoes for some will last into the future' (DES, 1987, p. 29).

To use poetry as illustration of a set theme virtually denies the range of responses indicated by de la Mare above, and again pins a poem down to the teacher's interpretation of its implications. Such a practice fails to allow pupils room to think and feel into a poem for themselves, circumscribing their responses from the outset.

However, there is an even greater loss when poetry is subjected to inclusion in project or thematic work. What is lost sight of is that experience of literature for its own sake which alone seems to develop children into enthusiastic readers. What I mean by this is the experience of comparing one poem with another that pupils have enjoyed recently or by the same author, of reflecting on their own similar experiences of life and literature, in short, of 'anticipating and retrospecting' (Benton and Fox,

37, p. 106). It is easier for children to develop a life-long love of reading literature
if it is presented as something of value and interest in its own right. When covert
utilitarian purposes dictate its presence in a lesson and fix its possible meanings,
pupils quickly deduce that poetry is just another teaching tool like a textbook and
moderate their interest accordingly.

The practice of 'using' poetry for other ends, which is still so popular at the primary
level, embodies a hitherto unrecognized 'hidden curriculum' which is very disturbing:
a poem does not have to be worth reading for its own sake to be acceptable; its
value lies in how far it links with the current theme or topic. This exploitative
approach reduces imaginative literature with all its potential emotional and intellectual benefits to an arid functionalism. It thereby presents young children with an
insidiously dangerous model. This exploitation of poetry simply mirrors and
reinforces the values of the commercially exploitative world that exists outside the
school gates and can only help to prepare our pupils to accept exploitation as the
norm, not as something to be resisted.

It is clear that in the last two decades 'the unique value of literature [which] can
be discovered only through its unique disciplines' (Bolt and Gard, 1970, p. 148) has
been sacrificed on the altar of utilitarianism. Only regard poetry as an end in itself,
though, and what follows is liberation from such restrictions as described above. A
poetry lesson can then legitimately be quite self-contained and does not have to lead
anywhere or stimulate anything except an interest in poetry and pleasure in reading
it.

SOME SUGGESTED LESSONS

There are a great many ways of devising poetry lessons, even after we have abandoned stimulus and illustration as guiding principles of selection and organization.
Because our material, the poetry itself, has such a teeming variousness — in mood,
subject-matter, tone, length, seriousness, form, style, attitude — our poetry lessons
need never become predictable. What follows are some suggestions for lessons which
are by no means to be regarded as exhaustive. You will notice that the selection of
poems is not guided simply by subject-matter, but by poetic form, author, and
popularity. The degree of active involvement of the pupils alters, too. Some lessons
go for more 'performance' than others. These variations are dictated by our respect
for each poem's own special qualities.

1. Read a mixed bag of poems, by different authors, on different subjects and of
   different lengths and difficulty — one long, several short, some very slight, one
   deep or demanding. This is the easiest way of doing it. James Reeves suggests
   that it also allows our pupils the utmost freedom of response, as meaning is not
   pinned down by selection on the basis of thematic similarity.
2. Read three or four ballads (or folksongs or sea shanties or sonnets) of differing
   moods, perhaps one from the Robin Hood cycle ('The Death of Robin Hood'
   is very long and takes all of 25 minutes), and a humorous one like 'Get up and
   Bar the Door'. Brief comments from the teacher can help to pinpoint differences
   and similarities between the poems. Your introductory comments might briefly
   tell the pupils something about the origin of ballads, how they survived and
   how universal they are.

3. Read five or six (or six to twelve, depending on length) poems by the same author. Bring him or her to life with a few biographical details. Robert Louis Stevenson, John Clare, Wordsworth, Blake, Emily Brontë (or a poet you have a particular liking for and knowledge of) are all of interest to the middle-school age range. Some lives, like Thomas Hardy's and Christina Rossetti's, are uneventful in a way that would not be very appealing to children of 7–13.

4. Read some poems on the same broad subject (e.g. cats, winter, war, Hallowe'en, the sea, etc.) but which conjure different pictures and express different attitudes. Make brief comments again on the differences or similarities between each poem's presentation of the subject, like 'Now, we have a more serious view of cats, unlike the lively and humorous ones we've just read'.

5. Let children individually choose a favourite poem from an anthology and read it aloud in turn in class, having practised it first at home. Again the teacher can pinpoint differences between choices. One lesson won't be enough to hear every child read. Repeated once a month throughout the term (or each day for a week), this gives each child a chance to take part.

6. Have a choral presentation of a dramatic poem, that is, one with choruses, refrains and dialogue, such as 'The King's Breakfast' (A. A. Milne) for 8–9-year-olds, 'The Wife of Usher's Well' for 11–12-year-olds.

7. Have a brief request session in the last five minutes of a lesson or devote a whole lesson once in a while to reading again children's favourite poems from the preceding 8, 10 or 12 weeks' lessons.

8. Have the children fold their arms, rest them on their desks, rest heads on arms, close eyes and listen to an atmospheric, magical poem read really evocatively by the teacher — one like de la Mare's 'Silver', Stevenson's 'Windy Nights' and Kipling's 'The Way through the Woods'.

9. Read a variety of humorous and comic verse. Compare what makes us laugh or smile in each case, or better still make no comment. Very little comment is sensible here as humour tends to die a quick death if it has to be explained in any detail.

10. Read one long narrative poem, *The Pied Piper of Hamelin* for 9-year-olds, *The Ancient Mariner* for 12-year-olds, *The Wanderer* for 13 and over. By reading the poem aloud to the class we can choose something beyond our pupils' own competence to read for themselves on their own.

11. James Reeves suggests that with older pupils (13 and over), just occasionally it would be appropriate to talk them through a poem that is much loved by the teacher, and gives as an example Keats's 'Ode to Autumn'.

12. Occasionally we might withhold a poem's title. After the poem has been read two or three times and feelings and thoughts about it have perhaps been shared, pupils can be asked to make their own suggestions for titles. I did this many years ago with Arthur Waley's translation of the Chinese poem about homecoming. My 11-year-olds came up with really feeling titles like 'The Sad Return', 'Loneliness', 'Desolation'. Benton and Fox rightly suggest (1987, p. 144) that this undemanding task requires 'a kind of concentrated comprehension' and yet it avoids all the drawbacks of comprehension-type questioning.

COMPREHENSION EXERCISES

Perhaps the most serious pitfall in teaching poetry is that of turning the lesson into a comprehension exercise. As already suggested, discussion, paraphrase, analysis — all the major components of oral comprehension work — are not recommended when reading poetry in the primary school. It goes without saying that written exercises on poems ought to be taboo. Although I am loath to say 'never', I think it is bad psychology to associate poetry in pupils' minds with the chore of comprehension exercises, whether oral or written. Enjoyment makes a very hasty exit.

What is certainly true and not often realized is that there are ways of deepening our pupils' appreciation of what they read without having to resort to old-style comprehension work. As we shall see later in this chapter, it is possible to devise a gentle form of questioning that will enable pupils to engage closely with a poem. Chapter 7 also offers a range of specific suggestions for deepening appreciation. We must always bear in mind, though, the dangers of overdoing any of these suggestions. The pedagogical outcome of a lesson should never be predictable for pupils. Whenever a poetry lesson approaches, all they should be able to anticipate is a pleasurable experience.

Comprehension brings us back again to the kind of understanding of a poem that the teacher as an adult possesses, and which is castigated earlier in this chapter. It doesn't matter that our pupils do not share our mature grasp of *The Ancient Mariner*. It is enough that they enjoyed the story and sat through a reading of it without fidgeting. After all, 40 minutes of sustained concentration is a tall order for some children. However, the choices of verse that one makes for 6–8-year-olds are far from the length and gravity of our greatest literary ballad. 'The House that Jack Built' (anon.), 'The King's Breakfast' (A. A. Milne), 'Mr Nobody' (anon.), 'The Tide in the River' (Eleanor Farjeon), 'The Months of the Year' (Sara Coleridge), 'The Jumblies' (Edward Lear) are all so straightforward and simple that they require no talk or discussion, nor are they likely to prompt feeling reminiscences, though children do like to share their anticipated pleasure — 'I've read this before, Miss. It's really good'.

EXPRESSIVE READING

The most crucial technique we have to develop is to learn to read poems really expressively. This means that we must cast all inhibitions aside. Practise at home, if necessary on friends and relatives. Inject real feeling into your reading; use pausing and emphasis, tone and pitch, to gain the maximum effect. Some comic poems like A. A. Milne's need dramatic emphasis and even use of accents. Magical poems like de la Mare's 'The Listeners' and Kipling's 'The Way through the Woods' need control over timing if we are to tingle pupils' spines. It all comes with practice. We can all improve in time just as long as we do practise at home beforehand. We also have to dispense with embarrassment and shyness — you can't afford these as a teacher, anyway. These days some colleges of education (most notably Nene in Northamptonshire) actually offer courses in what is called 'Spoken Literature' (see Harrison, 1984).

It would be easy to dismiss the simplicity of what I am recommending. Certainly our training as teachers encourages us to think in terms of the myriad activities we can devise for a lesson, not what we, as a person and a voice, can offer our pupils. However, authorities such as Clive Sansom stress the importance of teacher as reader: 'through the teacher's voice, the children can catch the wonder and delight of poetry in a way no other method can give' (1978, p. 118).

If you think you are a weak reader, then practise. You can also resort to records or tapes of others reading, although this isn't really advisable especially with primary children. Tapes are too distant and disembodied, and can dissipate the immediacy of the poem's impact, whereas the living voice of a responsive human being alive in body and spirit in front of the class makes for a directness that can move a class to laughter or to tears.

I propose now to look at two poems by Walter de la Mare to show what I mean by expressive reading. 'Five Eyes' is suitable for 6–9-year-olds.

FIVE EYES

In Hans' old Mill his three black cats
Watch his bins for the thieving rats.
Whisker and claw, they crouch in the night,
Their five eyes smouldering green and bright:
Squeaks from the flour sacks, squeaks from where
The cold wind stirs on the empty stair,
Squeaking and scampering, everywhere.
Then down they pounce, now in, now out,
At whisking tail, and sniffing snout;
While lean old Hans he snores away
Till peep of light at break of day;
Then up he climbs to his creaking mill,
Out come his cats all grey with meal —
Jekkel, and Jessup, and one-eyed Jill.

As this poem has its setting in a mill, it is useful to start off by clarifying by means of questions just what a mill is and what it is used for. We also need to find out that our pupils know what cats are kept for when not kept as pets. The first line of the poem has no punctuation at the end of it. This is a helpful guide because it suggests there is no reason to pause at the end of the line. Make sure your breath is big enough to carry over into the second line without a break. Then pause after 'rats'. The third line needs to be said clearly and distinctly to convey all the deliberation of cats getting into a position of readiness. I would emphasize the long vowels in 'smouldering' by speaking the word slowly. A brief pause at the colon before changing in tone completely. The word 'squeaks' requires a highish pitch to suggest a rat, and the next three lines should be speeded up considerably to contrast with the previous stillness of the cats. 'Then *down* they *pounce*, now *in*, now *out*' has a pouncing rhythm to show the cats are actually doing their job and it needs a little emphasis in the reading. Then after 'snout', stop abruptly and read the next two lines much more leisurely to contrast the stillness of Hans with his cats' activity.

'Snow' is a beautiful, descriptive poem also by de la Mare. It lacks the drama of 'Five Eyes' but has its own inimitable fragility. It is suitable for 9–12-year-olds.

Snow

No breath of wind,
No gleam of sun —
Still the white snow
Whirls softly down —

Twig and bough
And blade and thorn
All in an icy
Quiet, forlorn.
Whispering, rustling,
Through the air,
On sill and stone,
Roof — everywhere,
It heaps its powdery
Crystal flakes,
Of every tree
A mountain makes;
Till pale and faint
At shut of day,
Stoops from the West
One wintry ray.
And, feathered in fire,
Where ghosts the moon,
A robin shrills
His lonely tune.

This needs to be read in a soft voice with a sense of the hushed atmosphere of a snow-covered world. The only difficulty is that caused by the punctuation in the middle of the poem. Stop after 'roof' as the dash tells us to do. Carry 'everywhere' in meaning over into the next line: 'everywhere it heaps . . .'. Pause at 'flakes' before taking a breath for 'Of every tree/A mountain makes'. Then the 'one' ray that stoops from the West needs emphasis; after all, it is *only one*. The final image, so ordinary in actual fact, so radiant and mysterious in de la Mare's rendering of it, requires a change of tone to awe and wonder.

However, even if we do not try to become good readers, these poems will still work with most of our junior-age pupils. But they do succeed with all pupils on every occasion if presented with verve and vigour, and a bit of thought given over to the actual mechanics of the reading.

FIRST READING

The next most important consideration is the first reading. It is important that pupils have a textbook or duplicated sheet in front of them, which they can follow as the teacher reads to them. This reinforces the idea of reading as a process and connects the pleasure visually with print. This is very important if we are introducing poetry in order to encourage our pupils in their own further reading for pleasure. Moreover, it is impossible for volunteers to read after you if they haven't their own copies in front of them — and you *will* definitely be inundated with volunteers. It's only fair to allow half a dozen or so to re-read, either the whole poem or a verse each.

Sidney Bolt and Roger Gard (1970, p. 36) underline the importance of pupils following from a text in front of them while the teacher reads. It means that no pupil

is reading on his own. His reading of the page is reinforced by the teacher's: the emphasis and tone of the teacher's voice brings out structures and implications which might otherwise require excavation. Moreover, the class stays together throughout the reading, instead of splitting up into a horde, migrating through the book, with rapid readers spurring ahead and slow readers straggling miles behind in the rear . . . The experience therefore is very similar told orally without benefit of text. Nevertheless, the presence of the text does make a crucial difference at certain times, one of which is when irony is in question. It is a text for the teacher, just as it is for the pupil. Although the teacher speaks the words, they are not *his* words. The teacher, therefore, can speculate about what the words mean in company with his pupils and if irony is involved he stands in the same relation to it as they do.

What is imperative is that we as teachers do the first reading of the poem to the class. This is because we will already be well acquainted with it, having read it at home beforehand. More than that, we will have given it a certain amount of careful thought and practised our reading of it. In other words, only we can give the poem a really expressive reading at this stage. And that reading will make our pupils' first encounter with the poem a really memorable one. An expressive reading conveys meaning by inflexion and tone alone, making explanation redundant.

We must not forget that this reading is likely to be our pupils' first encounter with the poem and however slight the poem is, it gains their interest more rapidly if the first reading is an expressive one. Even a good pupil reader of mature years will not convey meaning half so well as a teacher, and may well stumble in places simply through lack of prior knowledge.

We teachers, then, should always do the first reading aloud of our chosen poems to the class. After that, we should certainly invite volunteers to read aloud their favourite one or parts thereof. In my experience, pupils are almost desperate to read something they really enjoyed. If the poem you have chosen is a demanding one and you intend to encourage some talk about it, then the pupils ought to be asked to re-read the poem silently to themselves. Only after that silent reading start to promote talk. After all, the pupils have only just met the poem for the very first time. If you are actually going to go so far as to ask questions, then the class must be given time to read the poem several times in order to become better acquainted with it. If we wish all our pupils to have the chance of answering and showing their appreciation — not just the bright ones who may well grasp most of a poem's implied meanings on a first reading — then a silent reading by all is imperative, followed perhaps by a second reading by the teacher.

QUESTIONING

If, at the secondary level especially, you feel duty bound to ask questions, do try not to. But if you absolutely must, there are gentler ways of doing it than using a battery of comprehension-type exercises. At the secondary level, Benton and Fox suggest using questions of an open, general nature 'inviting the reader both to attend to the words and to frame and value the individuality of his own experience' (1987, p. 24). They single out four areas for comment — on language, form, observation and feeling. For example,

On Language
   What words, phrases or lines stood out — for whatever reason — when you were reading or listening?

On Form
   Can you say anything about the shape of the poem, how the words were laid out on the page?

Do you notice any patterns?
What effect does such a shape have on you?

(Ibid.)

At the junior/middle level, broad, open questions on the *language* of a poem are possible even with the youngest juniors. Such questions can become a way of deepening appreciation while the class is still in the process of sharing its enjoyment of a poem. For example, 'Are there any words or lines or expressions that you really liked or were impressed by?' is a question that helps to focus attention clearly on the language of the poem while still respecting pupils' own personal responses. It is not a question we are likely to want to ask very frequently as few of the poems we read to 7-year-olds will have anything particularly noteworthy about their language. But now and then it is helpful to highlight the importance of the language of a poem, for it is the words and their particular order and arrangement that make a poem memorable.

At the early secondary level, it may do no harm just occasionally to ask rather more questions closely related to the text; in other words, to study a poem. In doing so, it is a good idea to make sure one has a mixture of carefully sequenced questions, some straightforwardly factual, some deductive, that is, requiring inferences rather than citing what is directly stated. When the questioning is over, always complete the 'work' on the poem with a volunteer or two reading the *whole* poem aloud again. After analysis must come synthesis. Do not leave your pupils' last impression of a poem at the dissected, fragmented stage, like pieces of chopped-up meat on a butcher's slab. Put it together again for the sake of the pupils' response to the totality that is a poem — its music as well as its meaning — which, however thorough we have been in our questioning, we can never plumb utterly.

Questioning can add variety to our approach but should only be an *occasional* technique for finishing a lesson (i.e. follow-up work) and not our regular way of doing it. Otherwise we shall taint poetry with the same instrumentalist and materialist odour that has invaded other aspects of the English subject area. The hidden curriculum of 'use/exploit' in order to promote talk, writing, etc., applies especially to the prose literature, usually in extracts, that children get in school. None of it is ever allowed to speak for itself to each individual pupil. I remember being besotted with *Wuthering Heights* as a teenager and used to re-read it at least two or three times a year until, by the time I was interviewed for a place at university, I was quite expert on it. I had not studied it for any exams nor had it been presented to my class in the form of extracts with emphasis on the themes that the teacher saw in it. My pleasure in it was very personal and I should not have wanted to divulge why to any teacher. Fortunately, in those days teaching methods were more tactful.

Encouraging intellectual curiosity and further reading are surely among our main aims in teaching. They certainly over-ride whatever is the latest 'good cause' that teachers are intent on using literature to explore and debate. I speak as someone committed in my personal capacity to many good causes, but it is not my place to condition pupils into accepting my views by raising 'issues' I think important.

Back to the vexed business of questioning. As with all things in teaching there are a number of dos and don'ts. Here are a few helpful tips. First, always avoid questions that require yes/no answers. They are useless because they do not promote any thought. They come too pat and lead nowhere. Secondly, never ask a class their opinion of a poem. This serves no useful purpose and actually encourages disaffection. Eric Morecambe's 'Rubbish!' is a real cul-de-sac answer! Liking is actually immaterial to promoting the *understanding* of a poem, which setting questions is concerned with. Primary children usually like everything we read to them; it's simply that some poems are *more popular* than others. Next, always keep questions to the minimum.

It is important, too, to sequence our questions very carefully, with the easiest at the start. This ensures commitment from the whole class, even its less able members, who will actually be able to understand and answer early questions. We should try, if possible, to include deductive questions. As one of the higher-order intellectual skills, deductive thinking (drawing inferences, seeing what is implied rather than directly stated) is more difficult than simple recapitulation of statement. It should, therefore, be left till last. It's also much easier for all pupils, including the less able ones, to have a go at the more difficult, deductive questions if the earlier questions have helped to deepen their understanding of the poem. For this reason, questions ought to lead back into the poem and not away from it.

But, whatever else you do, try to refrain from asking absolutely obvious, simple-minded questions like 'How many gipsies stood at the castle gate?' in 'The Wraggle Taggle Gipsies'. The number (three) is irrelevant to the poem and such a question does nothing to deepen the pupils' grasp of why the lady runs away to join the gipsies, leaving her 'new-wedded lord' as well as all the material possessions the poem so lovingly catalogues — golden rings, goose-feathered bed, sheets, fashionable shoes, silken gown. Comprehension-type questions of this nature are simply mechanical.

If questions must be asked at the secondary level, then I would suggest the occasional use of something along the lines of the following as appropriate for first and second years or top-middle-school pupils. The poem is 'The Wraggle Taggle Gipsies':

1. How does the gipsies' music affect the lady when she hears it? (Simple factual recall — she cries; it has awakened her emotionally.)
2. What state or mood do you think the lady is in before the gipsies come, as suggested by line 4 of the first verse? (Straightforward interpretation of figurative language — she's unhappy or in an emotionally arrested state as 'her heart is like snow'.)
3. What exactly does the lady give up to run off with the gipsies? (Factual recall — various material things as well as her new husband.)
4. What details suggest the lady's life has been very comfortable up to the point when the gipsies appear? (Factual recall coupled with interpretation of detail.)
5. What do you think her life will be like with the gipsies? (Interpretation of details of physical hardship as well as opinion and inference — something possibly more intangible.)
6. How does her husband try to persuade her to return to him? What do you think he ought to have said, but didn't? (Factual recall of material things he tempts her with and inference — no reference to love.)
7. Why is it, do you think, that the lady goes off with the gipsies and rejects her comfortable life and her new husband? (Deduction, evaluation and opinion.)

READING, THINKING AND FEELING

A poetry lesson in the junior school should, quite simply, be 20–40 minutes of shared enjoyment in reading poems. This is the point I wish to stress. It is reading that is crucial here, not talk or writing — especially not writing. A poetry lesson is for listening, reading, thinking and feeling. The reading need lead nowhere, neither stimulate nor provoke anything other than an interest in reading more poetry together as a class. It is, in other words, a discrete lesson, that is, one that is self-contained. This runs counter to what we have been told in our training. But experience and the evidence in Chapter 1 support the view that reading poetry for itself alone has far-reaching, intangible effects, not least of which is that it encourages a love of reading, a recognition that reading and pleasure can go hand in hand.

Once we have introduced and read aloud expressively our selection of poems to our class, we should as a matter of course invite pupil-volunteers to chose the one they most enjoyed and, individually, read it aloud to the rest of the class. They don't have to move from their seats. And never mind if one poem is read more often than another.

Repetition is a compliment. In fact, it is a good idea to set aside one lesson every so often for the reading again of favourite poems from previous weeks' or terms' lessons. It is true that the more a piece of literature is re-read, the more the reader can see in it. Re-reading is the simplest of strategies, but it too can help to deepen appreciation, as Walter de la Mare (1953, p. 497) explains:

> At every reading of a poem, though it may have been familiar from early childhood, some hitherto hidden delicacy of rhythm or intonation may be revealed. Indeed, what is read on the printed page is merely so many words. It is the reader alone who out of them can create a *poem*, and this poem changes for him as he himself changes with the years.

As I have already suggested, the poetry lesson, if it does anything, promotes reading, thinking, and feeling. Do not be afraid if children respond quietly, even silently, to what a poet has said, and said in his own inimitable way. We all need the chance sometimes to reflect in awed and grateful silence. Children's 'work' in a poetry lesson is largely personal and internal.

The poetry lesson has the potential to be one of the profoundest experiences pupils are ever likely to have at school and yet it is, paradoxically, one of the easiest lessons to set up and prepare for. In fact, the less we intervene as teachers, the more the poet's own thoughts have a chance to percolate into our pupils' minds and souls. No great range of materials or supplementary ideas on our part is called for. All that is actually needed is a textbook or duplicated sheets printed with poems we like. Obviously, if we choose duplicated sheets, then the typing and lay-out must be clear and easy to read, bearing in mind that some 6–8-year-olds are still finding the mechanical business of reading something of a hurdle. In consideration of this, it is better perhaps to find some poetry books to use with the infant and youngest junior classes.

VISUAL AIDS

No visual-display material is needed, as poems creat their own pictures in the individual mind of the reader. There is no equipment, no open spaces to find, either. And what is more, there is no 'teaching' as such to do. Nothing could be more straighforward and simple.

The preparation at home — examining a wide variety of poems so as to make a successful selection and practising an expressive reading aloud — is where our work as teachers lies. The only time visual material is helpful is when we occasionally read poems all by the same poet in one lesson. It adds variety and interest to our lesson to provide a few biographical details in order to bring the poet to life. Then it is really helpful to our pupils to put up on the classroom walls some portrait posters or postcards to show just what he looked like, where he lived, etc. The National Portrait Gallery holds postcard portraits of most English poets.

With Wordsworth, for example, the fact that he lived in the Lake District is crucial to the emotional content of his poetry and therefore a picture or two of the lakes at their most scenic (taken from a travel brochure perhaps) would also be valuable, especially for urban children with no experience of mountainous regions. William Blake was a painter and engraver as well as a poet and, like children, illustrated his own poems. Some of these illustrations are available from the Tate Gallery.

What we should avoid is trying to provide pictures that will remove the effort of recreating the mental picture the poem encourages us to make. Just like writing itself, reading is an active, making, creating process, so that exterior visualization of the subject of a poem intervenes between the child and his effort of recreation. It makes him passive and lazy. Worst of all, it gives him a 'realized' version that comes between him and his experience of the poem. Children do actually enjoy the abstract process of visualizing and making their own response without teacher intervention. After all, we are simply allowing them to be responsible and free in their response to literature. And who is to say that a child's picture is any worse than a teacher's because it is different? We all bring different preoccupations and experiences to our response to literature. Ultimately, the popularity of the poetry lesson lies in the respect and trust we accord our pupils' own visualizing powers.

SEATING ARRANGEMENTS

For poetry to be successful it also requires, at least initially, a whole-class teaching situation. This means it is very difficult in 'open-plan' schools where 'individualized learning' holds sway and where constant activity and its attendant noise is the order of the day. Poetry must be read aloud to the whole class so that a shared experience is possible. The shared feelings are the more intense for being shared. A traditional class arrangement, even down to the minutiae of desks facing the teacher so that all children focus on the teacher reading, is essential to encourage attention and to give the teacher potential eye contact with every pupil. Without the attention of all our pupils we cannot develop their interest (or motivation) nor that special atmosphere that a poetry lesson will evoke when all minds are concentrating as one on a poet's words.

For that reason, a poem needs peace and quiet, as well as full attention, to work its magic on our pupils' minds and hearts. Our first reading cannot, therefore, take place in anything other than silence within the classroom and as far as possible outside it. Abandon doing poetry if workmen are digging up the playground outside your windows. Reduce all possible distractions to a minimum. There can be no wandering off, nor intruders from other areas.

Such undisturbed quiet is not an end in itself, but a means to securing our pupils' access to a poet's thoughts. Some poems are such delicate, almost reticent, little artefacts that anything less than full attention will not allow them to make any impression on our pupils. Arthur Waley's translation of the Chinese gem entitled 'Homecoming', Robert Frost's 'A Tuft of Flowers', and Thomas Hardy's 'On Midsummer Eve' (all suitable for top-middle pupils — 12 and over) are all cases in point. How flat and dead they would fall if subject to the noise and activity that 'performance poets' experience. In fact, noise and movement during a poetry lesson restricts the kind of poetry we can read to our classes, limiting us to the loud, instantly attention-grabbing attractions of humorous verse, ruling out deeper and more delicate pieces.

SUMMARY

It is important to make the bulk of our poetry lessons discrete, self-contained 'reading-as-pleasure' lessons. If we don't, we simply 'exploit' or 'use' poetry for other ends and risk such a hidden curriculum influencing our pupils. The basic and regular format of the lesson should be reading aloud with talk and questions from pupils generated by the interest in the poems, followed by pupil-volunteers reading. We are then free to vary that format from time to time, with visual material of a biographical nature and with a range of follow-up work, including choral reading, as we shall see in the next chapter.

Chapter 4

Choral Speaking

Just as songs are meant to be sung and seem pretty thin gruel without their accompanying music, so poetry is meant to be spoken aloud (and listened to), not just read by the eye and heard by the inner ear. In its early history, poetry was an oral art, akin to music. Primitive societies that had not yet developed writing always possessed their own poetry, orally composed and delivered. The sharing with others in the tribe or collective group made for much of the poetry's power to move its listeners.

Since the advent of literacy, poetry has become a closet activity, read silently by individuals — an occupation for a solitary moment. This has, in its turn, affected the kind of poetry poets have chosen to write. It has become much more introspective, meditative and complex. There is nothing inherently wrong in this. Indeed, complex poems actually repay close attention and only yield up all their implications after detailed study. Since the advent of public examinations, poetry in school has also been much subjected to close and detailed study. And this approach, fitting perhaps for sixth formers, has percolated down most inappropriately to third, second, and even first years. It is inappropriate for such young children because study requires poetry of a certain kind — that which can be studied; in other words, poetry that is complex, serious (if not solemn), that is susceptible to close and detailed analysis. And so even pupils who have just transferred to secondary school get further and further away from the sort of spoken verse they all so much enjoy as young primary pupils.

As the Opies reveal in their many books, it is very young primary children who still chant, intone, sing, speak (in other words, vocalize) poetry — in the form of nursery rhymes, skipping rhymes, rhyming adjuncts to playground and street games. Rhymes live on in children's play if nowhere else and are still a potent source of delight. It shouldn't be difficult, therefore, for primary/middle teachers to bring this love of speaking verse into the classroom.

James Reeves (1958, p. 21) defined the choral speaking of poetry (or verse) in school as 'the *organised* speaking of poetry aloud'. In other words, it is active participation by the pupils under the direction of the teacher. He also describes it as 'the acting of poetic form' (*ibid.*) We shall see what this means later when I make suggestions about how to divide some poems for choral purposes.

It is a truism that young children are especially responsive to poetry because they enjoy sound and rhythm so much. They are in the primitive phase of their development so that words have a magical potency, especially when combined with a strong musical beat or well-marked rhythm. The speaking aloud of poetry is useful vocal practice for them, which we should not scorn but, on the other hand, we should also beware of making it the be-all and end-all of our poetry lessons. However, it is much more than simply vocal practice. It is also a means to poetic appreciation. This last point is stressed by both James Reeves and Clive Sansom, the only recent (1958 and 1978 respectively!) advocates of choral speaking in schools who have written helpfully on the subject for teachers. Their two books cannot be recommended too highly. What they mean by 'poetic appreciation' is that to speak a poem well can only be done with feeling and understanding.

RHYTHM RHYMES

Before teachers tackle choral speaking in a poetry lesson, Sansom recommends that they first do much reading aloud of poetry to the whole class (as already suggested in earlier chapters) so as to foster the children's love of poetry. He and Reeves also recommend as an essential preliminary the use of rhythm rhymes 'to guide children's physical and emotional response to rhythm' (Sansom, 1978, p.117). It is my view that even if guidance is necessary, the children may well need to practise choral speaking on easy little rhymes before launching into the oral delivery of longer and syntactically more complex poetry and verse. Clive Sansom and his wife, Ruth, have compiled several booklets of delightful rhymes for this purpose, and it would be a loss to one's pupils not to include them as the best of them have all the qualities of traditional nursery rhymes. Some are so simple that even infants and hesitant readers among 7-year-olds love to speak them (see *Rhythm Rhymes*, by Ruth Sansom, A & C Black, London, 1964, and *Speech Rhymes, Counting Rhymes* and *Acting Rhymes*, by Clive Sansom, A & C. Black, London, 1974–5).

There are also books designed specifically by speech therapists for practice with children who have a speech impediment. Though written by experts in speech training, their rhymes and jingles lend themselves perfectly to choral practice because they encourage that clear enunciation that can in itself be so enjoyable for early work in choral speaking. *A Book of Rhymes and Jingles*, by W. Kingdom Ward (A. & C. Black, London, 1954), is a useful example. It contains the following rhythm rhyme-cum-tongue-twister called 'Ducky-Daddles' that is suitable for both infants and youngest juniors:

> Ducky-Daddles
> Loves the puddles.
> How he waddles
> As he paddles
> In the puddles —
> Ducky Daddles!

Trippingly on the Tongue, by Mona Swann (Macmillan, London, 1951), is an excellent booklet of rhythm rhymes, although hard to come by, having been last reprinted more than 35 years ago. It has many indispensable examples including 'Feather Game', (p. 19) and 'Stitching Game' (see later), which exercise both the 'f' and the voiced and breathed 'th':

Feather Game
Puff, puff,
Puff the fluff
And fly, feather, fly;
Puff, puff,
That's enough —
It's far, far off in the sky.

These little rhymes develop confidence in speaking, promote clarity of speech as well and, as an added bonus, are *fun* because many of them come close to being tongue-twisters, when uttered aloud. Once confidence has developed, children can move on to 'dramatic speaking'. In other words, they should be encouraged to put in emphasis, alter tone and inflexion. They will find this easy to do if they are practising with rhythm rhymes because they offer a very small compass and easy thought-patterns. If no intellectual demands are made (by way of difficult vocabulary and syntax), the child's mind is then freed to concentrate on expressiveness.

EXPRESSIVE READING

But no child is going to speak expressively if the class teacher doesn't set a good example of expressive and lively reading. It is crucial that the children's first experience of a poem is through an expressive reading. It is this which generates interest. In the context of the primary and middle school this means that

the foremost part of the teacher's equipment is to be able to speak verse in such a way as to give pleasure to those who hear . . . Verse speaking can be learned by anyone whose voice is not badly defective and who is prepared to take a bit of trouble.
(L. A. G. Strong, 1946, p. 14)

The importance of practising one's reading aloud beforehand at home, and of annotating one's own book or duplicated sheet so as not to forget what decisions one made at leisure in the quiet of one's home about one's pauses, change of tone, speed, etc., need to be stressed again. The bustle and stress of the school day can easily force such delicate matters out of one's mind, if they haven't already been committed to writing.

Here are two examples of what is meant by annotation to promote expressiveness. Mona Swann's 'Stitching Game' (1951, p. 20), which incidentally provides useful exercise for both the breathed and voiced 'th' (so often expressed as 'f'), is a lively rhyme much enjoyed by infants. As it involves two speakers we could try to adopt two different voices. If that is too difficult, then the 'my' in the second line should be given some stress to indicate an opposing viewpoint:

'My thread is too *thick*!' ⎫	Say with surprise or exasperation.
'*My* thread is too thin!' ⎭	Slight stress on 'thick'
'So this is the thing we'll do;	explanatory tone
We both will ask mother	carry this line over quickly to the next
To give us another,	pause slightly

And with it a thimble, too!'   Pause slightly after 'with it' and raise voice for 'thimble' because they are asking for something extra.

If we give thought as to how to speak a poem or rhyme, we shall encourage our pupils to do so, too. Some words or phrases lend themselves to emphasis; others require a pause before being uttered; still others, a different inflexion or tone of voice. The whole point is to convey meaning more effectively without sacrificing the rhythm. Clive Sansom's 'The Dustman' (1974b) is very lively and much loved:

Every Thursday morning   slight stress on 'every'
Before we're quite awake   slow, quiet, as if waking up
Without the slightest warning
The house begins to shake.
    With a Biff! Bang!   }
    Biff! Bang! Biff!   }   quick, clear
It's the dustman who begins
    Bang! Crash!
To empty all the bins
Of their rubbish and their ash
    With a Biff! Bang!   }
    Biff! Bang! Bash!   }   loud, clear, quick

These are lovely noisy rhymes which can be given just that extra fillip by some careful thought. The first line can be said with a little annoyance creeping into the voice, and perhaps a little stress on *every*, while the second line can be said more slowly and quietly than the first line, as if the speaker has indeed not yet properly woken up. Such a reading at the start helps to contrast with the noise of the rest of the rhyme. The refrain, which stresses the racket the dustman makes, should be said clearly and quickly.

Even simple rhymes like these two benefit from careful thought and preparation. Never be loath or too busy to practise them at leisure beforehand. Nothing is more likely than an expressive reading to lead children from indifference to poetry into a newly found interest in it and in reading it. If your pupils are already enthusiastic converts to poetry, then not to practise beforehand is to let them and their interest down. In my experience a good, lively, even dramatic reading by the teacher can encourage pupils to overstep the bounds of the lesson, so to speak, by going in their own time, voluntarily, to the school or public library to borrow books of verse. Pupils of mine regularly borrowed the duplicated sheets we had read in class so that they could take them home to copy out their favourites into personal anthologies they had started to compile in their own time, such was the interest generated. Further voluntary reading and writing can only be beneficial for the child's own language development.

WAYS OF DIVIDING POEMS AND GROUPING PUPILS

It is important to stress at the outset that choral speaking does not mean the whole class speaking a whole poem in unison. That is designed to kill poetry or even good verse stone dead. Thirty voices speaking at once lose their natural flexibility and become slow and monotonous. The individual feels he is not personally involved and ceases to think or imagine for himself and so stops trying to convey meaning. The chant takes over, which is undesirable for poetry although permissible for the chore of learning things by rote like tables. It is advisable, therefore, to avoid at all times *long stretches* of whole-class unison speech.

Clive Sansom (1978, p. 117) suggests there are three ways of tackling poetry speaking in the classroom:

1. Group speaking using the whole class under the teacher's direction.
2. Group speaking using small independent groups.
3. Individual speaking.

Poems chosen for choral treatment should naturally fall into different sections — for individual speakers, for small groups, and/or the whole class. This is why it is so important for us to read and prepare beforehand. However, it is a crucial rule that the division of a poem should only be dictated by *the form of the poem* and not by other considerations, like involving as many pupils as possible. For example, question and answer poems such as 'Where Are You Going To, My Pretty Maid?' or 'The Key of my Heart' (with its suppressed questions) separate logically into two groups (or two single speakers):

Where Are You Going to, My Pretty Maid?

(*group of*) *Boy(s)*	'Where are you going to, my pretty maid?'
(*group of*) *Girl(s)*	'I'm going a-milking, sir,' she said.
B	'May I come with you, my pretty maid?'
G	'You're kindly welcome, sir,' she said.
B	'What is your father, my pretty maid?'
G	'My father's a farmer, sir,' she said.
B	'What is your fortune, my pretty maid?'
G	'My face is my fortune, sir,' she said.
B	'Then I cannot marry you, my pretty maid?'
G	'Nobody asked you, sir,' she said.

The Key of my Heart

Boy	Madam, I will give you a new lace cap
	With embroidery on the bottom and insertion on the top,
	If you will be my bride, my joy and only dear
	To walk and talk with me everywhere.
Girl	Sir, I will not accept of your new lace cap
	With embroidery on the bottom and insertion at the top.
	I won't be your bride, your joy and only dear
	To walk and talk with you everywhere.

. . .

'Soldier, Soldier', another question and answer poem, requires a narrator or narrative group in addition to its two speakers:

Soldier, Soldier

Girl	Soldier, soldier, won't you marry me
	With your musket, fife and drum?
Boy	Oh, no, sweet maid, I cannot marry you
	For I have no hat to put on.
Narrator/or small	*So up she went to her grandfather's chest*
narrative group	*And she brought him a hat of the very, very best*
	And the soldier put it on.

. . .

'Who's That Ringing?', in part a question-and-answer poem (suitable for infants), has a refrain in addition to its two speakers. This suggests a way of involving the whole class:

Speaker 1	Who's that ringing at the front door bell?
All	Miau! Miau! Miau!
Speaker 2	I'm a little black cat and I'm not very well.
All	Miau! Miau! Miau!
Speaker 1	Then put your nose in this bowl of mutton fat.
All	Miau! Miau! Miau!
Speaker 2	For that's the way to cure a little pussy cat!
All	Miau! Miau! Miau!

This whole-class involvement can become an excellent opportunity for what James Reeves (1958, p.33) calls an 'exercise in vocal expressiveness'. Once the class has practised saying the refrain in unison, they should be encouraged to see how each line of the refrain can be said in a different tone of voice to reflect the cat's changing fortunes. Line 2 is introductory; line 4 can be spoken pitifully; line 6 longingly; while line 8 can suggest he's fully cured by being said in a strong and vigorous tone. Otherwise it is difficult for such a simple refrain to avoid taking on a monotonous sing-song. Ballads like 'The Riddling Knight' and sea shanties like 'The Golden Vanity' (for 10–13-year-olds) often need a narrator or small narrative group, two or three solo speakers who have dialogue to speak, and the whole class to speak the chorus or refrain.

Some poems are cumulative in their effect, starting with one or two short lines in the first verse, adding extra lines to each consecutive verse until they end with the last verse of twelve or more longish lines. 'The House That Jack Built' (anon.) and 'The Train to Glasgow' (Wilma Horsbrugh) are like this. A cumulative rendering would begin with one speaker, another joining in on the second verse until finally ten or more speak the last verse together. However, a word of warning: if you are working with 6–7-year-olds, and particularly with those children who are still unsure of their reading skill, this cumulative approach may be too hard. There is no reason why you shouldn't make a slight alteration. After all, the point of choral work is not that it should test reading ability but that it *should make poetry enjoyable*. Assign a different speaker for each verse as you would for a cumulative reading, but simply require each speaker to speak his or her verse singly (at least for the first two or three readings). That is enjoyable in itself, as long as you bear in mind the golden rule that among 6–7-year-olds and weak or early readers the verses should be apportioned according to reading ability — the ablest allotted the longest verses at the end, the weakest given the shortest and therefore easiest verses at the start of the poem. Try not to leave the weak readers out simply because they're weak, unless they specifically indicate an unwillingness to have a go. Most children, however weak, are desperate to read aloud a poem (or part of one) they enjoyed hearing.

There are, of course, poems which actually require this division into a succession of separate voices. In other words, they fall naturally into this form. 'The Bonny Bride of Kent' by Eleanor Farjeon starts and ends with a narrator but within that frame has a series of different suitors suggesting just how they individually might improve the bride's life for her. It's a poem for at least eight speakers, including the narrator. As the narrator's lines resemble a refrain and are short and uncomplicated, they can be spoken by the rest of the class in unison while the separate suitors are spoken by individuals. In that way the whole class can be involved without forcing the poem out of its natural form.

The anonymously written 'Cock Robin' lends itself to the same presentation. It isn't often, however, that one poem will manage to involve the whole class, nor should the teacher force the poem to do so against its own grain, so to speak. That is not to say that only a few members of the class will ever read. There is nothing to stop you allowing every individual member of the class to read a rhyme like 'The Dustman' if such is their wish. If 'Soldier, Soldier' were divided between only one boy, one girl and a narrator, there is no reason why it shouldn't be presented ten times, so that all have a chance to be involved. However, to avoid the (unlikely) possibility of boredom setting in from such frequent repetition, have another poem or two as stand-bys, limit readings to three or four repeats and then move on to a different poem for those who haven't yet had the pleasure of reading. It is important to give everyone a chance to read, should they so wish, not just the noisy pupils or the good readers.

WHEN NOT TO DIVIDE

What we should never do is *unnecessarily* divide a poem, because this will produce a fragmented impression in the minds of the children even if it involves more of them. I have in mind the 'senseless vandalism' that Clive Sansom (1978, p.130) refers to of having different speakers for narrative and direct speech:

Speaker 1	'The time has come,' (direct speech)
Speaker 2	the Walrus said, (narrative)
Speaker 1	'To talk of many things' (direct speech)

Such a presentation is unnecessary and destroys utterly the continuity of the poem and ruins its atmosphere or mood. The poem becomes reduced to a mere vocal exercise when it should be an enjoyable experience of reading aloud *with meaning*.

Some poems should never be divided in any way: poems that are personal, lyrical or reflective and poems whose compactness or continuity of thought or idea would be fatally damaged by division. For these, unison presentation by the whole class is also inappropriate. But that does not rule out unison speaking by small groups of children. For example, the eerie atmosphere of R. L. Stevenson's 'Windy Nights' would collapse completely if it was subjected to the battery of a whole-class reading. Its light, quick, airy rhythm would change to a slow plod. But a group of two or three children can certainly convey the magic of that invisible entity we call the wind. The mysteriousness of Walter de la Mare's 'Someone' would be destroyed by division and also needs unison presentation by a small group if its rhythm is not to become facile and insistent.

SPEAKING WITH MEANING

It isn't just the number of children speaking that affects the reading, as James Reeves is careful to point out. Even a group of two or three could speak in a lifeless, mechanical fashion if they have not been encouraged to speak *with meaning*. Even though choral speaking indirectly exercises such reading skills as correct pronunci-ation, this should *not* be our principal reason for tackling it. The emphasis must be placed on understanding the meaning of the poem and attempting to convey that meaning through the medium of the voice. Correctness is secondary. Slovenly speech that slurs words is undesirable, of course, because it hinders proper comprehension on the part of the audience. This normally takes care of itself, as children display a strong tendency to self-correction, especially when speaking aloud. Prior practice with speech rhymes is invaluable in improving weakness or slovenliness.

If speaking with meaning is our first aim, then long before the first reading aloud the mind of the readers must be focused on the meaning above all. The teacher can do this easily by introductory comments which encourage the class to visualize the poem or to share its feelings by referring to similar experiences in the children's own lives. Even some exploratory questioning would be in order because, contrary to reading poetry for pleasure, only poems or verses that are fully understood should be presented chorally. For example, to grasp fully the meaning of 'Soldier, Soldier', and convey that understanding adequately through the voice, one's pupils would need to realize (either through questions or comments) that the soldier isn't very fair or honest. He leads the girl on, in her quest for a uniformed husband, to give him all sorts of useful civilian garments and it's only when he's fully equipped that he casually reveals he's already married. He could and should have told her at the outset this crucial fact about his situation. However, such honesty would not have gained him her grandfather's outfit. How should the boys speak the soldier? As greedy and cunning or as someone who simply realizes he's on to a good thing and is prepared to try his luck — an amiable rogue?

Each verse of 'Where Are You Going to, My Pretty Maid?' requires a different tone from each speaker. The gentleman begins by asking *casually* where the maid is going. She replies *factually*. He then asks *politely* if he may walk with her. The maid replies equally *politely* (perhaps secretly pleased). He asks *with interest* what her father does. She replies *factually*. Then *much more keenly* he asks what her fortune amounts to. The maid replies *proudly* that her face alone constitutes her fortune. The gentleman *reluctantly* (or *snobbishly*) rejects her. The maid has the last word and *haughtily* rejects him. As the bracketed alternatives suggest, there is no definitive reading of this verse — it is the way I should decide to read the poem to my class as their introduction to it prior to a choral reading. They might well decide on some other emphasis and would be free to do so. However, it does need variety of tone throughout, because otherwise it will simply take on a sing-song chant, especially if they have already become acquainted with it in music.

In 'The Key of my Heart' the lady finally agrees to marry the young man after refusing him four times. What produces her acceptance is the offer of his *heart*, not a range of precious or pretty material things. Does this mean he is too timid or shy to offer himself at the start, thinking that he personally is not sufficiently worthy? Does the lady's tone change through the poem, betraying impatience and even annoyance as she rejects all his material temptations? Or does she speak encouragingly, her tone suggesting he try again because there *is* definitely something he could offer that she would consider? It is answers to questions of this kind that will inform a dramatic reading because the answers the pupils arrive at will determine the inflexions of their voices. It is easy to see that with understanding the readings can be truly dramatic.

SPEAKING NATURALLY

We should aim to produce and to encourage in our pupils as *natural* a voice as possible. That means our speaking should be as close as possible to natural speech while not ignoring the rhythm of the poem. This especially rules out adopting plummy accents. It is important, too, not to over-emphasize syllables or pronounce too carefully in a way one would never dream of doing in ordinary speech — saying, for example, 'fount*ains*' (fountins), 'pant*ed*, (pantid), 'sudd*en*' (suddn) and 'pave*ment*' (pavemnt). There is also a danger in allowing pupils to exaggerate the rhythm and metre, so that a poem as delicate and eerie as de la Mare's 'Someone' becomes a jingle. This is very easy, even for teachers to do. It is also imperative not to allow pupils to stress unimportant words or parts of speech like prepositions and definite articles. All these warnings are unnecessary if one's pupils fully comprehend what they are reading.

GIMMICKS

Sansom and Reeves warn against the use of what they call gimmicks like background music and sound effects, because in Sansom's words (1978, p. 139), 'We cannot add to a work of art without subtracting from it'. Such gimmicks tend to suggest a certain insecurity on the part of the teacher. Just as no one ever suggests that a piano concerto by Brahms or Beethoven needs words to enhance it, so poetry requires no musical additions to improve it either. It makes its own music as well as its own meaning. It even creates its own pictures in our imaginations. Today there is a strong tendency to treat poetry like some commercial product that needs window-dressing to make it attractive to its potential consumers. As I have emphasized throughout this book, teachers need nothing more than lots of poems and a good reading voice. The poems themselves will do the rest, especially with something as active and participatory as choral speaking.

INDEPENDENT SMALL-GROUP WORK

Once the class gains some experience of choral speaking under the teacher's direction, it will be possible to separate pupils into small groups to work on the presentation of a poem independently of the teacher. This can be very beneficial in that each group of about five pupils will have to discuss a poem together and form their own opinions about how to present it. In the course of discussing how to present a poem chorally, children actually engage, albeit indirectly, in an elementary form of literary criticism. They have to examine the words and their implied meanings very closely, deduce mood and emotion and then work out how to present their conclusions vocally. This can be quite a demanding task. So, if we feel that we cannot justify doing choral speaking to our head teachers on the simple grounds of the pleasure or even vocal practice it affords, we can insist that children are having to think critically when engaged in discussing how to speak certain lines and verses.

Although in this kind of independent group work the teacher occupies a less prominent position, it doesn't follow that we have nothing to do. It actually involves as much organization and preparation beforehand as working with the whole class under the teacher's direction. Clive Sansom recommends, for example, that as a matter of course we must annotate our chosen poem or poems with the different speakers' parts clearly marked and also that we read the poem(s) aloud to the class during the week before the lesson. It goes without saying that we should also try to set the scene beforehand, as usual, by some introductory comments relating the poem to similar experiences in our pupils' lives or by encouraging them to imagine the poet's experience and share it with him. This is certainly essential, at least the first few times we embark on independent group work. It means that each group's job is simply to discuss and practise the actual *speaking* (emphasis, tone, inflexion, etc.) of their parts.

It can be argued, however, that a valuable learning experience is lost if children are not allowed at least occasionally to be given a poem totally unannotated by the teacher, so that they have to decide for themselves where the divisions ought to come. This may well be a useful learning exercise but we must bear in mind that, in effect, it will considerably expand the amount of time spent on the poem, causing it to run over into at least two lessons, maybe more. One alone will probably be needed for working out the divisions of the parts, another for debating and then practising the presentation of it. This is where the law of diminishing returns comes in. To spend more than one lesson of 45 minutes or more on only one poem quickly leads to boredom, certainly among primary and young secondary pupils. Pleasure makes a very hasty exit. If we wish to retain spontaneity and interest, then it seems that for most of the time pupils engage in independent group work they ought to be helped by being given a 'score' of the poem with the speakers' parts clearly indicated. Some practitioners of choral work, like John F. Danby (*An Approach to Poetry*, Heinemann, London, 1967, p.56) would even recommend that appropriate expressions be indicated as well. If the essence of choral work is, as Danby insists, *effective speaking as a group*, then there is no reason why we should not even add appropriate expressions to our score. Choral speaking is about 'accuracy of attack, where the combined choir is speaking, variation of speed and variation of volume' (*ibid*, p. 58).

While the groups are working independently, the teacher cannot sit back and take an entirely recessive role. We ought to move from group to group listening and tentatively offering helpful suggestions which may or may not be adopted, arbitrating perhaps between conflicting interpretations, not by edict but by suggesting a closer look at certain lines. This is sometimes easier to do than at others. It's a useful lesson for children to learn that there aren't always cut-and-dried answers and that sometimes different readings of the same poem are possible. After a tight time limit (so as to galvanize mental activity) of, say, ten or fifteen minutes of discussion and practice, the children should re-group as a whole class and each group 'present' its poem to the rest. The other groups should be invited to listen critically. This is easier to do if the class has been working in separate groups on the same poem.

PASSIVITY

Pupils should be encouraged to listen critically, ready to give praise or make sugges-tions for improvement and with their reasons why. Listening is an essential part of the process of choral speaking and a crucial skill for educational advancement. Let there be no mistake. A child is not passive when listening. He is in fact concentrating. Just because teachers cannot measure degrees of concentration that is no reason to deny children the opportunity to learn to listen. There is a tendency in education circles to assume that unless children are actively 'doing', they are not learning or responding. Marjorie Hourd, an early exponent of progressive ideas in education, was herself worried by this tendency as it ignores the quieter pleasures of literature.

> The teacher takes a poem, reads it and the class listens; that I imagine would be called passivity. Then he gets the class to talk about it, to act it, to draw it; this is activity. But some poems were not written to be acted or drawn; they may be purely lyrical in quality or wholly undramatic. In other words, it is the intrinsic nature of the thing being taught which should determine the method to be used in dealing with it.
>
> (Cited in Sansom, 1978, p. 120)

Where poetry lessons are concerned, we must never forget that because we cannot see or assess what is going on inside a child's mind or heart, it doesn't follow that its mind is blank or its heart is empty. Physical stillness is often a precondition of mental activity.

SAYING AND DOING A POEM

It is clear that what we do with a poem in the classroom should reflect that poem's unique qualities. Like Marjorie Hourd, most authorities agree that lyrical poetry suffers from activities that attempt to externalize response like acting, drawing and even group choral work. James Reeves (1958, p. 24) has some sharp words about a choral presentation he once heard of Hardy's delightful lyric, 'Weathers'.

Ballads, however, are highly dramatic poems and can even lend themselves to a semi-dramatized form of choral speaking, if we are of a mind to have a go at something a little more adventurous. It will certainly add even greater variety and flexibility to our battery of techniques for handling poetry in the classroom. John Danby (1967) has an excellent chapter on 'The Doing and Saying of Poems' in which, as an example of what he means by this, he annotates that superb medieval ballad, 'Sir Patrick Spens'. Danby indicates the speaking parts, the appropriate expressions and the actions possible within a classroom space. What follows is a summary of his suggestions for a successful lesson using this technique based on a lesson done in a normal classroom. If it strikes you as too demanding, then just use the text of the poem for choral speaking and leave out the 'doing'. However, as 'Sir Patrick Spens' is a ballad for lower secondaries or top middles (or very able top juniors), the pupils will not be too young and excitable to organize. Nor does this kind of 'dramatization' require theatrical skills on the part of the teacher.

Sir Patrick Spens

The King	The King sits in Dunfermline town
	    Drinking the blude-red wine;
	O where will I get a skeely skipper
	    To sail this new ship o' mine?

Narrator	O up and spake an eldern knight, Who sat at the king's right knee —

Lord   Sir Patrick Spens is the best sailor
               That ever sailed the sea.

King (writing letter with huge flourishes in the air, and sealing it with a ponderous fist)

               Oh, I will write a braid letter
               And seal it with my hand,
               And send it to Sir Patrick Spens
               Who's walking on the strand.

Messenger (who has taken three paces to Sir Patrick during the last line of the King's speech)

               To Norroway, to Norroway,
                 To Norroway o'er the foam.
               The king's daughter of Norroway
                 'Tis thou maun bring her home.

Narrator   The first word that Sir Patrick read
               Sae loud, loud laughéd he;
                 (*Sir Patrick does so*)
               The next word that Sir Patrick read
                 (*Sir Patrick stops and stares*)
               The tear blinded his e'e.
                 (*Sir Patrick takes out his handkerchief*)

Sir Patrick (angrily)

               O who is this has done the deed
                 And told the King o' me?
               To send us out at this time o' year
                 To sail upon the sea.
                 (*Sir Patrick turns to his gallant crew*)
               Be it wind, be it wet, be it hail, be it sleet,
                 Our ship must sail the foam;
               The King's daughter of Norroway
                 'Tis we must fetch her home.

Narrator (the gallant crew hoist sails during the first line and rock rhythmically backwards and forwards during the second and third lines, and stand out in their files facing across the classroom to where, in the next file but one, the 'lords of Norroway' are seated)

               They hoisted their sails on Monday morn,
                 With all the speed they may,
               And they have landed in Norroway
                 Upon a Wodensday.

               They hadna been a week, a week,
                 In Norroway but twae,
               When that the lords of Norroway
                 Began aloud to say:

Norway Lords
               Ye Scottish men spend our kinges gold,
                 And all our queenes fee!
Crew   Ye lie, ye lie, ye liars loud,
                 Full loud we hear ye lie!

Sir Patrick (the crew has seated itself in high dudgeon)
               Make ready, make ready, my merry men a',
                 Our gude ship sails the morn.

Sailor   Now ever alack, my master dear,
                 I fear a deadly storm.

               I saw the new moon late yestreen
                 Wi' the old moon in her arm,

And if we go to sea, master,
I fear we'll come to harm.

Narrator (during the second verse of the Narrator's speech those of the class who are not in the ship make fitting storm noises)
They hadna sailed a league, a league,
A league but barely three,
When the lift grew dark, and the wind blew loud
And gurly grew the sea.

The anchors brak, and the top masts lap,
It was sic a deadly storm;
And the waves came o'er the broken ship
Till all her sides were torn.

Sir Patrick (he rocks from side to side with his hand on the helm and his crew do likewise)
O where will I get a gude sailor,
To take my helm in hand
Till I get up to the tall top mast,
To see if I can spy land?

Second Sailor O here am I, a sailor gude,
To take the helm in hand,
Till you go to the tall top mast;
But I fear you'll ne'er spy land.

Narrator (the sailor at the helm continues to rock, and the crew with him. The background noises of the sea and wind grow louder)
He hadna gane a step, a step,
A step but barely ane,
When a bolt flew out of our gudely ship
And the salt sea it came in.

Sir Patrick Go fetch a web o' the silken cloth,
Another o' the twine,
And warp them into our ship's side,
And letnae the sea come in.

Narrator (the Scottish lords who file next to the crew, get up during the second verse, walk up and down the aisle in a finical manner on tiptoe, and are washed overboard back into their seats on the last line of the verse)
They fetched a web o' the silken cloth,
Another o' the twine,
They warped them round that gude ship's side,
But still the sea came in.

O loth, loth were our gude Scots lords
To wet their cork-heeled shoon!
But long or a' the play was played
They wet their hats aboon!

And mony was the feather bed
That fluttered on the foam,
And mony was the gude lord's son
That never mair cam' home.

(The ladies and maidens sit in the files on the side of the class farthest away from the ship. They must suit their actions to the Narrator's words)
The ladies wrang their fingers white,
The maidens tore their hair,
All for the sake of their true loves,
For them they'll see nae mair.

The Ladies	O lang, lang may we ladies sit Wi' our fans into our hands. Before we see Sir Patrick Spens Come sailing to the strand.
The Maidens	And lang, lang may we maidens sit Wi' our gold combs in our hair, Awaiting for our own dear loves, For them we'll see nae mair.

All Class (most mournfully)
    Half ower, half ower to Aberdour,
    'Tis fifty fathom deep,
    And there lies gude Sir Patrick Spens
    Wi' the Scots lords at his feet.

The saying and doing of poems is an approach which relies essentially on quick memories. The aim of the lesson is that the ballad should be successfully said and done three or four times within a 40–50 minute lesson. Because of this, Danby suggests that it is not necessary for the teacher to read through the poem from beginning to end first. Instead, the teacher should simply read the King's speech (verse 1) and then ask for a volunteer to say the King's lines. If there is no response, the teacher should read it again. By the second or third reading there is usually someone who has it *more or less* by heart. This more or less is important. We should not bother about odd errors, minor substitutions, or small verbal variations when memory fails. Archaic phrases may stick or they may well disappear to be replaced by more everyday expressions — 'lift' becoming 'sky', 'gurly' changing to 'burly', and 'the morn' turning out as 'at dawn'. Such was the process by which ballads were passed on from one speaker to another and from generation to generation. It is a useful exercise in itself as it demonstrates the ballad tradition to perfection. The main thing is that the verses should be quickly memorized. After the King's part has been taken, the teacher should go through the rest of the poem, part by part, calling for volunteers. The only pupil to have the script should be the Narrator, as he or she has most lines to speak. The different speakers/actors might be allowed small slips of paper on which to jot down helpful notes or cues. The poem is then read through once by its speakers so that they know what they have to do and can start their performance. The first performance will not be perfect and may well be halting and tentative but it will be sufficiently interesting to warrant another go at it. Successive attempts will show considerable improvement. By the third or fourth performance the children should speak with clarity, vigour and confidence.

Danby's suggestions for placing the 'actor/speakers' presuppose a traditional classroom situation. Whatever arrangement you have, the King should be placed in full view of the class at the front with the Messenger and the Lord on either side. He needs to sit on something elevated (teacher's desk?) to give him his proper importance. The Narrator should be out of the way of everyone else in an elevated corner of the room. The Narrator's voice is important and must be clear, dramatic and compelling. He has to lead the others in the rhythm when the words spoken have to be accompanied by appropriate actions. The rest of the characters in the tragedy can be arranged in groups as follows: the Crew with the First and Second Sailors, the Scots Lords, the Norway Lords, the Maidens, and the Ladies.

We do not need to adopt this particular technique every time we read a ballad with our classes. It simply offers us a lively and interesting variation on the choral-speaking approach to poetry in the classroom. Indeed, it is important to bear in mind that we avoid an excess of choral speaking itself, however popular we find it to be. If we overdo it, we take the edge off our pupils' pleasure in it. We should regard choral speaking as one of a range of possible follow-up activities.

Infants and Youngest Juniors: 5–7-year-olds

At this very young age, when children have just graduated from nursery school, poetry must be concrete, vigorous and rhythmical. Nursery rhymes are still a potent source of pleasure, partly because of their strong rhymes and rhythms, but also because of their sheer love of language, especially the *sounds* of words, however nonsensical. The 5–7-year-old shares this appreciation with pre-school children.

> There was an owl lived in an oak,
> Wisky, wasky, weedle,
> And every word he ever spoke
> Was fiddle, faddle, feedle.

Teachers should not feel embarrassed at the simplicity, even silliness (to the adult ear), of much of the verse that will be popular at this stage. Young children find a magical element in the mere sound of language — in alliteration and nonsense inventions like 'wisky, wasky, weedle'. Indeed, the pre-school child has a tendency which the 7-year-old has lost to invent his own (sometimes nonsense) rhymes and move about intoning them as if making a spell, as all parents and Chukovsky (1971, pp. 64–5) can testify. It has no doubt to do with his growing control over, and feel for, the linguistic medium which defines our humanity. It also stems from his dawning sense that it is, quite literally, a marvellous skill to be in possession of. But, essentially, very young children are truly alive to the wonder of sounds alone. They have in fact the poet's feeling for the sheer sounds (not only the meaning) of words. Like wine-tasters, they savour those sounds in a purely physical way.

This means, of course, that very young children are unusually receptive to poetry. It's a shame, therefore, that poetry reading for pleasure is so largely neglected in our primary schools. Our training emphasizes that the golden rule in teaching anything is to start from where the children are, to move from the known (and understood) to the unknown. Nothing could be easier in the case of poetry. Nursery rhymes are in fact the first poetry our pupils are likely to have come across in their brief lives. They have almost universal currency still. And an excellent introduction they prove to be. Indeed, as teachers, we cannot go wrong if we make sure we incorporate these traditional rhymes into our poetry lessons with the infants and youngest juniors, even if they already know some of them off by heart. After all, you don't just kiss a girl once, as my husband would say! If reading matter is really enjoyable, then one goes back to it time and again. This is certainly true of children, even much older ones, who never seem to tire of re-reading their favourite novels. I remember well a 12-year-old I taught at secondary school who had read *Charlotte's Web* eleven times!

THE IMPORTANCE OF NURSERY RHYMES IN EARLY LEARNING

Language Development

The importance of nursery rhymes cannot be exaggerated, especially the unobtrusive but crucial part they play in fostering children's language development. It is now realized, for example, that the traditional songs and rhymes the baby imbibes along with its mother's milk (and long after it's been weaned) are of vital importance in developing early listening skills. Chukovsky, the great Russian educator, children's writer and pioneer researcher into pre-school children's language, pointed out as long ago as 1919 that the influence of traditional nursery rhymes on young children (between the ages of 2 and 5) is to enrich their grasp of the vocabulary and structures of their native tongue. This isn't all. There are even greater benefits. Modern research findings, like those referred to in John Brierley's books, support Chukovsky's insistence that intellectual development and language development are inextricably linked:

> We must not forget also that part of our task in helping the child acquire knowledge of his spoken language is the constant enrichment of his speech with more and more new words. Since a child's mental growth is closely connected with the growth of his vocabulary, it is easy to see how important this task is. In this sense, to teach a child to speak well means also to teach him to think well. One is inseparable from the other.
>
> (1971, p. 17)

It is clear that, in the pre-school stage of language development, children learn language, like most other skills they acquire, through *imitation*. What they imitate are the norms made known to them through adult speech. Parents and teachers who have had pre-school children will know how at first they apply these norms (or rules) absolutely rigidly: 'The bird flied away, Mummy'. But in most languages the general rules governing grammatical forms have exceptions because of the living way in which languages evolve. But the child violates these in its inflexibility. Before they learn the correct forms, children make many (and, to parents, endearing) mistakes, some of which are new and perfectly intelligible inventions. The reader is recommended to consult Chukovsky's invaluable book, *From Two to Five* (University of California Press, Berkeley, 1971) for a wealth of examples.

It is, of course, extremely important that what the child hears via adult speech, and also in the literature that is read to him, *strengthens* his grasp of his native language. For children who come from a linguistically restricted home background, it must be the job, indeed the duty, of the school to make up for what is missing. These children more than any other need desperately to improve their hold on the vocabulary and structures of their own tongue. It often seems a daunting job when presented in this way to trainee teachers, but we need to go no further than nursery rhymes to find a most useful if not indispensable tool. Chukovsky was writing about the pre-school (kindergarten) phase when he insisted that 'the proper training of young children in poetry is a most important part of their education', (*ibid*. p. 82). What he says is just as applicable to the linguistically deprived child in the infants and first-year juniors. As always, it must be a case of first things first.

It is clear that verse and poetry — that which has a strong rhythm and rhyme — has an irresistible attraction for all young children. They love to hear it and memorize it, however young they are. At present, I am amazed at how many nursery rhymes my 2-year-old son can recite from memory, ones like 'Jack and Jill' containing vocabulary he has not met in any other context: 'crown', 'caper', 'trot', 'plastered' and 'vinegar'. The memorableness of the verse form is what makes these unfamiliar words stick much more readily than reading them in prose would.

It is impossible to over-emphasize the importance of nursery rhymes in our early poetry work at the primary level. One of the great rules in teaching is to try to start from where the child is. Nursery rhymes help us fulfil this dictum to the letter, as these traditional songs belong essentially to the pre-school *oral* language environment. Rare indeed is the child who has gone through the first five years without hearing at least *a few* of the rhymes ('Round and Round the Garden'), lullabies ('Hush-a-bye, Baby'), and songs of babyhood. If mother doesn't sing them, then Granny will. Long before they can walk or talk most babies have enjoyed the delicious experience of being bounced up and down on mother's knees while she sings 'This is the Way the Farmer Rides', or of being tweaked on the toes as she chants 'This Little Piggy'. The close physical contact accompanied by rhythm and melody makes for a joyous experience for both mother and baby. But, without wanting to devalue the joy, it is so much more than joy. Unbeknown to the mother, they are actually engaged in an educative process which confirms the old adage that learning begins on the mother's knee. The rhythmic movement, the physical contact and the sound are inseparable. As a result, the baby gradually learns to associate a different part of its body or a different movement with different sounds — '*Down* into a ditch' (from 'This is the Way the Farmer Rides') with the movement of dropping down between mother's knees. Even though the baby cannot articulate such words, it is *learning* meaning all the time and beginning to recognize and build up (internally) a vocabulary. Any mother can tell you that her baby or toddler understands much, much more than it can express.

It would be a mistake to shy away from nursery rhymes because we suspect, rightly, that pupils already know many off by heart. There are a great many they won't know and will actually enjoy being introduced to. Peter and Iona Opie calculated that in their two collections, *The Oxford Nursery Rhyme Book* (1967) and *The Puffin Book of Nursery Rhymes* (1977), there were about 1,000 rhymes in all, 800 in the first and over 200 in the second. And this was discounting the 150 most common ones that they claim most of us 'know' or have in our heads if only we could remember them. Such is the wealth of English traditional verse! Our pupils can't possibly know it all. Even if they did, they would not be averse to hearing their favourites again and again. The 7-year-old, like the pre-school child, does not find repetition boring.

A great many educators and writers have stressed the immense value of nursery rhymes. For example, they are not all simple little jingles. Many of them have a wide vocabulary and make few concessions to their young listeners' linguistic immaturity. Yet understanding is rarely impeded by this. The context and freely used synonyms make sure that the child is not left in complete ignorance:

Jack and Jill
Then up Jack got and home did *trot*
As fast as he could *caper*.
They put him to bed and *plastered* his head
With vinegar and brown paper.

The House that Jack Built
This is the priest all shaven and *shorn*
That married the man all *tattered* and torn.

The many tongue-twisters found among traditional verses are a great source of hilarity for pupils, even within the formalities (such as they are) of a poetry lesson. For teachers, they provide invaluable material for pupils' practice in clear enunciation. Such practice tends to have its own inbuilt self-correcting mechanism too, so that we do not need to do much prodding. I can think of nothing else in the English curriculum area that makes teaching so easy and learning so painless and thoroughly enjoyable!

The wealth of riddles, many going back as far as Anglo-Saxon times (over 1,000 years old), is truly remarkable. They offer that element of the brain-teaser so beloved of children at this age. They stretch children to think, to ponder analogies, to solve a problem, in fact:

A house full
A hole full
You cannot gather
A bowl full. (mist)

As round as a butter bowl
As deep as a cup
All the Mississippi river
Can't fill it up. (A sieve)

One of the most beautiful of them is the following, from the Anglo-Saxon period:

In marble halls as white as milk,
Lined with a skin as soft as silk,
Within a fountain crystal clear,
A golden apple doth appear.
No doors are there to this stronghold
Yet thieves break in and steal the gold. (An egg)

As you can see, it is not difficult to demonstrate that English traditional verse is far from being suitable only for the pre-school child. Its tremendous range and variety is one of its chief glories.

Their Valuable Psychological Function

The effects of nursery rhymes are just as valuable as they are varied. I have already mentioned the essential enriching of the child's own language that nursery rhymes unobtrusively perform. They also serve an undeniably important psychological function for the young child. It seems that they help to boost his self-esteem. We hear much of this term in educational circles yet it is rarely, if ever, applied to all children. It is clear, though, from observing working-class children that many do lack that rightful confidence without which educational progress is slow. The presence of simpletons, like Simple Simon going for water in a sieve, and such impossible happenings as the man in the moon burning his mouth by eating cold pease porridge initially cause laughter, as indeed they are intended to do. If the child laughs it is because he has recognized the *silliness*. To recognize foolishness in others is to laugh at them, from a position of intellectual superiority: 'I wouldn't be so silly,' thinks the child. Chukovsky had much to say on this topic (1971, p. 102), because of its importance:

> This childish self-satisfaction is served by all sorts of songs and stories about simpletons who act contrary to the established order of things . . . for every 'wrong', the child realises what is 'right', and every departure from the normal strengthens his conception of the normal. Thus he values even more highly his firm, realistic orientation. He tests his mental prowess and invariably he passes this test, which appreciably increases his self-esteem as well as his confidence in his intellectual abilities; this confidence is most essential to him in order that he may not become discouraged in his chaotic world . . . The main importance in children's play with topsy-turvies [nursery rhymes about stupidity or impossible happenings] lies in this verifying and self-examination.

Developing Imagination

Together with fairy stories and folk tales, nursery rhymes also feed and enrich the child's imaginative life. It is not hard to understand why. Although their characters are always recognizably human or animal, the rhymes display a *world* where the extraordinary and bizarre prevail. Old ladies sweep cobwebs from the sky; a maid hangs her washing on the moon to dry. There is, also, a magical quality to many of them that is quite beyond the power of words to assess — which is as it should be, let me hasten to add. What an awful world it would be if everything could be quantified!

The Role of Nursery Rhymes in Bringing Order to a Chaotic World

The baby and young child are avid for knowledge. It is by means of these simple but invaluable rhymes that he or she learns to give names to, and therefore to pin down, the apparently chaotic world with which he or she is surrounded, and to impose some kind of order on it:

> The developing interests of the young child are reflected in the many nursery rhymes about everyday things the child can recognise, about other people and animals he may meet, about the sequence of going to bed, getting up in the morning, eating and dressing with which he is familiar, about the weather, his mother's work in the house and a number of other phenomena within his experience. Through familiarity with the rhymes, he learns the words necessary to identify and classify many objects and living things he meets; thus he begins to bring a measure of order into the complex world which surrounds him.
>
> (Newton and Handley, 1971, p. 28)

Practical Help in Learning

It is plain from all that has been said so far that nursery rhymes are an invaluable if gently unobtrusive educational resource for young children. And it really doesn't matter which ones we choose to read to and with our classes for them to serve the purposes mentioned above. However, many do appear to teach much more obvious and useful lessons, like the series of sequence rhymes on the days of the week, months of the year, seasons and numbers.

> Solomon Grundy
> Born on Monday,
> Christened on Tuesday . . .
>
> One, two, three, four, five,
> Once I caught a fish alive . . .
>
> January brings the snow,
> Makes our feet and fingers glow . . .
>
> Spring is showery, flowery, bowery;
> Summer: hoppy, croppy, poppy;
> Autumn: slippy, drippy, nippy;
> Winter: breezy, sneezy, freezy.

If pupils at 7 still find such sequences difficult to master, then these rhymes offer the perfect mnemonic. Most adults can testify that they do work. I'm sure many, like me, would be lost without that little rhyme which recalls correctly the number of days in each month:

> Thirty days hath September,
> April, June and November . . .

There are even traditional rhymes which pass as nonsense verse that help children see just how confusing written communication can be if it lacks that boon called punctuation. The actual verses come unpunctuated, and readers are asked: 'How can these strange wonders be?' and then invited to 'add some commas and you'll see':

> I saw a pack of cards gnawing a bone
> I saw a dog seated on Britain's throne
> I saw a queen shut up within a box
> I saw a shilling driving a fat ox
> I saw a man lying in a muff all night
> I saw a glove reading news by candlelight
> I saw a woman not a twelvemonth old
> I saw a greatcoat all of solid gold
> I saw two buttons telling of their dreams
> I heard my friends, who wished I'd quit these themes.

Not all nursery rhymes offer such practical help, nor would I want to concentrate on their utilitarian benefits, though these should not be neglected either. What it is important to realize is that they are there to be drawn upon when needed. One thing is crystal clear. Children love nursery rhymes partly because so many are humorous and just good fun. Humour is a marvellous spice in that it makes palatable at much more advanced ages that which would seem babyish without. I often used 'I saw a pack of cards' when teaching punctuation to first and second years at the secondary level, much to their amusement and enlightenment.

The meaning of nursery rhymes seems to exercise children's emotions *not one jot*. Children who are so often upset by cruelty to animals seem not to notice that the farmer's wife in 'Three Blind Mice' offends doubly by taking advantage of handicapped creatures — or so a humourless, self-appointed censor might insist! This should not give us cause for concern — it is almost as if at this age young children are determined to enjoy themselves. I suspect that it is the element of the chase that possibly so thrills them in 'Three Blind Mice'. The rest is missed.

THE IMPORTANCE OF PROVIDING A WIDE VARIETY OF VERSE

So many simple verses really tickle children's fancies. They enjoy hugging a quiet, little chuckle to themselves as much as emitting a loud guffaw. This means, of course, that we do not have to go overboard by providing raucously funny material all the time. We must always make sure that the range of verse we read is wide. In that way our pupils will not develop a limited view of what makes for enjoyment in poetry reading. Too many teachers today concentrate entirely on the one area they know succeeds with pupils, namely, comic verse. I would not want to deny the pleasures it affords and, as I have suggested already, much of the traditional verse in anthologies of nursery rhymes is humorous. However, this is not true of all of it. Some of it is serious, sad or even profound like 'Who Killed Cock Robin?', 'Poor Old Horse' and 'A Man of Words and not of Deeds'. Where young children are concerned, what makes a poem truly memorable is not so much the presence of humour as a *distinctive* rhythm. If this were not so, lovely rhymes like 'Twinkle, Twinkle, Little Star' would not be as popular as they are.

THE APPEAL OF RHYME AND RHYTHM

Moving on from nursery rhymes, we cannot go far wrong if at first we make sure we select poems with this distinctive rhythm. I discovered when I taught young juniors recently that poems whose rhythm imitates, say, a train's movement or noise like 'The Train to Glasgow' (Wilma Horsbrugh) and 'Clinkerdump' (by the same author) are much appreciated:

> *The Train to Glasgow*
> Here is the train to Glasgow.
>
> Here is the driver,
> Mr MacIver
> Who drove the train to Glasgow.
>
> Here is the guard from Donibristle
> Who waved his flag and blew his whistle
> To tell the driver,
> Mr MacIver,
> To start the train to Glasgow. . .

> *Clinkerdump*
> Clinkerdump, clinkerdump, rattlecomeree,
> I live in the train and you can't see me,
> But whenever the wheels go round and round
> You hear me making my monotonous sound:
>
> Clinkerdump, clinkerdump,
> Clinkerdump, clinkerdump,

> Clink, clank, clinkerdump, clank,
> That's me! . . .

The first of those two poems offers the added bonus of building up into a crescendo as it goes along, rather like 'The House that Jack Built'. The first stanza or verse is very short (one brief line); the second adds a line or two; the third adds a few more until the final stanza is 12 or more lines long and requires a huge mouthful of breath to get it out properly. For children who have only recently learned to read or are still not reading fluently, the later verses can be hard work to *follow* let alone to read aloud, yet so enjoyable is the poetic experience that motivation to work at it is high. Even the poor readers among my 7-year-old pupils were desperate to persuade me to let them read a stanza. 'The Holiday Train' (Irene Thompson) refrains from imitating the movement of a train and opts instead for reproducing that excited repetition and impatience so typical of the young child travelling:

> 'Here is the train!
> Here is the train!
> Let us get in!
> Let us get in!'

It is one of the easiest of all poems for the new reader to tackle because each stanza consists of only four lines of no more than four syllables, while the first and third lines are repeated. For all its obvious simplicity, it is an incredibly effective little piece for conveying the excitement that so exhausts parents while it keeps the children all agog.

Rhythm rhymes like those written by Clive and Ruth Sansom are short and sweet, highly rhythmical and easy to read. Some of them, as suggested in Chapter 4, resemble tongue-twisters (a natural link with nursery rhymes), which gives them a testing, teasing quality beloved by all junior children. The following example by Mona Swann exercises the compound vowel sounds ō–ŏŏ and ĭ–ōō:

> Snow, snow,
> Where do you go?
> I don't know
> Where I go.
>
> You knew, dew,
> Didn't you?
> Yes, I knew.

The next lively example, which concentrates on rhythm, is by Christina Rossetti, the nineteenth-century poet who wrote many poems of great beauty, delicacy and sensitivity. 'Mix a Pancake' is typical of her work in its simplicity:

> Mix a pancake
> Stir a pancake
>   Pop it in the pan.
>
> Fry the pancake
> Toss the pancake
>   Catch it if you can.

This little rhyme cries out for actions or movements to accompany the words, as well as perhaps lending itself to some simple group speaking. Whenever a short rhyme features dialogue, like 'Ten Little Mice' (only six lines long), or refrains as in Clive

Sansom's 'The Engine Driver', we can begin to encourage a little group or unison speaking without imposing excessive strain either on ourselves or our pupils. As we saw in Chapter 4, choral speaking has to be enjoyable or it is not worth the candle:

Narrator	Ten little mice sat down to spin.
	Pussy came by and she peeped in.
Pussy	'What are you doing, my jolly ten?'
Ten Mice	'We're making coats for gentlemen.'
Pussy	'Shall I come in and cut off your threads?'
Ten Mice	'Oh, no, Mrs Pussy. You'd bite off our heads.'

FIND A PLACE FOR POETRY WHICH REFINES THE SENSIBILITY

However tempting it is to stay with the easy, lightweight and comic material, it is clear that we must attempt to introduce our pupils occasionally to more challenging poetry. For one thing, it adds variety to our lessons and therefore robs them of any possible predictability. Even at 7, children are not too young to read something with more depth and complexity to it than what we have considered so far in this chapter. As I said in connection with nursery rhymes, seriousness and depth will stretch our pupils and nourish their burgeoning thoughtfulness and sensitivity. For these special qualities, Christina Rossetti, R. L. Stevenson, Walter de la Mare, Eleanor Farjeon, and some of the post-war poets like James Reeves and Charles Causley, are especially useful. Though often simply written, their work at its best has a resonance that is the mark of intense feeling and great writing combined.

The seriousness of these deeper poems does not make them solemn. Indeed, they are often quite exhilarating in their perceptiveness and their impressive choice of words and images. For example, Eleanor Farjeon's 'A Dragonfly' is a gem of delicate description:

> When the heat of summer
> Made drowsy the land,
> A dragonfly came
> And sat on my hand.
>
> With its blue jointed body,
> And wings like spun glass,
> It lit on my fingers
> As though they were grass.

R. L. Stevenson's 'Escape at Bedtime' captures to perfection the wonder and imaginative delicacy of the small child, for whom the world is clearly a magical place. The adults ('they' in the poem) in his life are more prosaic:

> The lights from the parlour and kitchen shone out
>   Through the blinds and the windows and bars;
> And high overhead and all moving about,
>   There were thousands of millions of stars.
>
> There ne'er were such thousands of leaves on a tree,
>   Nor of people in church or the Park,
> As the crowds of the stars that looked down upon me,
>   And that glittered and winked in the dark.
>
> The Dog, and the Plough, and the Hunter, and all,
>   And the star of the sailor, and Mars,

These shone in the sky, and the pail by the wall
Would be half full of water and stars.

They saw me at last, and they chased me with cries,
    And they soon had me packed into bed;
But the glory kept shining and bright in my eyes,
    And the stars going round in my head.

Thomas Hardy's tender description of a small deer at night in the snow looking into his cottage window communicates a similar sense of the breathtaking wondrousness of the natural world. With a delicate timidity matched only by the creature itself, he describes an encounter that seems almost magical:

The Fallow Deer at the Lonely House
One without looks in tonight
    Through the curtain-chink
From the sheet of glistening white;
One without looks in tonight
    As we sit and think
    By the fender-brink.

We do not discern those eyes
    Watching in the snow;
Lit by lamps of rosy dyes
We do not discern those eyes
    Wondering, aglow,
    Fourfooted, tiptoe.

Finally, Walter de la Mare's 'Then' conveys compassion for the watchman calling the time all through bitter winter nights:

Twenty, forty, sixty, eighty,
A hundred years ago,
All through the night with lantern bright
The Watch trudged to and fro.
And little boys tucked snug abed
Would wake from dreams to hear —

'Two o' the morning by the clock,
And the stars a-shining clear!'
Or, when across the chimney-tops
Screamed shrill a North-East gale,
A faint and shaken voice would shout,
'Three! — And a storm of hail!'

To be deep a poem does not necessarily have to be difficult, as these few examples prove. From time to time it is important that our lessons contain something linguistically and conceptually more meaty and demanding, something to talk about perhaps, something that will nourish the child's life and stir his deeper emotions and sympathies.

Chapter 6

Reluctant Readers

Reluctant readers among top-middle and junior-secondary pupils tend also to be *poor readers*, if indeed 'reluctant' isn't actually a euphemism for weak or backward readers. This weakness has a lot to do with the fact that such children have not yet discovered that reading is an immensely pleasurable experience. During their earlier struggles to master the skill, it has probably seemed to them simply a mechanical process and an end in itself. It may well have been presented to them at the primary-school level as merely a technical hurdle to be jumped, not as a means to a hugely enjoyable and even useful end. Indeed, the research conducted by Frank Whitehead and his team into children's reading habits, published under the title *Children and their Books* (Macmillan, Basingstoke, 1977), suggested that this was so.

A POEM'S LENGTH IS AN IMPORTANT CONSIDERATION

It is my contention that reading poetry and good verse can convince reluctant readers that bothering to stick at reading practice and actually to master the skill is a worthwhile activity because it opens up such worlds of genuine fun and pleasure. This is where we must start with reluctant/poor readers — with the pleasure principle uppermost. This will demand, at least at first, poetry that is humorous, easy and short. Length of poems is an important consideration for weak readers. Nothing is more likely to be off-putting than a poem which goes on and on, and this is true even of comic poems and ones on subjects much loved by pupils. Length simply overtaxes concentration and then interest rapidly flags. So, in the early stages of poetry lessons with poor readers, the shorter the poems are the better. Limericks, epitaphs, riddles, rhyming proverbs, some merely of two lines, none more than six to eight lines.

> *Epitaph*
> Let the wind go free
> Where'er thou be,
> For 'twas the wind
> That kill*ed* me.
> (Anon.)

Riddles

See it go along the street,
Carried by no human feet,
Town or country, feast or fair,
A crown no King or Queen can wear.

I begin
Tall and thin
I end in a muddle
Sat in a puddle.

An Inscription on an Old Sun-dial
Time wastes our bodies and our wits,
But we waste Time, so we are quits.
(Anon.)

Traditional — Scribbled on the Flyleaf of an Old School Book
This book is mine
This boot another.
Touch not the one
For fear of the other.
(Anon.)

A Toast
Here's to the happiest days of my life
Spent in the arms of another man's wife
                        — my mother.
(Anon.)

Proverbs
Man's work lasts till set of sun
Woman's work is never done.
(Anon.)

Rain
There are holes in the sky
Where the rain gets in,
But they're ever so small,
That's why the rain is thin.
(Spike Milligan)

The Pessimist
Nothing to do but work!
Nothing! Alas! Alack!
Nowhere to go but out!
Nowhere to come but back!
(Trad.)

Children gain an enormous sense of achievement in mastering, however haltingly, one whole piece of verse, in getting it mentally under their belt, so to speak. Even if all that this means is simply listening to it being read aloud by the teacher and following it in their books or from duplicated sheets. The shorter and easier the poem is, the more likely a poor reader is to volunteer to try to read it aloud himself to the class. It's vital that we attempt to foster a sense of personal achievement at this early stage if we want *these* pupils in particular to persevere with mastering this long-delayed skill.

This does mean, of course, that we have to leave till much later material that is more emotionally suited to this age range. Our difficulty as teachers with such older pupils is that, although they will display such very young reading ages, much of the material suitable for 6- and 7-year-olds will be too babyish for 11–13-year olds. The onus is on the teacher to read widely and to develop a repertoire of material accessible to such a difficult group of pupils. Not only is *the Ancient Mariner* not suitable because its length makes it too demanding even of concentration and listening skills, but neither are the nursery rhymes that are still a source of fun and delight for 7-year-olds. But that shouldn't rule out *parodies* of nursery rhymes. They use the original's easy rhythm and yet have a witty or comic twist, as in:

> Mary had a little lamb,
> She ate it with mint sauce,
> And everywhere that Mary went,
> The lamb went, too, of course.

This and many others are to be found in *The Faber Book of Verse and Worse*, edited by Arnold Silcock (London, 1971), a wonderful source book of comic material for all older pupils, but especially for reluctant readers, whether weak or genuinely reluctant, that is, unwilling.

THE APPEAL OF WORD-PLAY

The appeal of this kind of verse for top juniors (or lower-secondary pupils) lies no doubt in the fact that at this age children are inordinately fond of word-play, however weak they may be individually as readers. Most parodies (like the one quoted above), limericks, etc., make use of puns, some extensively. I have met teachers who would shun such material as too difficult for 11–13-year-olds who are also poor readers. This is a grave mistake, if only from the point of view of motivation. What is more, weak readers are not necessarily dim-witted. Many that I taught in the past had very agile brains and all enjoyed the word-play contained in most jokes, like those in the *Crack-a-Joke Book*, (Puffin, Harmondsworth, 1978), which were all contributed by children.

The following examples are not beyond the capacity of even the weakest readers amongst 11–13-year-olds to appreciate, and are certainly no more demanding than jokes.

> *Dr Bell*
> Dr Bell fell down the well
> And broke his collarbone.
> Doctors should attend the sick
> And leave the well alone.
> (Anon., 18th century)

> *Epitaph on a Dentist*
> Stranger! Approach this spot with gravity!
> John Brown is filling his last cavity.
> (Anon.)

I have read this next one to pupils as young as 9 who were tickled pink at the rapid succession of puns:

> *Epitaph on a Brewer*
> Here lies poor Burton
> He was both hale and stout.
> Death laid him on his bitter bier

> Now in another world he hops about
> (Anon.)

A teacher needs to make clear before starting to read the following one (a limerick) that the class understands that 'inter' means 'to bury'. The pun will then take care of itself:

> *Double Interment*
> There was a young fellow from Clyde
> Who fell down a sewer and died.
> The next day his brother
> Fell down another
> So now they're interred side by side.
> (Anon.)

What especially appeals to junior/middle school children in this last one is the combination of crudity (not to be recommended for its own sake) and cleverness.

THE APPEAL OF THE SURREAL

There is more to humour, of course, than the appeal of word-play (crude or not). There is also a surreal or zany element in much English verse, stemming from Edward Lear and Lewis Carroll, which seems to be popular across the whole middle-school age range (9–13) and especially attractive to 11–13-year-olds. Much of Spike Milligan's verse is in this vein:

> You must never bath in an Irish stew
> It's a most illogical thing to do
> But should you persist against my reasoning
> Don't fail to add the appropriate seasoning.

I suspect that in the next example it is the desire to defy the constraints of reality that tickles the fancy of pupils so much:

> *The Perfect Reactionary*
> As I was sitting in my chair
> I *knew* the bottom wasn't there,
> Nor legs, nor back, but I just sat,
> Ignoring little things like that.
> (Hughes Mearns)

Much traditional (anonymous) verse has this quality, too:

> As I was going down the stair
> I met a man who wasn't there.
> He wasn't there again today:
> I *wish* that man would go away!
> (Anon.)

Traditional verse is so richly varied, you will find that the surreal element is not only present for purely comic effect. Sometimes it expresses very serious themes or intuitions, but in such an oblique way that the seriousness is distanced and never threatens to overwhelm the reader. For example, the fear of the unknown and even of child abduction seems to inform 'My mother said I never should, /Play with the gypsies in the wood', but it is expressed with almost goonish humour in lines like:

My father said that if I did
He'd rap my head with a teapot lid.

On the other hand, 'A man of words and not of deeds' offers no humour at all, just a succession of surreal images that are highly evocative:

A man of words and not of deeds
Is like a garden full of weeds;
And when the weeds begin to grow,
It's like a garden full of snow;
And when the snow begins to fall.
It's like a bird upon a wall;
And when the bird away does fly,
It's like an eagle in the sky;
And when the sky begins to roar,
It's like a lion at the door;
And when the door begins to crack
It's like a stick across your back;
And when your back begins to smart,
It's like a penknife in your heart;
And when your heart begins to bleed,
You're dead and dead and dead indeed.

THE NEED TO EXTEND THE IMAGINATIVE RANGE

A word of warning, however. It is also important to plan ahead a programme for weak readers (even if we find we fail to progress along it as quickly as we expect), just to make sure that we do actually attempt to introduce less trivial and less slight material from time to time. To let our pupils stay with the lightweight for a whole year or even a whole term is not in the long run in their best interests educationally. Request sessions can always redress the balance back to humour if they so wish. However, you may be surprised to find more serious pieces actually figuring among requests. It's a mistake to assume that material that isn't trivial or slight must be grave, or even that serious must equate with solemn. More serious poems and verses tend, by and large, to offer greater personal fulfilment to the child in that they stimulate the imagination, enrich the inner life and appeal at a deeper emotional level. As long as such pieces are not too demanding linguistically or syntactically (that is, in their vocabulary and sentence construction) or in their length, they will extend the emotional and imaginative range of the reluctant reader. I have in mind traditional verses like 'A man of words and not of deeds', James Reeves's 'Slowly', Eleanor Farjeon's 'The Tide in the River'. None of them is demanding, but all three of them offer a little more to think about than the humorous examples do:

Slowly
Slowly the tide creeps up the sand,
Slowly the shadows cross the land.
Slowly the cart-horse pulls his mile,
Slowly the old man mounts the stile,

Slowly the hands move round the clock,
Slowly the dew dries on the dock.
Slow is the snail — but slowest of all
The green moss spreads on the old brick wall.

The Tide in the River
The tide in the river,
The tide in the river,
The tide in the river runs deep,
I saw a shiver
Pass over the river
As the tide turned in its sleep.

FINDING POETRY THAT HAS BOY-APPEAL

Once reading ability has improved a little and interest has been generated, we should begin to inject the odd longer poem into our poetry programme, something like the traditional *Casey Jones* and *The Three Jolly Welshmen* or John G. Saxe's *The Six Blind Men of Hindustan*, all of them still vigorous or comic. At the very least, longer poems help to improve listening skills and develop concentration. When concentration has improved we can introduce poems that are not so undemanding (lingusitically, metrically or emotionally) as long as the poems we choose are still strongly rhythmical, vigorous and *masculine*.

The last point is important. It is no exaggeration to say that most poor readers at the secondary or top-middle level are boys. One of the reasons why boys tend to regard poetry as effeminate stuff is that they have never been exposed to the kind of poetry they would find attractive — that is, poetry about heroic figures, death-defying or death-dealing exploits, self-sacrifice and adventure. I am reminded of a relative's child who at the age of 9 had to be sent to a remedial reading centre once a week but whose reading matter, once he had mastered the skill, moved from the *Crack-a-Joke Book* of one liners to Arthur Waley's long and densely packed plain-text translation of the Chinese classic, *The Adventures of the Monkey King* (Unwin, London, 1979), which this child re-read many times over.

It may be unfashionable to be interested in war and battles, but many boys collect miniature soldiers and play war games at home — better an interest in battles distant in time and place than more near-at-hand violence such as teenage vandalism and mugging. It's not as if English poetry glorifies war. It doesn't. The realities of battle – blood, pain and death – are well to the fore in some of the sea shanties, while the Robin Hood ballads from the Middle Ages feature, for all their sense of the joyous defiance of authority, the thorny problems of life like the treachery and deceit of supposed friends and allies. It may be that some feminists would object to giving boys masculine poems, but the poems I have in mind do not flinch from a realistic grasp of the grim price men pay (and have paid through the ages) for their masculinity.

Battle poems are not necessarily jingoistic or even nationalistic. Indeed, one of the more worthy features of English literature is that its great national battle poems are much more likely to celebrate notorious defeats and individual loss than glorious victories. This particular English characteristic started over 1,000 years ago with the Anglo-Saxon poem 'The Battle of Maldon' — which the Anglo-Saxons lost. Probably the most well-known of these poems is Tennyson's 'The Charge of the Light Brigade', with its compelling rhythm and incantatory reiteration of 'Into the valley of death rode the six hundred'. Equally famous in their time, though not so well-known today, are 'The Revenge, a Ballad of the Fleet' (also by Tennyson) and 'The Burial of Sir John Moore at Corunna' (by C. Wolfe), the Dunkirk of the Peninsular War.

It took Orwell to remind us, if we had forgotten, that it is the English spirit (unlike anything to be found on the Continent) to remember our defeats rather than our victories. Indeed, it is a source of bewilderment to foreigners how Englishmen tend to laugh at references to 1066, the last occasion when the country was successfully conquered by invaders. A sobering thought. Of all the engagements of the Second World War, the one that always springs to mind first is Dunkirk, which was almost a rout.

All this is not to suggest that we offer nothing but fighting material to our backward readers. Far from it. It is to insist, however, that without poetry that celebrates courage, daring and vigorous action (on the side of right) we will find it difficult to attract boys — especially backward boys — to read at all. It is worth bearing in mind that of the 115 poems in Kaye Webb's *I Like This Poem* (1977), only 17 were sent in by boys, who mainly chose comic pieces. We will not be able to fill a term with comic verse alone, despite its plentiful supply in English literature and its popularity with pupils. So, for the sake of *variety*, as well as boy-appeal, sea shanties and poems about dangerous/heroic exploits are important ballast.

Casey Jones, which has already been mentioned, is a very good example of this. It was written to commemorate a nineteenth-century American railwayman's pride in his work and his ultimate self-sacrifice to save his passengers. Other work ballads, like 'The Great American Railway', about the arduous work of laying the tracks, are equally vivid and realistic in the picture they paint of dangerous, real-life working conditions. Such poems celebrate human skill and endurance.

At this late stage in their schooling, reluctant readers need desperately to be put in touch with as much as possible of what they missed at the junior level. Luckily, many of the traditional verses that are so memorably strong on rhyme and rhythm are also pretty vigorous and concrete. In other words, they have to be accessible both lingistically and emotionally — a harder match for teachers to make as poor readers advance in years. This is why so many of these children lose out, especially at the secondary level, because the match becomes almost impossible the older they become.

POOR READING ATTAINMENT DOES NOT EQUATE WITH LACK OF SENSITIVITY

You will notice that I do not recommend poems about gangs and delinquency for reluctant boy readers. This omission is not accidental. Such verse exists and such themes tend to loom large in prose material for remedial readers, especially at the secondary level. In recent years, it has become a commonplace assumption that poor readers at the secondary school must also, by definition, be lacking in sensitivity. In other words, embryonic delinquents. Having myself taught many remedial pupils in an inner-London comprehensive, I find this assumption grossly offensive. I can recall third-year remedial girls objecting to material that my head of department had deemed suitable for the likes of them. They couldn't explain what was wrong with it, simply that they didn't like it. 'It's not nice, Miss', they insisted. They were quite right. I could see, as an adult, that much of the material verged on the 'sick' and certainly offered nothing positive or wholesome to these young people.

To offer remedial pupils material about gangs and delinquency, or horror and unpleasantness (on the mistaken assumption that it will appeal), merely marginalizes such children even further, children whose only problem is low reading attainment. To equate poor reading performance with lack of sensitivity or mental agility is to blame the child for its weakness. The blame or fault could just as well lie at the door of the school and the method that was used initially to teach reading to the child.

To teach English poetry to our pupils is, willy-nilly, to induct them into their cultural heritage. An able reader moves with ease into its possession. More than any other child, the poor reader needs the teacher's conscious help to enter into possession of his full cultural birthright. To palm him off with marginal material is to deny him access to what could and should be his as much as anyone's. Indeed, to go further, if one's older pupils *were* actually lacking in sensitivity, it would be a lamentable teaching strategy to set out to reinforce that deficiency.

THE USEFULNESS OF NARRATIVE VERSE

Stirring Victorian and Edwardian poems, like Henry Newbolt's 'Drake's Drum', Hardy's 'The Night of Trafalgar', Kipling's 'The Smugglers', and Alfred Noyes's 'The Highwayman' (the length of this last one may preclude its use with reluctant readers until considerable improvements in listening skills and reading ability have been made), are popular with all pupils, but particularly useful for reluctant readers because of their powerful atmosphere (of daring, defiance of authority, of naked courage) and their rhythmic and alliterative compulsiveness. Such poems are hugely enjoyed by top juniors and so by extension will also be attractive to reluctant readers at the upper-middle level. 'The Highwayman' was selected by a pupil (a girl, incidentally) for inclusion in Kaye Webb's collection *I Like This Poem* (1977), though it has been out of favour with adult anthologists for many decades. More recently, it has reappeared in an excellent anthology for primary schools called *Passport to Poetry*, by E. L. Black and D. S. Davies (Cassell, London, 1980).

Narrative poetry is one of the most effective kinds of poetry for catching the interest of *all* pupils. It appeals largely because it tells a story, however briefly, sometimes with the added attraction of dialogue, but always with the pace and verve that is conferred by rhythm and rhyme. This need for rhymed and rhythmical verse is vital. My students in training used to consider it important to introduce their pupils, even the backward ones, to *un*rhymed poetry. This was because these students had an ulterior motive in presenting such poetry to their pupils. They intended ultimately (usually not more than ten minutes later) to set their pupils the task of writing their own poems. As these students had no skill themselves in composing poetry and little idea of the enormous range of different rhyme schemes and metrical forms available to a budding poet in English, the only advice or help they could offer their pupils in such a difficult undertaking was that poetry doesn't have to rhyme. This never took into account the fact that the more immature the reader is, in years and experience of literature, the more difficult it is for his ear to detect the poetic music in unrhymed forms. Even blank verse, which is the most rhythmical of the unrhymed forms, is hard for young readers' ears. Unfortunately for pupils, the only kind of unrhymed verse students had in mind and presented to them was 'free verse', which is devoid of rhythm as well as rhyme and is intended for *trained* adult ears. So, for instrumental reasons, primary/secondary pupils are offered, as a regular diet, free verse which is the nearest verse there is to *prose*. Is it any wonder that primary/secondary pupils on such a diet are not convinced that poetry has anything special to offer them?

However, *stories in verse* are thoroughly gripping. It's not just the intrinsic merit of the story itself, but the rhythmical form in which it is couched that gives it its appeal. Reluctant or poor readers are especially helped through a story by its strong rhythm and rhyme, which gives the story an irresistible propulsion, like the *Bar Room Ballads* (Benn, London, 1960) of Robert Service, an Englishman who emigrated to Canada early this century. His verses are set in the Wild West and the Yukon goldmining fraternities and, like 'The Shooting of Dan McGrew', display compulsive rhythmical qualities:

> A bunch of boys were whooping it up in the Malamute Saloon;
> The kid that handles the music-box was hitting a ragtime tune;
> Back of the bar, in a solo game, sat Dangerous Dan McGrew
> And watching his luck was his light-o-love, the lady that's known as Lou.

There are many twentieth-century narrative poems that would be particularly attractive to older boys who are also poor readers. For example, Charles Causley's 'Death of an Aircraft', which is about wartime heroism in Crete, and Kipling's 'Danny Deever', about a squaddy due to be hanged, a poem that is conducted entirely in dialogue. W. H. Auden's *Ballad* ('O What is the sound') is a mysterious but age-old story of betrayal of a young man to the military. It would also submit to a choral presentation by abler readers. All these poems can be found in *Narrative Verse* by Paterson (Longman, London, 1967).

THE NEED TO KEEP FOLLOW-UP WORK SIMPLE

One must exercise severe restraint over the urge to devise follow-up work for reluctant readers, be it choral speaking or anything else. It is really inappropriate at the stage at which these really weak readers find themselves to be set tasks, even quite simple ones like a choral presentation. It has to be a case of first things first. Until our pupils' reading ability has markedly improved, a poetry lesson must not be conceived as a means to another, even more demanding, end. It should be perceived by our pupils as a purely pleasurable experience, worth having for itself, not for where it will lead. There is, after all, a hierarchy of skills and they must be taken and exercised in order. This is what secondary teachers of older but exceptionally weak pupils forget. The earlier but basic stages have not been mastered. While reading precedes writing, simple writing tasks precede 'creative' writing tasks. If it is deemed proper that these pupils have to do something after a poetry lesson, then only the simplest tasks are advisable, like keeping personal anthologies, into which each child copies from time to time a favourite poem. Follow-up work of this nature is examined in Chapter 7.

REFINING OUR PUPILS' INTERESTS AND SENSIBILITIES

Once we have caught and begun to foster the interest of our reluctant readers in good verse by examples that are vital, vigorous and concrete, it is time to go on to refine that interest. Good teaching means never standing still, so to speak. Now begins the gradual process of introducing from time to time poems that are more delicate or sensitive than anything you have read to your class before — something like Charles Causley's 'Miller's End', a delicate ghost story with a final twist that makes one shiver, and 'My Mother Saw a Dancing Bear' (also by Causley), which is a most touching account of a practice only recently dead and gone. It is a poem that will develop empathy as well as a quiet thoughtfulness. Both of them are to be found in *Figgie Hobbin* (1983) an excellent collection of humorous as well as serious poems by Causley.

It is incumbent upon us to make room, if only occasionally, for poems that are imaginatively and emotionally richer than the normal poetic fare we offer. When we do so, it is important not to embed them in a lesson full of poems that are lightweight and humorous as that would be likely to evoke an inappropriate tone. In other words, the seriousness and profundity would be undermined if not completely nullified. It is a good idea, therefore, to start a lesson with a delicate or sensitive poem and prepare the ground by appropriately serious comments. In that way, we create a receptive atmosphere. Later in the lesson, the seriousness can be lifted by introducing some slighter, lighter poems, with no damage to the first poem. However, we should not be afraid of devising now and then lessons that consist of nothing but serious, sensitive pieces.

Chapter 7

Follow-up Work

If you have read this far, I hope you are now convinced that we must make sure we devise the bulk of our poetry lessons as 'poetry-reading-aloud-and-speaking' lessons, leading nowhere except to a pleasurable and enthusiastic re-reading of the poems by pupil volunteers. This may sound a contradiction of this chapter's title, and may well dismay many teachers who like to be seen to be 'doing', that is, taking pupils beyond the starting-point of the lesson. To stay with the poems, within their bounds, is too easy and doesn't seem to prove one has had sufficient ideas about developing one's materials. This will have been hammered into us as student teachers and it tends to spill over into all areas of the curriculum indiscriminately. The point is that some areas of the curriculum, most notably literature, require entirely different handling from the norm. Poetry isn't a strictly cognitive area and there are real dangers in attempting to treat it as if it were.

Our prime purpose in introducing a poem to children is *to allow it to speak for itself directly to our pupils.* For that reason we need as little elaborate presentation or follow-up work as possible, as little teacher intervention (by way of comprehension-type questioning) as we can manage. We must try not to get in the poem's way of its potential readership. In other words, the less elaborate our approach the better. Even re-reading can take different forms, like choral speaking, recitation and performance.

The usual follow-up work, however, consists of writing and discussion. After years of doing this myself, I now feel it is a grave mistake, even at the lower-secondary level. It is important to avoid such developments, at least as a regular thing. Once or twice a term is more than enough.

If we constantly 'use' poems to 'stimulate' children to write their own or to discuss 'issues', then we debase the coinage that is poetry and, however unobtrusively, set before them a model of exploitation — 'nothing is of any value in itself, only in as far as it can be used to produce something else'. This is a much more insidious 'hidden curriculum' than the racism and sexism we hear so much about, since it duplicates the commercially exploitative world outside the school gates and can only go to make our pupils its ready victims or servants. Conditioning indeed! The school's job is surely to suggest a better way of doing things — to inculcate a love of learning for its own sake, a love of reading for pleasure or information, a recognition that some things like literature generally, and poetry in particular, cannot be pigeon-holed by reductionist approaches like 'issue based' discussion or topic-based integrated studies or stimulus fodder.

Although the varied metrical forms, subject-matter and style are sufficiently different from poem to poem to rule out monotony, it is a good idea occasionally to vary the outcome of our lesson, so that our poetry lessons never become predictable. It is important to find a range of follow-up work that is possible but which doesn't turn the poems into mere tools, which doesn't, in other words, subject them to the crassest kind of instrumentalism. For example, it is now normal practice to introduce a poem as a mere stepping-stone or springboard to something else. However, it is not difficult to devise *tasks that reinforce the poem's appeal, that take the pupil back into the full experience of the poem* even if other skills than reading and even other mediums (like paint) may be involved.

PERSONAL ANTHOLOGIES

One of the simplest but most enjoyable things to do is for each pupil to keep a personal anthology or booklet in which to write out his or her favourites as the weeks pass. I found that some children will do this quite spontaneously anyway. One 9-year-old boy compiled his own anthology of all the poems he most liked in my lessons and included a few he had read elsewhere and a few he had composed himself. Another boy was always asking if he could take my duplicated sheets home just for an evening so that he could copy out his personal favourites.

Compiling an anthology of personal favourites is of great benefit to each individual child for a variety of reasons. It enables pupils to exercise skills other than listening, talking, and reading (either silently or aloud). Writing neatly and copying correctly are important in developing handwriting fluency. Copying also helps co-ordination between eye, brain and hand, which needs practice. Pupils also have to make decisions, something that is hard to do when all the poems in a lesson have been equally enjoyable.

Moreover, at the end of a couple of terms, the child possesses a booklet that is his own which he can keep. The enjoyment experienced in class can actually be revived and relived in the quiet (or not so quiet) of his own home. His favourite poems are his, to take away from the class and mull over and re-read as often as he chooses. A personal poetry anthology actually extends the child's area of choice over his reading matter, making him less dependent on the teacher and on the school or local library.

LEARNING BY HEART

Learning a poem or part of one by heart actually gives to the child the pleasurable reading experience as *a permanent possession*. Even personal anthologies can be lost or mislaid. And paper, especially when well-thumbed, wears out. But the music, the magic, the imaginative fillip of a poem that has been memorized a child can draw on as from a well in the most unlikely places and unexpected situations. Learning by heart has been out of favour for many years now. It deserves to be revived because it is educationally worthwhile and valuable.

Writers on brain studies also stress the importance of memory work in aiding the growth of the fine structure of the cerebral cortex. Experiments with rats quoted in John Brierley's *The Growing Brain* (NFER, Windsor, 1976) suggest that anatomical and chemical changes take place in the brain during a period of learning, especially in very young rats. These changes were manifested in greater brain weight and in a largely increased number of nerve connections. The greater the number of nerve connections in the brain, it seems, the greater is its capacity. The vital importance of *early* learning through memory and repetition cannot, therefore, be overstressed. It is certainly true that, given the opportunity, pre-school children quickly develop an amazing facility to learn nursery rhymes off by heart and even to memorize, word for word, prose stories read to them, refusing to allow omissions or deviations from the word order they know. In a brief article in *The Sunday Times* (1988), Brierley, a former HMI, actually recommended a return to rote learning. This is both on account of the scientific researches referred to above and because it can have inestimable personal and spiritual benefits:

> By not encouraging our children to learn poems and hymns by heart early in life, we are closing the door on an important source of enrichment and satisfaction. It does not matter if they do not understand every word. Understanding will come later and in later life will give them much pleasure and perhaps nourishment of the spirit.
>
> (*Ibid.*)

In other words, to commit to memory a beautiful piece of writing can sustain and succour children (and the adults they later become) when least expected or when perhaps they most need it.

Learning by heart gives children *freedom of choice* — they are not dependent on a teacher and the presence of a poetry book before they can revive their personal pleasure. With the abandonment of learning by heart we have thrown away self-sufficiency in education. The child has to rely more and more on the teacher. The less children learn by heart (like tables), the more dependent they are on teachers, books or machines to do their thinking, reasoning or calculating for them. Even though I am a teacher, I think that this can only be a dangerous state of affairs. So, never be afraid of promoting learning by *heart* once in a while as a natural and happy conclusion to a poetry lesson. Note that the operative word here is learning by *heart*, in other words, learning on the basis of pleasure, joy, love. What I am not suggesting is the rote learning of some barely liked piece of verse chosen by the teacher, as a useful exercise for memorization and recitation. Though opinion is divided on memorization, with most teachers against it in any guise, there are others, poets and ex-teachers like James Reeves and Leonard Clark (in Blackburn, 1966), who stress its value but only if it is the committing to memory of poems that were received with pleasure and thoroughly enjoyed. To others like Stevie Smith (1966), rote learning of great poems is essential for a budding poet. Indeed, many children will voluntarily learn by heart poems they have enjoyed at school. Those who do not will be denied the real benefits that accrue from this simple practice.

Once your pupils have started their own anthologies and written out eight to ten favourite poems, they should be able to choose at least one reasonably short poem to learn by heart at home to recite to the class. This will be no chore. Children usually jump at the task with alacrity. The sense of achievement alone that stems from this is worth promoting. All children need to gain a genuine sense of achievement from their work at school. Learning by heart is not hard but it does require and develop sustained effort and application — personal strengths children will need later as adults and without which little of consequence can ever be achieved.

ART WORK

Copying out poems can be taken one step further by bringing in art. Young children often spontaneously illustrate a poem they have copied out, usually in the style of an illuminated manuscript. Such a development is worth setting as a task at some point in the course of a term's poetry reading. As always, it is important to choose appropriate poems to submit to visualization. Not all do. The golden rule is also to vary the kind of work, from the small scale to the large.

There are some narrative poems so full of interesting characters and incidents that they actually lend themselves to the making not just of paintings but of a large-scale wall frieze. *The Pied Piper* and the Prologue to Chaucer's *The Canterbury Tales* are two which spring to mind immediately as being very well served by this form of illustration. The change from one medium to another need not mean that the poem gets lost *en route*. Indeed, the opposite should be the case. Painting characters from the Prologue keeps the poem to the forefront of the lesson as the children have to return to it to check details of dress, appearance and event. Neither does the poem disappear behind a welter of talk on issues that only the teacher perhaps sees as prominent in the poem. The vivid reality of a poem — its impetus, its varied characters, its different incidents — is still forcefully 'there' and is amply rendered into art as a joint class (or small-group) enterprise or individually.

Not all poems lend themselves to visualization — the more sensitive, purely emotional and lyrical a poem, the less it is susceptible to translation into graphic art because of its essential abstractness. But narrative poems (which includes ballads and sea shanties, epics like *Beowulf*) and descriptive poems like *Prefabulous Animiles* by James Reeves do lend themselves to translation into the medium of paint and coloured pencil as long as one doesn't overdo it. It would be a mistake to lay on art after every lesson featuring narrative or descriptive poems. Poetry followed by art work only retains its novelty and compelling interest if it does not become a regular, often-repeated feature of one's approach. James Reeves (1958, p. 55) also makes a point of stressing the dangers of overdoing it, while offering helpful guidance as to what kind of poetry is best suited to illustration:

> Obviously this can be carried too far. A drawing of a slug or a snail after reading 'Old Shellover' (de la Mare) would be of very little use; but making a drawing can, given the right material, assist the full comprehension and realisation of a poem. To make a drawing inspired by something in the opening lines of Coleridge's 'Christabel' or de la Mare's 'Nicholas Nye' is one way of stimulating the pictorial sense and demands a more than usually careful and responsive reading of the poem.

PERFORMANCE

As I do practise what I preach, I cannot now recommend performance and the following sections from personal experience. I kept my own follow-up work to a minimum, as I have recommended to you. In other words, I never went beyond choral speaking, learning by heart, keeping personal anthologies and occasional art work. This was because I wanted to assess how effective poetry is in itself in speaking directly to our pupils. I was, therefore, obliged to cut out all the extras that usually accompany poetry lessons and are far from 'optional'. Teacher training is obsessed with the integration of subjects (in the footsteps of Plowden) and is hostile to the idea of discrete or self-contained lessons. It was essential for me to find out the educational value of my ideas and so for that reason I kept follow-up work to a minimum. Naturally enough, the school I was in had its own ideas as to what constituted valuable follow-up work and that is dealt with in Chapter 8.

This preamble is to make clear that what follows in this and the following sections of this chapter is not based upon my own personal experience. I have drawn upon the experiences of other teachers, especially those recorded in *Not Daffodils Again* (Calthrop and Ede, 1984). But I shall recommend only ideas that seem to me to be valuable in that they actually help to promote further interest in reading poetry. I am not interested in ideas that distract attention away from poetry and lead it into other areas. As far as I am concerned, the Plowden emphasis on integration in learning is unproven, runs counter to what the philosophers of education like R. S. Peters have to say about forms of knowledge, and is always damaging to an interest in poetry for its own sake.

The following ideas all involve a whole-school approach — something much more demanding and difficult to organize than what I have so far suggested.

Assemblies

One valuable idea is to devote a week's morning assemblies to willing staff to read their favourite poems to the whole assembled junior school. A brief explanation at the start of each reading as to why that reader has made her particular choice should allow teachers to recall childhood memories or personal feelings. It's a sort of 'Desert Island Poems'. Not all the staff may be willing to take part at first, but many will actually be spurred on later by the interest generated or by their own class's reiterated, 'When is it your turn, Miss?'.

The children can also be involved. One morning out of the five can be given over to their chosen readings. In Brockwell Junior School, Chesterfield (Derbyshire), the whole idea took off so well that what was initially planned for a week lasted a whole fortnight. A third-year junior class took the children's assembly with the theme of 'The Circling Year', taking the school through a year in poetry and music. One teacher was sufficiently excited by the project to recite from memory and in dialect that famous Stanley Holloway recitation, 'Albert and the Lion', to the great delight of all the pupils. This sort of promotional assembly offers an ideal opportunity to allow the histrionic capacities of the staff full sway.

It also offers an excellent opportunity to show the complete anthology in which one's chosen poem appears, and to mention briefly similar pieces in the book in the hopes that if it is on the school's book-club list or in the school library, there will be some interested buyers or browsers. Brockwell Junior School can testify to the success of this approach in generating immense interest among staff and pupils alike.

Presentation — in Choral Speech and Drama

It is also possible to arouse interest by organizing an entertaining 'poetry afternoon' at which each junior class selects and presents a poem to the rest of the school. The audience for this can (and ought to) include the infants and as many adults, like kitchen staff, ancillary helpers, school secretary, head, as are needed to make it more of an occasion. The selection of poems to be presented should be made by pupils as well as staff, as children can hardly get involved in something they do not like. It is important, too, to exercise care in the selection of the poems so that those chosen are susceptible to movement, mime, drama or choral speaking.

There has to be a strict time limit if infants are in the audience and young juniors are involved in the presentation (say, 30 minutes in all), so as not to overtax concentration. Props and costumes (if any) should be kept to a minimum as too many extras inhibit children. The main danger inherent in such an undertaking is that too much rehearsing will dissipate pupils' interest and spontaneity. Cromford Junior School (Derbyshire) found this so successful they decided to repeat it once a term.

A Poetry Week Culminating in a Poetry Concert or Soirée

This exercise involves the ultimate in performance in that parents, in other words, the public, are invited to attend. What you fill your poetry week with prior to its culmination in the concert will depend on staff interest, talent and availability. What it need not involve is too much rehearsal and repetition for the big night, as that can lead to boredom.

The school that tackled this gargantuan task head-on was an 11–16 comprehensive. The English department, who devised the project, involved all the first-, second-, and third-year pupils. This is the sort of project that can start as a simple idea but in the event can blossom as thoroughly as you would like it.

One of the first events (and a popular idea) was to involve the senior staff, such as the headmaster, deputies, heads of science, etc. (all those apparently uninterested in poetry) to read and talk about their favourite or Desert Island poems to the children involved. Then the English department organized various competitions for which the headmaster donated prizes. Every pupil prepared for and then entered the verse-speaking competition and the handwriting competition. Most pupils were persuaded to enter the verse-writing competition — a much more difficult task. A local poet was engaged to judge the finals of the verse-speaking competition at the concert. The drama club dramatized *The Pied Piper*. Children who had won prizes in local or national poetry competitions were honoured and included in the concert reading their prize-winning entries. A few weeks' concentrated poetry work culminated in an evening which was long remembered with real pleasure.

It is often difficult to know how to enhance and to develop the enthusiasm that one's lessons inspire. As far as poetry is concerned, *sharing* one's favourites with others is one of the simplest and most effective ways of doing it. In this instance, as in so many others, simple ideas are usually the best. Some of the whole-school projects outlined above offer further ideas for building on the momentum that one's lessons have generated.

A POEM AS A PROJECT

The following approach is my adaptation of suggestions made by John Cheetham in an article entitled 'Quarries in the primary school', to be found in *Writers, Critics and Children*, edited by G. Fox (Heinemann, London, 1978 p. 189–197). In that piece, Cheetham calls into question the project method which is so widespread in primary schools because, in his view, it leaves literature out of account, concentrating on what is purely factual. It appears that in the course of four years of visits to schools in his capacity as senior adviser with special responsibility for the teaching of English, he had never once seen a project based on a piece of literature. It is clear, however, that such work could deepen children's appreciation of a text and increase their understanding of themselves. He notes that, although primary schools are 'obsessed with the teaching of reading . . . children are not exposed to literature often enough and for long enough' (*ibid.* p. 192). Once the hurdle of learning to read has been overcome, schools appear not to know where to take those new and growing reading skills. What he goes on to recommend is a way of extending reading experience and deepening enjoyment of a text that should be more widely employed by teachers.

'Project' is an awkward, even inappropriate, word as it smacks of integrated-studies work and of a factual input and output. By 'project' Cheetham does not mean using, say, *The Pied Piper of Hamelin* as a springboard for investigating the different methods of rat catching or as an occasion for examining the incidence of bubonic plague in our history. A project on *The Pied Piper* would involve these incidentally as part of its background, but would not concentrate on them as part of the *work* the pupils would have to engage in. By the same token, *The Ancient Mariner* would not involve children in factual work on the migration of birds or the navigational difficulties of different geographical regions. Literature is not to be treated as an excuse for history, geography or social studies. It is to be examined on its own terms, as language and as experience.

Cheetham's suggestions are for the class exploration of a novel. I have substituted a narrative poem and added some ideas of my own. The elements we would wish to explore are as follows:

1.   The story — the particular episodes or moments that capture the children's imagination.
2.   The different characters and their relationships one to another.
3.   The connection between the people and incidents in the poem and the children's own lives and experience.
4.   The physical settings and changing moods of the text.
5.   The language and form of the poem — its particular memorableness.

These elements need not necessarily find their natural expression in talk or writing. Pupils may explore 5, for example, by a choral presentation of part of the poem.

Where Cheetham takes the children's novel *The Wheel on the School*, by Meindert de Jong, to look at in detail, I shall make suggestions for *The Pied Piper of Hamelin*. The work prompted by a poem will, by virtue of its greater brevity, not last as long as that which a novel gives rise to. It would be a mistake to force the project to last for half a term when it has exhausted its framework within three or four weeks. But however long the project lasts, the work must constantly require the pupils to come back to the text as their point of reference.

There are two main phases to the work:

A. Basic

The poem is read by the teacher for the enjoyment of the class. After a first or even second reading, some talk will be in order about various aspects of the poem. There will certainly be class teaching by the teacher on matters that need elucidating. For example, pupils need to know that rats are one of the most damaging of pests. They eat or foul vast amounts of food each year and, moreover, constitute a danger to public health by spreading disease. This is the place to mention that the Black Death in the fourteenth century, which killed about half the population of Europe (an estimated 25 million people), was spread by rats. Because of this and because rats multiply at an alarming rate, one of the services that local councils provide, for which we pay in our rates, is a pest control department. We do expect them to see to this problem properly. All this input will be, and will remain, oral. New words will be clarified and recorded.

B. The Project

The emphasis should be on creative work inspired by the poem, in such areas as follows:

1. Themes related to the children's own lives:
   (a) The importance of keeping one's word.
   (b) Being greedy and selfish.
   (c) Helping people.
2. Art work:
   (a) Paintings of the Piper himself (see stanzas v and vi) and possibly of the Mayor.
   (b) A class frieze of the story in the form of a collage.
   (c) Individual pictures of the magic land that the Piper's music promises.
3. Drama/choral presentation.
4. Writing. This can cover a range of tasks from purely imaginative to more personal accounts.
   (a) Imagine you are the Piper (or the lame boy); describe the day you (he) came to Hamelin, what happened, and how you felt at different points during the day.

(b)   Have you ever broken a promise or has anyone ever failed to keep their word to you? Explain what happened and how you felt about it.

As Cheetham insists, 'Of paramount importance in all this are the searching questions carefully devised by the teacher' (*ibid.* p. 197), which should be put formally in a class situation so that no one misses out. For example:

1.   Why did the Council refuse to pay the Piper the small sum he asked for (1000 guilders) when they had actually promised him 50,000 guilders?
2.   How would you have behaved if you had been the Mayor or a councillor? Why?
3.   Did the disappearance of the children change anyone in Hamelin? How?

All these suggestions for work are, of course, devised and directed by the teacher. Such control shouldn't rule out the children's own enthusiasms determining at least some of the work they do within the project. We should always be sufficiently flexible, especially when it comes to writing tasks, for example, to allow elbow room for the possibility of a deeply felt personal response from an individual child. It is hard to know how to cater for this, but framing one of the writing tasks in a broader, more general way might help. Something like 'Describe a day in the life of the lame boy after the disappearance of his playmates' might perhaps give more room for manoeuvre to some children.

Other long narrative poems that would be worthwhile to tackle as a project include *Beowulf* (10+), *Sir Gawain and the Green Knight* (12+), *The Ancient Mariner* (13+), and 'The Death of Robin Hood' (11+). As with all the other examples of follow-up work in this chapter, it is important not to overdo the project approach to a poem. Once a term seems to me to be often enough.

Chapter 8

Write Your Own

Throughout this book I have inveighed against the current and widespread practice of using poetry as a 'stimulus' for promoting writing. You may, therefore, be wondering why a chapter has been included on the topic. I still wish to stress that, in my view, and for the reasons given earlier, writing should not be a regular feature of one's poetry lessons, which are solely for reading and speaking.

However, I am forced to bow to the inevitable in that I know that setting poetry-writing tasks is regarded as essential by some teachers, so that what I have said in opposition to the practice will not stop them. I am prepared to concede that an occasional 'write-your-own' task can do little harm. It must be well prepared and should never resemble a poetry-writing session I once witnessed. The student on teaching practice went into a class of 13-year-old girls with a short poem, Charles Causley's ballad, 'Timothy Winters'. She read it once, asked a couple of perfunctory questions which took less than a minute of their joint time and then set their writing task. She told the pupils that they were to write their own poem about a deprived child. Her only advice was, 'Remember, a poem doesn't have to rhyme', advice that strangely contradicted the jaunty rhythm and careful rhyme scheme of the poem she'd just read. During the rest of the double period the girls occasionally protested that they didn't know what to write. The student simply repeated her instruction and advice. This is not the way to do it, either regularly or even very occasionally. What this chapter aims to do is to share with you some reasonably successful 'write-your-own' lessons I have taught to pupils ranging in age from 8 to 13.

FREE VERSE

But first, a few general points. Like most students and teachers, the teaching-practice student made no attempt to suggest which specific non-rhyming form her pupils might employ, when she proferred her simplistic advice. They could have adopted 'blank verse', a rhythmical non-rhyming form, Shakespeare's choice for his plays. However, that would have entailed her providing some instruction in the metrical nature of the iambic pentameter. They might also have chosen 'haiku', a simple Japanese form.

This, too, requires instruction, as it involves a tight little pattern of seventeen syllables. Anglo-Saxon alliterative verse was also a possibility.

In my experience, though, it is 'free verse' of twentieth-century American origin, akin to abstract painting in its complete overthrow of technique, that most students have in mind when they offer the unhelpful advice, 'Remember, a poem doesn't have to rhyme'. What I find so fatuous about this advice is that it blithely ignores the fact that the bulk of English poetry does, nevertheless, employ rhyme and has seen fit to do so for nearly a thousand years. The little that doesn't rhyme, like that which does, goes in for a high degree of patterning and utilizes much of the battery of rhetorical techniques and poetic devices available to the poet writing in English. For if rhyme doesn't make for poetry, what does? When is poetry not poetry and when is it merely verse? When is it doggerel? What separates Eleanor Farjeon from Pam Ayres? These are questions that, if we as teachers are determined that our pupils should write their own, we must be prepared to address ourselves to.

For how far can we assess what our pupils have written, without answers to these questions? Once poetry has abandoned rhythm, rhyme and metre, when does it become prose? The answer to this last question may well be when it is 'free verse'. Of all the non-rhyming forms, 'free verse' most resembles prose in that it dispenses with the music and obvious patterning that makes poetry so distinctive and memorable, particularly at the primary level. The contemporary poet, Vernon Scannell, who has himself written a very helpful guide to poetry for the ordinary reader, would agree:

> The fact is that while pleasing poems have been written in free verse, a great deal of what, in this form, passes for poetry is in fact prose — and often miserably inferior prose — arranged on the page to resemble the shape of verse.
>
> (1987, p.50)

I suspect that it is this closeness to prose which makes 'free verse' so attractive to teachers. It is seen as an easy model to imitate because like prose it requires no instruction in technical matters. (I for one happen to think that prose writing does require 'instruction' in technical matters, but that is another question and not one to be considered here). If this closeness to prose is what recommends it to teachers, why do they not set a prose-writing task in the first place? Why must it masquerade as a poetry writing task?

In an article in *The Times Educational Supplement* (1978) on teaching poetry, Leonard Clark, children's poet and HMI, once described children's own poetry writing as 'chopped-up prose'. It would surely be better for children to try their hands at real prose rather than such fragmented writing as Clark had in mind. After all, prose makes considerable intellectual demands on pupils, much more so than 'poetry' that uses no techniques and doesn't have to rhyme. Prose requires a linear, rational development and logical connections to be perceived between apparently separate statements. Links of reason and consequence, of condition and concession, are important components of prose writing, though whether these appear or not in a child's writing is dependent on the type of task devised by the teacher.

It is as if poetry is deemed to be superior to prose in some mysterious way. This is manifestly not so. Actually, in the history of the world, poetry belongs to the early, primitive phase of Man's development. The most primitive of communities like the Bushmen and Australian Aborigines have their poetry if only in the form of oral chants. Communities do not develop prose writing until they are much more highly organized and sophisticated. Complex prose, like that of the great philosophers and novelists, belongs to societies that have achieved a high level of civilization.

All this is not to suggest that we write poetry off as primitive. It is obvious that Shakespeare's sonnets and Keats's odes, in their scintillating deployment of difficult rhyme schemes, their skilful use of rhetorical devices, all united in the service of expressing ambiguous feelings and complex thoughts, are highly wrought artefacts. Such poetry, produced in highly advanced societies, is likely to be extremely sophisticated. What I am trying to say is that good poetry and good prose are not mutually exclusive. Good prose is, in its own way, as skilful and as artfully constructed as good poetry. For that reason, when setting writing tasks teachers should not scorn prose as the perfect medium for some children to express themselves in.

It is a fact that some children cannot or will not write poetry. It is also a fact that some children, especially those between the ages of 6 and 10, possess an amazing facility for skilful rhyming and accurate scansion. Yet by a strange irony the current practice in primary schools is, perversely, to shunt all pupils into the narrow vein and dead end of 'free verse' or 'chopped-up prose'. To illustrate what is possible, the following is a poem composed by a 9-year-old working-class London child in 1961 (long before 'creativity' was the order of the day), a child who was not particularly academic but had been deeply impressed by classical mythology:

> *Pluto*
> Bare are the trees
> Frosty is the breeze
> And the hedgehog is tightly curled.
>
> The grass gives a quiver
> And the king comes hither
> The King of the Underworld.
>
> He is daring and bold
> In his chariot of gold
> With black horses' wings unfurled.
>
> He has come from the deep
> A wife to seek
> A wife with beauty pearled.
> (Wilma Dettmer)

If some pupils can cope with the tricky but satisfying business of making poetry rhyme (and in no facile way), then we should not deny them the opportunity of so excelling. The ubiquitous promotion of 'free verse' that comes in the advice the student offered seems designed to reduce all children to the lowest common denominator. Because some can't rhyme, none shall. However, there *is* another way out of this dilemma. If some pupils feel they cannot write rhymed poetry, they should be allowed, or encouraged, to use prose instead. If education is genuinely to respond to the needs of *all* pupils, then different provision must be made for the different talents of pupils.

For those teachers who worry about the possible élitism in this, let them rest assured that it's not the most intellectually able pupils who will carry off the poetic honours every time. In my experience, the case is quite the reverse. The most able child I have ever taught simply couldn't write poetry of any kind, rhymed or unrhymed. Her prose, however, was brilliant, even at the age of 11. It was mature and sophisticated, full of complex sentences and rare conjunctions. It is true too that less able children tend to be unhappy with writing their own poetry. But for some of those less academic but not backward pupils in between these two extremes, the writing of rhymed, or highly patterned or tightly structured verse can be a boon. It can help such children to express themselves well, probably because of the succinctness of the poetic form and the discipline that the brevity imposes.

READING IS WORK

Having conceded as much, I am still worried by the automatic assumption that is inculcated in us by our training that the reading of poetry (or of literature) should be *used*, capitalized on, to promote something else, that is, writing. For one thing, this ignores the fact that writing is so much harder than reading and *inwardly* digesting and appreciating. Indeed, it seems to downgrade the act of reading. Because children have enjoyed reading some poems and have responded to the rhythm and rhyme, it doesn't follow that they are either *able* to write themselves in a similar vein or on a similar subject or actually *wish* to do so. Responding to poetry is active in a very private way. 'Work' in a poetry lesson is of an interior, personal kind and cannot be quantified or tested. Reading is not a *lesser* activity in comparison with writing.

Modern theories of reader-response make great play with the fact that we all take different things from literature. We notice different aspects, emphasize different features and respond according to what we bring personally to the text. Responses can be so divergent that the author's intention becomes simply one of the many meanings the text can generate. Whether we agree with such theories or not, we know from our own experience of reading and of children's reading that what assumes importance for one child or reader in a text will not be the same for another. This is not to suggest that we or children simply find in a text things that are not there. Texts are such rich, many-faceted artefacts, which also interact with a reader's personality and interests, that the reading of them is a creative and expansive process. The imagination of the reader is required to work, his emotions and understanding are put on the alert, his past experience comes into play. To assume that children are not working when reading and are not working *until* they are made to put pen to paper is to ignore what the reading process is, and the real demands it makes on each individual reader.

USING POETRY AS A TOOL

There is more to my qualms about 'write your own' than what I have said hitherto. My main reason for writing this book, and what worries me still about the almost universal commitment in schools to 'write your own' *on a regular basis*, is the 'hidden curriculum' of exploit and use that this practice subjects poetry to. It is, in fact, destructive of poetry to use it constantly as a tool and not to read it for its own intrinsic worth. Its value lies in what it is inherently, not in what use it can be put to, or what it can stimulate.

Ultimately, such an exploitative approach has even more far-reaching implications. It presents children with an insidiously dangerous model at a formative stage in the development of their own sense of values. Exploitation simply mirrors and reinforces the values of the commercially exploitative world that exists outside the school gates and can only help to prepare our pupils to be its ready victims or exponents. If ever there was a 'hidden curriculum' it is this. It is surely the school's job to counteract such influences, not to duplicate them.

The notion of 'stimulus' and 'response', which underpins the way in which poetry is used to promote writing, derives from Pavlov's experiments with his dogs and Skinner's behaviourist ideas. Such conditioning may work with dogs, a bell and a concrete object like a bowl of food. However, applied as it is today to the interaction of pupils' minds and hearts with good literature, it is unacceptably deterministic and reductionist in its crude behaviourism. Poetry is totally unlike a bowl of food in the varied reactions ranging from belly laughs to quiet thoughtfulness that it can provoke.

THE DEMANDS OF WRITING

As professionals and adults, it is easy for us to forget what a difficult task writing is. In writing, children are required to use all those agreed signs and signals that in speech are conveyed by the voice (through tone, inflexion, volume, etc.) and by extra-vocal things like a shake of the head or a shrug of the shoulders. To expect children to juggle with all these signs and signals, write complex sentences, employ a wide and varied vocabulary, and *create* an original poem as well is a very tall order. It is not one we should force or expect our pupils to do every day or even every week. Who can be truly creative *to order*? If it can be wrung out of children on a regular basis, then it is a very mechanical exercise and hardly deserves to be described as creative. I suspect that it is because teachers instinctively realize this that they refrain from setting the writing of rhymed poetry as a task and plump for 'free verse' as easier to manage. Yet what is the purpose of setting writing tasks in school?

The immediate end of writing tasks on a day-to-day, week-to-week basis at school is to help our pupils exercise and eventually master that highly complicated business of putting pen to paper and all that that entails. It is clear that this involves remembering all those agreed signs, usually called punctuation, giving thought to correct spelling as well as making these hard-to-direct marks on paper. It's a process of translation, just as difficult for a young primary pupil as an adult finds moving from one foreign language into another.

Writing is a method of giving form to thoughts and feelings and facts. Those latter predominate at first in all pupils' written work because they are concrete, solid and reliable. They look and sound very real. They are real. This is a very necessary reassurance if you are still at the stage of greeting with some degree of wonder the gradual transformation of a blank page of white paper with thin and fat, tall and short, spider-like markings. Children are right to perceive it as a magical development. It *is* a real high point in mankind's development. In the very early stages of their initiation into this wonderful skill, children find evanescent things like feelings hard enough to describe in an original way, let alone to pin down on paper. It is only through continued practice at the sheer technical business that is writing that allows mastery to be rapidly achieved. Hence, to overload a weak pupil of 11 with the taxing task of creating (if only in 'free verse') a poem when his command of the technical aspects of the skill is still severely limited is asking for trouble. Pupil disruption is inevitable. In other words, creation or invention in any form of poetry is inappropriate if pupils are not sufficiently advanced in their command of the skill to be able to do it largely without thought to its mechanics — at least, as second nature.

As suggested in an earlier chapter, writing can take many forms. Essentially the tasks we set should be appropriate for each individual pupil, that is, take into account his degree of mastery of the mechanics of writing. While composing a poem might be suitable for some, like the 9-year-old quoted earlier, it will certainly not be so for all in the same class. Some pupils may be best suited with a task like compiling, by means of *copying*, their own anthologies of favourite poems hitherto read in class. I am well aware that copying (like dictation) is not in favour at present, but it does serve several useful purposes as long as it is carefully supervised by the teacher. It gives children practice in developing that *fluent hand* that so many, even at the secondary level, still lack and without which success in exams will not be forthcoming. It also helps to develop an essential skill, the co-ordination of hand, eye and brain that again so many pupils lack, partly through insufficient practice. Copying is simply one helpful step along the path to writing mastery which all pupils have to tread.

Within educational circles it has become the norm for us to think our job is to provide opportunity for creativity (whatever that means) whenever writing in English is to be done. However, developing a greater and surer command of the mechanics of writing as a tool is really the main aim of devising writing tasks, particularly at the primary level. I found that even at the upper secondary level, if I overtaxed those pupils for whom the basic writing skills were still a struggle, by requiring poetry or invention, then all I got for my pains was disruption. The personal satisfaction that stems from attainable goals is an important factor in reconciling pupils to the need for constant perseverance and effort in acquiring this skill. No one learns to do it overnight. Creativity, whether in prose or poetry, is so vague a notion that pupils cannot detect what it is they are meant to attain or master. By and large, pupils do need to be able to perceive the parameters of the lesson. It is for all these foregoing reasons that I feel that the 'write-your-own' type of lesson is at present overdone in our schools.

Because of the difficulties inherent in it, therefore, a poetry-writing lesson should not be a regular feature of our English lessons. I found that it could be valuable for some pupils if it became a special event, a once-in-a-while lesson, never more than twice or three times a term. Indeed, if it is as well prepared beforehand as it needs to be, the teacher will not find the time or energy to lay it on more often than that. What is intended is something in which much more than just a poem or two is needed if the lesson is to be of any benefit to the pupils. It is the teacher's job to open up the subject that he or she wants the pupils to explore. Quite a few poems are needed for this, at the very least three or four, but if the poems are excessively short then as many as five or six. Some prose is often helpful, too, and certainly lots of talk, both the teacher's and the pupils' own. The talk has specifically to be focused on the poems, on their language and on the experience or picture that they attempt to evoke. Personal reminiscence is in order here from the teacher as well pupils. Only by such a thoroughgoing opening up of the subject-matter which the pupils will be expected to write about can the majority of them be enabled to see what we are looking for and so put pen to paper intelligibly. Before they do so, there is the additional and crucial matter of *instruction* in structure, rhyme schemes, patterning, etc., if anything other than prose is to be attempted by the children. As will be seen from the following specimen lesson, though I read poems I did not expect or ask my pupils to write anything other than prose. Even that was excessively difficult for some of them.

SPECIMEN LESSON 1

This was a lesson with 8-year-olds on 'Nature' and some of its tiniest and apparently most vulnerable creatures. My first step was to read to the class the following five short poems, which suggest what the world we all take for granted as the right size might look and feel like through the eyes of such tiny creatures:

The Leaves in a Frolic
The leaves had a wonderful frolic,
They danced to the wind's loud song,
They whirled and they floated and scampered,
They circled and flew along.

The moon saw the little leaves dancing,
Each looked like a small brown bird.
The man in the moon smiled and listened,
And this is the song he heard.

The North Wind is calling, is calling,
And we must whirl round and round,
And when our dancing is ended
We'll make a warm quilt for the ground.
                                    (Anon.)

Explorers
The furry moth explores the night
The fish discover cities drowned
And moles and worms and ants explore
The many cupboards underground.

The soaring lark explores the sky
And gulls explore the stormy seas
The busy squirrel rummages
Among the attics of the trees.
                        (James Reeves)

The Fly
How large unto the tiny fly
    Must little things appear!
A rosebud like a featherbed,
    Its prickle like a spear;

A dewdrop like a looking-glass,
    A hair like golden wire;
The smallest grain of mustard-seed,
    As fierce as coals of fire;

A loaf of bread, a lofty hill;
    A wasp, a cruel leopard;
And specks of salt as bright to see
    As lambkins to a shepherd.
                    (Walter de la Mare)

The Ladybird
Tiniest of tortoises
Your shining back
Is like an egg of red
With spots of black.

How lightly you walk
Across this land
Of valleys and crevasses
That is my hand.

Your tiny black legs,
So small, so thin,
Their touch is like a feather
Upon my skin.

There, spread out
Your wings and fly.
No frailer creature
Beneath the sky.
(Leoma Rushton, aged 9)

The Caterpillar
Brown and furry
Caterpillar in a hurry,
Take your walk
To the shady leaf, or stalk,
Or what not,
Which may be the chosen spot.
No toad spy you,
Hovering bird of prey pass by you;
Spin and die,
To live again as butterfly.
(Christina Rossetti)

Before I began to read I set the scene with comments like those in the foregoing sentence. Once I had finished my first reading I embarked on a second and then we all examined each poem in some detail to see just what pictures it conjured up for us, the readers. Then I talked to the class about a Chinese proverb, 'To an ant the most ferocious creature is not a tiger but a chicken', and asked for explanations as to what it meant. I then took the implications of that proverb to see how they appeared in a vivid piece of English prose. I read a substantial passage from *Gulliver's Travels* in Brobdingnag, where Gulliver was a tiny being and all the other characters were giants. In such a context, a pair of wasps resembled flying tigers. This passage was greeted with much interest and provoked much talk. (Incidentally, many children went on to borrow *Gulliver's Travels* from the class library.) We then compared notes as to what we thought things like a petal or a dew drop or grass might look like to an ant or a fly. Only after a lot of thoughtful and sensitive suggestions from many members of the class did I then propose that the children try to write a paragraph or half a page from the eyeview of an ant or a fly or any tiny creature of their own choice. Imagine you are an ant. What would the world look like to you? All our joint reading and talking had taken 40 minutes, only about 15- 20 minutes was left for writing, which is just about right for 8-year-olds if they are to work uninterruptedly. The subject had been thoroughly opened up, yet there was still some room for personally interesting or striking details.

In case you think 15–20 minutes is not long enough and are tempted to allow pupils to spread themselves across half a morning or more, it's important to bear in mind that poetic authorities like Ted Hughes also recommend a set time limit as well as a set length for pupils to work within. Hughes (1967, p. 23) actually suggests 10 minutes and one page for 11-year-olds: 'These artificial limits create a crisis, which rouses the brain's resources: the compulsion towards haste overthrows the ordinary precautions, flings everything into top gear'. The results written within such constraints of time and length, all displayed interesting analogies, some that had been mentioned in class, some that had not. I suspect that the clear yardstick that all our reading and talk had provided helped the children, so that neither spelling nor sentence construction nor vocabulary suffered too much as they sought to organize their perceptions:

> If I was an ant, I would be careful not to go near a farm because if I did the chicken would gobble me up until he could eat no more.
> If I was a fly, I would fly but look where I'm going otherwise a spider's net would catch me and a vicious spider would come, even if I struggled it would be no good.
>
> (Aaron Sethi)

For an 8-year-old this shows an amazingly mature command of English. So many subordinate clauses is unusual in one so young, and when they are introduced by uncommon conjunctions like 'if' and 'until' it is even more striking and commendable. There is some precise vocabulary, in such words as 'vicious', 'struggled' and 'gobbled', all spelt correctly, too. The next example is less assured:

> The little spiders like me climb through the trees. The world is enormous and I am small. Through the grass on the wall, seeds are the same size as me. People are monsters and I am a little spider. I climb on tables. All the soups on the tables are boyling.
>
> (Nicholas Stantjesky)

This example reveals the child really getting down to the worm's-eye view as he perceives that seeds (not mentioned in our talk) resemble him in size. From such a minute perspective, even warm soup, an oddly domestic image, seems to threaten.

Although there could be no mistaking what I expected the pupils to write *in prose* for me, some children were still flummoxed by the task. It is a point worth bearing in mind when devising writing tasks that, while some children can immensely enjoy reading literature, they are quite unable to imitate even the subject-matter, let alone its poetic form. One boy wrote the following:'Ants ants Emagen to be a ants withe thes small litte lags and a small litte doo De Emgun to be a ants' (The Ants, Matthew Bellotti). It is immediately apparent that this child still has major problems of a basic kind, that is, in translating what he hears into their visual, written counterparts. Phonological correspondence is lacking at the very simplest level, for he links a singular indefinite article ('a') to a plural noun ('ants') — 'to be a ants'. He is not likely ever to hear such an expression. It is clear, I think, that this child required a much simpler task, something like copying out the one poem of the five we read that he liked the most, so as to accustom his eye to the visual correspondence of what he had received aurally.

However, this boy's twin sister displayed a much surer grasp of the skill of writing and not just at a basic level:

> Tiny, tiny, tiny me in a forist in a tree O Dear I am stuck in David Longs hair when I got out I went in to a house and in the Bath room I got smeard with tooth paste and I went out side agen and I saw a Bee I thoart It was a tiger and I got stung By it I tride

to have a ride on it then I fell into a Daisy it felt like a bed then I fell in to a forist it was rely a patch of grass

(Ruth Bellotti)

She obviously needs some instruction in when to capitalize, how to punctuate and how to spell some frequently used words like 'tried', 'again', 'thought', 'forest' and 'really'. But these technical aspects of writing are easy to rectify as they lie within the teacher's own area of responsibility and simply need her to do some regular instruction in them. Despite such functional weaknesses, the girl has grasped fully what the task required and sticks to it from start to finish. She is so small she can hitch a ride on a bee, use a daisy as a bed and find that a classmate's hair as well as grass resembles a forest. What also impressed me was her command of some very precise and accurate vocabulary like 'smeared' and 'patch'.

When I discussed this girl's writing recently with a group of students in teacher training, many found it lacking in originality. This is because the child had reproduced some of the examples we had raised in our talk as well as Gulliver's tiger simile. Several other children did, too, and it is hardly surprising as it's a very graphic image. After all, *Gulliver's Travels* had made a tremendous impression on the class. Borrowing at this age is something of a tribute to the source. We cannot expect an 8-year-old to come up with freshly minted, entirely personally derived comparisons throughout her piece of writing. She is still manifestly grappling with the sheer mechanics of writing. To make such demands of such young children is to put them on a par with *adult, professional* writers. This is demonstrably absurd.

I certainly didn't seek originality. What I was looking for were goals more attainable at this particular level — the ability to find precise and accurate vocabulary, to handle coherently the many examples we had mentioned in our talk, and to shape them into a cogent, unified whole. I also wanted them to write a reasonable amount in the limited time available. Gwen, too, included the tiger image and some other ideas that had come up during discussion. Her piece is simpler in structure and shorter than Ruth's. She does choose, and spell correctly, some good vocabulary, for example, 'universe' and 'panther':

I'm a ant extremly small. And the universe so tall Imagine a buzzy bee it would be a tiger to me. And a black cat would be a panther. And a monkey to me would be King-Kong. And a lovely gold fish would be a terrible shark.

(Gwen Odeluga)

Though she wrote ostensibly in prose, it is plain that in the first half of her paragraph, Gwen is unconsciously making rhymes:

> I'm a ant extremly small
> And the universe so tall
> Imagine a buzzy bee
> It would be a tiger to me.

These rhymes in no way detract from the intelligibility of what she has to say nor are they forced or facile, yet such are the usual arguments for actively discouraging children writing in rhyme.

After another lesson, in which I read seven or eight poems about cats, a boy in the same class produced the following perfect little gem of a poem, written across the page as if it, too, were prose:

> Silent as he stalks
> The mouse is unaware
> That the cat is there.
> Run mouse! Run mouse!
> Scurry, hurry do
> Or the cat will catch you.
> (Micky Delaney)

It is obvious that children who can write like this without any instruction in rhyme schemes, structure or patterning are naturally talented. Many more can produce startlingly good work if the teacher provides direct and clear instruction in form and structure.

SPECIMEN LESSON 2

There are few more tightly structured non-rhyming forms than haiku, a Japanese poem of three lines which I used to teach to 12–13-year-olds when I was working at the secondary level. It is so brief, almost instantaneous, a form that it needs very careful thought as to how to introduce it to one's pupils. I decided on a pictorial approach. I had already acquired some reproductions (from a calendar) of classical Japanese paintings. For the purposes of teaching haiku, the more delicate these are the better. A also went to the British Museum and bought a dozen or so postcards of Hokusai and Hiroshige's work, which I later mounted on black card. The British Museum also has available for sale a magnificent poster of a tiger which was used to advertise an exhibition some years ago. Just before the actual lesson began, I pinned all this pictorial material to the cork display-boards in my room.

Since the *strangeness* of oriental art may well strike children first, before they are impressed by its beauty, and in order to forestall a possibly scornful response to its simplicity, I stressed how different Japanese art was from what they, the pupils, knew as art. I also drew attention to its apparent oddness and insisted that difference should not equate with inferiority. I need not have feared. My pupils were so bowled over by the beauty of Japanese art that some of them even persuaded their parents to take them to the British Museum to see the originals of the postcards I had displayed.

I then invited my pupils to describe the quality of the paintings, doing what amounted to a vocabulary exercise. I aimed to elicit and did (but, if necessary, to introduce) words like 'beautiful' (of course), 'graceful', 'elegant', 'delicate', 'refined'. One girl even came up with 'exquisite'! I talked about the light touch, deft execution and simplicity of these beautiful paintings, where a few strokes of the brush suggest a whole world. This made a perfect introduction to the poetry, which I pointed out was just as elegant, simple and delicate, and made a similar attempt to capture perfectly a scene in nature.

I had previously duplicated about six examples of haiku from Bashō's *The Narrow Road to the Deep North, and Other Travel Sketches* (Penguin Classics, Harmondsworth, 1966), which I read with the class twice. I then embarked on a detailed analysis of the haiku structure. Since these miniature poems are organized according to their syllables, it is necessary to ensure that all the pupils know what a syllable is. We talked about syllables, about monosyllabic and polysyllabic words, and did a good half-dozen examples together on the board, dramatically counting their syllables aloud. I then stressed that the haiku has to contain only 17 syllables and that it must be divided into three lines of 5–7–5 syllables each.

It was also necessary to explain that translations of haiku (like some of those on the duplicated sheet in front of them) often fail to achieve the right number of syllables per line, though I insisted upon a strict adherence to the pattern in their efforts. To show them it could be done, I had attempted a couple of haiku myself and read these to the class.

When we re-read Bashō's haiku and I discussed their content with the children, stressing the way in which a picture from Nature or a feeling is hinted at in one or two strokes; the way the poet tries to pinpoint a timeless moment by using the minimum of detail.

This introduction had taken 20 minutes, so for the rest of the lesson — 15 minutes — I suggested my pupils try writing at least two or three haiku on aspects of Nature, like the seasons. Some went so far as to produce five or six and some chose their own topics. Many were startling good, as may be seen from the following examples from the work of one class:

> I look at my hand
> I see valleys and mountains
> And paths to nowhere.
> > (Angela Brown)

> The Far Eastern Art
> With its lines so slight but firm
> Each sketch holds a thought.
> > (Sarah Webb)

> Frosty window panes
> A sugar coated glass sheet
> Now, slowly melting.
> > (Karen Jackman)

> Eyes are red and wet
> And hearts are sore and broken
> Longing for the past.
> > (Samina Khan)

> Minute snow flakes fall
> Soft but cold and wet to touch
> A dainty doily.
> > (Ann Vogt)

> Wax which is melting
> It flickers and glows in air
> String which holds a flame.
> > (Enza Barbarino)

I found this was a really useful exercise for heightening my pupils' awareness of the formal nature of poetry and the craftsmanship required of the writer. It helped them, too, to appreciate that a strictly disciplined framework can enable them to order their thoughts, feelings and ideas more clearly and succinctly than an unstructured impressionism can. Pupils whose work was not normally outstanding in any way excelled themselves. The tight structure put a fine pressure on them to search about for the exact word and to put it in the right place. It made them stop and think and re-organize in a way they would never have done for prose writing. Of course, the space in which they have to do this is very small, only three lines. But the brevity of the form is one of its recommendations, for young children cannot write in such a controlled fashion at any great length. Let me end this lesson with some examples from a generally much less able class than the one I have just quoted from:

> Ponds glazed with sunlight
> Icicles like crystal tears
> Glint as I go past.
> > (Tracy Bearham)

> A lonely puddle
> Suddenly came to life when
> A rainbow appeared.
> > (Lesley Wilde)

> The moon has risen
> A million stars appear
> To light up the sky.
> > (Yvonne Sibblies)

> Long elegant stem
> A pompom of fragile fluff
> Dandylion clock.
> > (Phaedra Kingman)

> Frost glitters soundless
> On the dry clear window pane
> Sharp, emotionless.
> > (Maria Bubb)

> A baby asleep
> Innocent beautiful
> Like a lovely rose.
> > (Parul Desai)

It is quite plain even from these by and large less arresting examples just how effective the haiku structure is in forcing pupils to be precise in their language. 'Glint' is a magnificent word, and in conjunction with 'go' and 'glazed' it introduces an alliterative pattern in the poem, just as the 't' of 'glint' and 'past' and the hard 'c' of 'icicles', 'like' and 'crystals' also alliterate. Tracey's haiku is an exceptionally accomplished piece of writing. Even so, some of the others display that same capacity to startle and surprise for which Bashō's originals strive.

SPECIMEN LESSON 3

My next example of a successful writing lesson came out of the reading of one very long poem that I selected specifically because it called up personal experience and reminiscence. I read this to two different classes, 9-year-olds as well as to top juniors. 'These I Have Loved', by Rupert Brooke, runs into several pages in the original. I selected a mere 30 lines that I thought would be appealing and comprehensible to modern children:

> These I have loved:
> > White plates and cups, clean-gleaming,
> Wet roofs beneath the lamplight; the strong crust
> Of friendly bread; and many-tasting foods;

Rainbows; and the blue bitter smoke of wood;
And radiant raindrops couching in cool flowers;
And flowers themselves, that sway through sunny hours,
Dreaming of moths that drink them under the moon;
Then, the cool kindliness of sheets, that soon
Smooth away trouble; and the rough male kiss
Of blankets; grainy wood; live hair that is
Shining and free; blue-massing clouds; the keen
Unpassioned beauty of a great machine;
The benison of hot water; furs to touch;
The good smell of old clothes; and other such —
The comfortable smell of friendly fingers,
Hair's fragrance, and the musty reek that lingers
About dead leaves and last year's ferns . . . Dear names
And thousand other throng to me! Royal flames;
Sweet water's dimpling laugh from tap to spring;
Holes in the ground; and voices that do sing;
Voices in laughter, too . . .
Firm sands; and the little dulling edge of foam
That browns and dwindles as the wave goes home;
And washen stones, gay for an hour; the cold
Graveness of iron; moist black earthen mould;
Sleep; and high places; footprints in the dew;
And oaks; and brown horse-chestnuts, glossy-new;
And new-peeled sticks; and shining pools on grass—
All these have been my loves.

After reading the poem twice, I asked the class to find any vocabulary in it they didn't understand. As I expected, 'benison', 'musty' and 'reek' all cropped up. These I explained. I then attempted to heighten the class's awareness of language precisely used and of description informed by close and detailed observation by giving time and attention to the poet's examples. The 'glossy-new' chestnuts were much appreciated, while 'the cool kindliness of sheets' evoked favourable comment. Others responded to 'the blue bitter smoke of wood'. We considered how hair can be described as 'live', how a smell can be 'comfortable', how water can be said to be 'dimpling' and how it can 'laugh'. The Bullock Report (DES, 1975, p. 132) makes it clear that it is vitally important to focus our pupils' attention sharply on the text itself before moving on to something else. To introduce a text as a mere springboard for writing or discussion of 'an area of experience to which it [the text] is related' (*ibid*. p.132) is to oversimplify the text's own richness. A close and attentive engagement with the text can help the children to find their own questions to ask. One query unprompted by me was how a machine can be described as beautiful and even 'unpassioned'. Only after thoroughly exploring the language of the poem, did I begin to hint at the task to come.

First, I talked about things I had loved when I was their age — autumn evenings just before Bonfire Night when the air seemed to be tinged with a burnt smell; bare electric light-bulbs hanging in the local greengrocer's shop, which seemed to cast a delicate glow in the autumn dusk; frosty mornings when you can actually see your own breath, as well as that thin layer of frost looking for all the world like feathery icing on twigs and branches; and so on.

They contributed, too, many of them eagerly and sensitively. I then gave them the rest of the lesson (20 minutes) to write in prose a page of what things they have loved in their own short lives. I set a minimum of six examples and insisted that they describe their loved things and not just say something like 'rain' and leave it as flatly and baldly as that. The trap I suspected most would fall into would be that of simply writing a list. However, few succumbed to this, largely because I asked them to go into some descriptive detail about each loved thing. The results were very pleasing.

Because it drew on genuine personal experience or preference, it engaged the children's interest from the start. Because it was relatively straightforward, it enabled them to cope with all that successful writing entails — spelling, sentence construction, vocabulary. I was particularly pleased with the following example, as this 9-year-old West Indian boy had produced nothing of any merit or length since the beginning of term. He was immensely and justifiably proud of the result, especially when I gave it a mark of 8 out of 10. He was in firm control at the beginning when he employed some fine verbs: 'rustling', 'trampling' and 'crackling':

These I Have Loved

I like snow in the winter when all the leaves have fallen rustling in the wind trampling through the snow kicking leaves around making snow men. And playing snow balls. Playing with my dog. I love the crackling of a fire all the flames going up then falling down. Then all the fireworks going up and down bang bang bang going up and down. I like the smell of leaves on the Ground. And the smell of chips. And all the frost you Blow your Breath comes out into the air. Then the sound of hooters beep beep beep when all the cars go by. It is nice watching all the snow Flakes coming down. And the smell of petrol in the petrol station and all the exhaust Fumes coming out of the cars. And the noise of Police cars 'ne dar ne dar'. And all the shouting everywhere about. The rustling trees. These are the things I have loved.

(Daniel Bennett)

The work produced by the top juniors was amazingly thorough. None wrote less than a page, some wrote more. The following are excerpts from some of them:

When I wake up on a winter's day I feel the touch of cold air. I like how birds chatter in the morning but then the crow spoils the chorus. But I especially like the crunch of leaves in autumn. Then I feel the leaves and throw them over my head.

(Patrick Bourke)

Reading an interesting book and wondering what will happen next and getting to know the characters in it because they all usually get up to mischief. Watching the clouds in the sky and watching them move into lots of different shapes.

(Claire Cassar)

I have loved to see flowers with raindrops and raindrops on webs, because it looks like a magic world.
I have loved trying to go to sleep the night before an exciting day.
I have loved planting a seed and watching it grow and thinking I have made this possible, making something in the world.

(Stephanie Ressort)

I always loved going into the woods and smelling the fresh smell of pines; the dewdrops in flowers; looking at the moon at night and the stars, lighting up the universe; going out when it has just snowed and when you step feel the crunch, and the crisp breeze; at Christmas, smelling the pine and looking at the crib; having the pleasure to see the expressions on people's faces when you give them a present; drinking lovely cool water of a spring; holding a little kitten whose life you saved.

(Monica Bazzani)

As is clear from these few examples, most of the children wrote in prose. I did not ask or expect them to do anything else. Still, one must be ready to admit that form and pattern exercise an irresistible pull for some children, who will try to imitate, if only subconciously, the form of the poem with which one introduces the lesson. Stephanie was the only pupil who tried to impose some sort of pattern on her list of reminiscences. Naturally enough she was not able to reproduce Brooke's heroic couplets but, in the event, and without her knowing it, her sentence-paragraphs resembled the long lines of a Walt Whitman poem! However, that was not the objective of my lesson, just an interesting by-product.

My objective was that *all* my pupils — 9-, 10-, and 11-year-olds — should be able to tackle the task with some degree of confidence and success, and with a clear understanding of what they were meant to achieve. The examples of work quoted are reproduced here as they were handed in to me, that is, without my later corrections. It is clear that the task was not so taxing that it caused the children's spelling, punctuation and general technical mastery to suffer. This is likely to happen when the task is either too demanding or too vague or too diffuse in its nature. One should always state clearly the nature of the task, while the examples of prose and poetry chosen to be read within the lesson should make the task even more unambiguous. The prior discussion must also direct the children's thoughts along well-defined lines, from which few of them will stray.

In all honesty, I should admit that Patrick's really accomplished piece of writing — 'the touch of cold air', 'the crow spoils the chorus' — declined rapidly into irrelevance, despite all my preparation and guidance. He obviously wasn't up to a sustained piece of writing at that time. However, those first four sentences do reveal a considerable thoughtfulness as well as sensitivity in his response to language which with more technical help and guidance will, I feel sure, develop more fully later on in his school career.

SPECIMEN LESSON 4

As was mentioned in Chapter 2, Shakespeare has immense potential for enriching our children's imaginative lives and their store of language. Because his poetry is in the form of five-act plays, it tends, by and large, to be reserved for secondary examination pupils. This is a pity because there are parts of his plays that are not beyond the appreciation of even young primary-school pupils. In fact, the greatest enthusiasm a lesson of mine has ever generated was when I taught *Macbeth* to a class of 9-year-olds. I propose, therefore, to look at a writing lesson based on a reading of the witches' spells from *Macbeth*. These and their conversation round the cauldron go down particularly well with 8–11-year-olds, especially at Hallowe'en. The prophecies to Macbeth and Banquo can be included as well for 11–13-year-olds or for really advanced younger readers:

When Shall We Three Meet Again?

First Witch	When shall we three meet again
	In thunder, lightning or in rain?
Second Witch	When the hurleyburley's done,
	When the battle's lost and won.
Third Witch	That will be ere the set of sun.

First Witch	Where the place?
Second Witch	Upon the heath.
Third Witch	There to meet with Macbeth.
First Witch	I come, Graymalkin!
Second Witch	Paddock calls.
Third Witch	Anon!
All	Fair is foul, and foul is fair:
	Hover through the fog and filthy air.
	(*Act I, Scene I*)
	(Glossary)
	Graymalkin: Witch's cat.
	Paddock: a toad or frog.

Round about the Cauldron Go

First Witch	Round about the cauldron go:
	In the poison'd entrails throw.
	Toad, that under cold stone
	Days and nights hast thirty-one
	Sweltered venom sleeping got,
	Boil thou first i'the charméd pot!
All	Double, double toil and trouble;
	Fire burn and cauldron bubble.
Second Witch	Fillet of a fenny snake,
	In the cauldron boil and bake:
	Eye of newt, and toe of frog,
	Wool of bat, and tongue of dog,
	Adder's fork, and blind-worm's sting,
	Lizard's leg, and howlet's wing,
	For a charm of powerful trouble,
	Like a hell-broth boil and bubble.
All	Double, double toil and trouble;
	Fire burn and cauldron bubble.
Third Witch	Scale of dragon, tooth of wolf,
	Witches' mummy, maw and gulf
	Of the ravin'd salt-sea shark,
	Root of hemlock digg'd in the dark,
	. . .
	Add thereto a tiger's chaudron,
	For the ingredients of our cauldron.
All	Double, double toil and trouble;
	Fire burn and cauldron bubble.
Second Witch	Cool it with a baboon's blood,
	Then the charm is firm and good.
	(*Act IV, Scene I*)

These spells (there are more in Act III, Scene I) are the sort of extract that can stand alone — and often do as they are in fact frequently anthologized — but I would recommend that we attempt to create a context for them. This means telling the story up to and including Macbeth's first meeting with the witches and their prophecies to him and Banquo, which is a good suspenseful point at which to stop. It doesn't actually take long as this fateful meeting occurs near the start of the play. For those teachers unsure of their own story-telling powers, Bernard Miles's *Favourite Tales from Shakespeare* (Hamlyn, London, 1976), with atmospheric illustrations by Victor Ambrus, is a perfectly good substitute (except that one of his factual details is wrong. Do check the play itself before you start). I kept this book conspicuously on my table for several weeks after this lesson and found it was regularly borrowed by pupils for silent reading when they had finished a set piece of work. Some simply finished the story of *Macbeth*. Others read all the stories in the book.

Once you have read the speeches in a good hag-ridden voice, you will find pupils dying to have a go at an expressive reading themselves. Each passage requires three speakers and offers possibilities of choral speaking. You can follow this up both with art work (paintings of the witches round the cauldron casting their evil spells) and with a simple writing task, such as re-telling the story so far in their own words. This may sound uninspired but it seems to me that the more demanding the material the pupils work with, the simpler the task should be. It is possible to set the class writing their own spells. I was asked to do it once with 8–9-year-olds and was not at all pleased with the result. Either the children were too young or the task was too difficult. A prose account of the opening of the story allows ample room for a personal response while grappling with Shakespeare's archaic and compressed language. Some of the children's descriptions of the witches' appearance were most impressive:

> The witches were old and wrinkled like shrivelled prunes.
>
> (Lee Cessford)

> It was a windy and a stormy night and was raining heavily when suddenly Macbeth and Banquo saw three ugly witches. They had crooked noses, green glowing eyes, skinny fingers, soot black hair, green knobbly arms and legs and black pointed hats and cloaks. They were all sitting round a deep black cauldron.
>
> (Susanna Abel)

The following girl starts her account off with great clarity:

> Once in Scotland while King Duncan was on the throne, there was a greedy man named Macbeth who was the thane of Glamis and wished to be king.
>
> (Niamh Friel)

The succinctness and control manifested in this opening sentence was not easy to achieve, given that Niamh uses as many as three subordinate clauses. Such a complex sentence looks and sounds effortless but from the pen of a child as young as 9 it represents a considerable achievement.

One boy actually caught the sense of suppressed excitement Macbeth must have felt after the witches' greetings to him as Cawdor and then king began to be confirmed by the messenger from Duncan:

> They disappeared so fast before he could say shazam.
> They rode through the dark. Two messengers came from behind bringing a private letter from King Duncan. Macbeth read it.
> It said to the Thane of Glamis, the Thane of Cawdor has been arrested, you are now Thane of Cawdor.
> So those witches were right.
> Just you wait till I get home, so I can tell my wife.
>
> (Michael da Costa)

Notice how Michael highlights Macbeth's thoughts by giving them separate lines. They are so important, they become paragraphs in their own right.

I would like to add that my class of 9-year-olds last year were so enthused by these excerpts from *Macbeth* that they actually asked to be set some of these difficult lines to learn off by heart. As in fact most of it is quite difficult, I set the two most famous pairs of couplets spoken by all three witches:

> 'Fair is foul and foul is fair;
> Hover through the fog and filthy air'

and

> 'Double, double toil and trouble;
> Fire burn and cauldron bubble'.

These inner-city children felt a tremendous thrill in afterwards being able to quote by heart a couple of lines of Shakespeare, our greatest poet.

There is a school of thought in some education circles that would regard such a tightly controlled approach to promoting children's writing as anathema. My students in teacher training were frequently appalled by it, preferring themselves to set a vague task with few, if any, guidelines so that the children's own 'creativity' would not be hindered or interfered with. Such a loose approach or 'method' seems to me to be fraught with difficulties, not least in that it produces unhappy and fractious pupils, because they have little or no idea of what they are meant to be achieving.

It is time to try a more carefully controlled, 'directed' teaching method. I cannot guarantee that your pupils will produce work as promising as that produced by my multi-ethnic classes in South London, but I feel certain that they will be much better than the results that emanated from the less-directed approach.

It is also a point worth stressing that in an 'uncontrolled' method, only the bright and already talented pupils stand a chance of showing what they are capable of. With a more controlled method, *all* pupils are helped and guided so that even the average and less than average have a chance to make a creditable offering. Such a method is essentially more democratic, therefore, since it is not biased in favour of those pupils with an innate talent.

Chapter 9

Resources

I have left till last a variety of lists that I hope will provide a quick at-a-glance source of reference for the hard-pressed classroom teacher. There is something rather schematic about lists but I offer them as a way of putting readers in touch with a range of resources that might have been submerged under greater detail earlier, or actually escaped mention altogether. However, these lists are not to be regarded as either exhaustive or prescriptive. They merely attempt to give some helpful indication as to what further material is available of the kind already mentioned in the course of this book.

ANTHOLOGIES

Once you embark on poetry reading in a regular way in class, you may find your class's taste for it rapidly outstripping available resources. You will certainly want to foster the interest that is generated. It is a good idea, therefore, to include on one's class library shelves a few wide-ranging and appealing anthologies so that your pupils have ready access to poetry for browsing whenever the appetite prompts and the time allows. A wet break does not sound like a propitious time for reading poetry, but I have known keen pupils settle down with a good anthology while others around them read comics or played board-games.

There are so many anthologies to choose from and schools have such limited funds available for buying new books that teachers may be forgiven for not knowing where to start and so not start at all. I would advise all those keen enough to begin to consult *Poetry for Children — a Signal Bookguide* by Jill Bennet and Aidan Chambers (Thimble Press, Stroud, 1984). As an annotated list it offers invaluable help in making appropriate choices, even providing information on the cost of each hardback and paperback edition. At the risk of attracting charges of needless repetition, I shall list below a few anthologies I would class among the best in providing for poetry across the 5–13 age and ability range. I shall start with anthologies for the youngest and indicate a possible age range as long as teachers realize that this does not imply mandatory age *limits* be applied to poetic reading matter. Older pupils love to dip occasionally into material for younger ones and vice versa. To attempt to colour-code poetry anthologies and thereby restrict access will inevitably nip interest in the bud.

5–8
Blakeley, P. (ed.) (1978) *Nonsense Rhymes*, A. & C. Black, London.
Foster, J. (ed.) (1984) *A Very First Poetry Book*, Oxford University Press.
Ireson, B. (ed.) (1970) *The Young Puffin Book of Verse*, Puffin, Harmondsworth.
9–11
Benton, M. and P. (eds.) (1979) *Watchwords*, Bk 1, Hodder & Stoughton, Sevenoaks.
Blishen, E. (ed.) (1985) *Oxford Book of Poetry for Children*, Oxford University Press.
de la Mare, W. (ed.) (1978) *Come Hither*, Kestrel, London.
Foster, J. (ed.) (1985) *A Second Poetry Book*, Oxford University Press.
Ross, D. (ed.) (1972) *The Illustrated Treasury of Children's Poetry*, Collins, London.
9–13
Causley, C. (ed.) (1978) *The Puffin Book of Salt Sea Verse*, Puffin, Harmondswoth.
Wilson, R. (ed.) (1987) *Out and About*, Kestrel, London.
11–13
Benton, M. and P. (eds.) (1981–2) *Watchwords*, Bks 2 & 3, Hodder & Stoughton, Sevenoaks.
McGough, R. (ed.) (1982) *Strictly Private*, Puffin, Harmondsworth.

Class or school-library shelves ought also to contain single-poet collections, even if only in cheap paperback editions. I refer readers to earlier chapters and to the general bibliography for information on such collections.

Finally, a handy book for teachers and pupils alike, because it enables one to locate a poem on a specific topic at a moment's notice, is Helen Morris's *The New Where's That Poem?* (Blackwell, Oxford, 1985).

ESSENTIAL READING

If teachers are going to embark on poetry teaching in any sustained and on-going way, then they will find themselves sooner or later in need of personal poetic support as well as more pedagogical guidance. One of the difficulties for the keen primary/middle teacher is the discouragement on finding that handbooks like this present one are very thin on the ground. It is also true that many of the most helpful of such guides are well over twenty years old and therefore out of print. However, public and college libraries still hold copies, while it is also possible to come across them on sale cheaply in secondhand bookshops.

One can do no better than to start with James Reeves's still indispensable guide/handbook for teachers, *Teaching Poetry* (Heinemann, London, 1958), which has chapters on what to teach and how to teach it to children of every age group from 5 to 16. It is packed with successful poems and a wide variety of simple ideas for handling poetry that respect each poem's unique qualities and yet, at the same time, never daunt the teacher-beginner. This is the most easy-to-read book there is on teaching poetry. The straightforward commonsense and delicacy with which Reeves discusses pedagogical niceties such as the differences in maturity of taste between able and less able first-year boys at the secondary level should make us pause for thought in an age of mixed-ability teaching. These are still pertinent observations.

Equally full of helpful pedagogical insights and also more recent is Calthrop and Ede's invaluable *Not Daffodils Again: Teaching Poetry, 9–13* (Longman, York, 1984). I strongly recommend the endpieces by the editors as moving tributes to the potential power of poetry in our pupils' and our own lives. If you are looking for a book that indicates what choices of poetry other practising teachers are making and what they do with their choices in their classrooms, this is for you. It really lives up to its subtitle 'Schools Council Programme 2: Helping Individual Teachers to Become More Effective'.

Benton and Fox's *Teaching Literature: 9–13* (OUP, 1987) includes prose literature as well as poetry, but teachers will find its suggestions for follow-up work, its lists of anthologies, and its discussions of individual poems of great help and interest even if the book appears to have been written with the English-subject graduate largely in mind.

For teachers involved in selecting suitable material for pupils of 11-years-old and over, Ted Hughes's *Poetry in the Making* (Faber & Faber, London, 1967) offers interesting examples of modern (largely unrhymed) poetry as well as very useful insights into a poet's way of working. He makes particularly valuable suggestions as to how to approach the task of promoting children's own writing of poetry.

Presenting Poetry: A Handbook for English Teachers edited by Thomas Blackburn (Methuen, London, 1966) is a very helpful book as it includes so many useful short essays, not just by teachers and ex-teachers such as HMI Leonard Clark, but also by poets like Stevie Smith and Charles Causley.

Once teachers have found some further pedagogical support and guidance and have established some durable approaches to classroom practice, they may wish to develop their own personal understanding of more adult poetry. I shall mention just a few of the many books available on this topic and confine myself to those that are written specifically with the non-specialist in mind. Yet again, the name that crops up is that of James Reeves. He has devoted his life to poetry, writing it for children, teaching it and making it more accessible to the common reader. All his books are worth looking at. Particularly useful is his brief and very readable, *Understanding Poetry* (Pan, London, 1967), exploring with non-specialists what poetry is and how it works. Invaluable, too, is his account of his own practice in *How to Write Poems for Children* (Heinemann, London, 1971). Equally valuable in that it is just as easy to read and is also written by a practising poet in a totally unpretentious way for the ordinary reader is Vernon Scannell's more recent *How to Enjoy Poetry* (Piatkus, London, 1987).

USEFUL ADDRESSES

There are two organizations concerned solely with promoting poetry:

The Poetry Society, 21 Earls Court Square, London SW5 9BU.
The Schools Poetry Association (SPA), David Orme, 27 Pennington Close, Colden Common, Nr Winchester, Hants SO21 1UR.

Other organizations with a wider remit for literature generally, and children's literature in particular, are listed below. Book Trust has a Children's Books Officer and is a mine of information, producing useful booklists on particular topics for specific age groups.

Book Trust (formerly the National Book League), Book House, 45 East Hill, London SW18 2OZ.
Book Trust Scotland, 15a Lynedoch Street, Glasgow G3 6EF.
School Bookshop Association (SBA), 1 Effingham Road, Lee, London SE12 8NZ.
School Library Association (SLA), Victoria House, 29–31 George Street, Oxford OX1 2AY.
The Youth Libraries Group (YLA) of the Libraries Association, 7 Ridgmount Street, London WC1E 7AE.

These organizations also publish regular booklets or magazines in which they review new books:

Books for Keeps, six issues a year, published by SBA.
Creative Language (formerly *Schools Poetry Review*) edited by David Orme. Three issues a year. Now published by Stanley Thornes, Station Road, Leckhampton, Cheltenham, Glos.
The School Librarian four issues a year, produced by SLA.

JOURNALS AND MAGAZINES

Several journals publish articles on children's literature, which sometimes include poetry for children:

Children's Literature in Education, four issues a year, subscription details from Mrs B. Collinge, 2 Sunwine Place, Exmouth, Devon.
Schools' Poetry Review, three issues a year, edited by David Orme, 27 Pennington Close, Colden Common, Nr Winchester, Hants SO21 1UR.
Signal, three issues a year, edited by Nancy Chambers, The Thimble Press, Lockwood, Station Road, South Woodchester, Stroud, Glos. GL5 5EQ.
The Times Educational Supplement has three *Children's Books* numbers a year, as well as weekly reviews.
The Use of English, three issues a year. Subscription details from Scottish Academic Press, 33 Montgomery Street, Edinburgh EH7 5JX.

WRITERS IN SCHOOLS SCHEME

Another way of creating a context for poetry in school is to organize a visit from a living poet. To do this, schools in England should contact their local regional arts association. Elsewhere in Great Britain, contact the National Arts Council. The Poetry Society organizes a Poets-in-Schools scheme, funded by W. H. Smith. Its education department also runs a children's poetry competition . Poets who will take part in events are listed in *The Authors and Illustrators List*, compiled by the National Book League — now the Book Trust.

LOCALITIES

I once took some A-level pupils from London to the Lake District to let them see just what it was that had inspired Wordsworth. They had been sceptical about 'getting worked up about a few hills', but the experience, blessed by some unexpectedly excellent weather, bowled them over. Wordsworth and his poetry took on a new lease of life.

In the same way, children's novelist, Cynthia Harnett, always makes her historical fiction more real by adding an epilogue in which she draws attention to actual places and buildings her stories have included and that can still be visited today. Such information tends to generate renewed interest in both place and period, especially among children who live within or close to the areas involved in her stories.

In the recent booklet, *Teaching Poetry in the Secondary School: An HMI View* (DES, 1987), HMI notes that not enough is done in school to create a context in which poetry can flourish. Literary pilgrimages, like the one I organized above, can definitely help. But there are simpler, easier and less time-consuming ways of doing it. One suggestion HMI makes is 'to draw pupils' attention to poets who live or have lived in the neighbourhood or may have used the locality in their work' (*ibid*. p. 18). This is such an obvious idea that I'm sure teachers who work in Cumbria and Stratford-on-Avon do make much of Wordsworth's and Shakespeare's connection with their area. There are, however, many other well-known poets who have much less mooted associations with places. I have, therefore, drawn up a brief list of well-known poets and indicated some of the localities they lived in at different stages of their lives, in the hope that such information may help to foster the interest of children living in the same areas today. I feel sure that it will generate increased enthusiasm among children in Warrington to know that Lewis Carroll was a local boy. Teachers might, as a result, find themselves taking the children on a literary pilgrimage to the vicarage where he was born.

Books to help in tracking down favourite poets and the localities they have lived in are *The Who's Who of Children's Literature*, compiled and edited by Brian Doyle (Hugh Evelyn, London, 1968) and, for greater detail, *The Oxford Companion to Children's Literature*, by Humphrey Carpenter and Mari Pritchard (OUP, 1984).

For a book that goes into greater biographical as well as topographical detail than Carpenter and Pritchard, I recommend you consult the poet Edward Thomas's *A Literary Pilgrim in England* (Webb & Bower, Exeter, 1985), recently republished with stunning photographs and other pictorial material. It is limited to only 16 poets, omitting R. L. Stevenson who appeared in the original and who is of particular interest to primary teachers, but it is well worth dipping into.

Belloc, Hilaire Born in Paris, educated Oratory School, Birmingham. From 1906 to 1910, he was Liberal MP for South Salford. Head of English Department of East London College, 1911–13.

Blake, William Born 28 Broad Street, Golden Square, Soho, London, 1757. Married Catharine Boucher, whose father had a market garden in Battersea, at St Mary's Church, off Battersea Square. Used to go for country walks in Surrey to little villages such as Newington Butts and Camberwell. It was on Peckham Rye that he had one of his many visions and saw a tree filled with angels. He was tried for sedition, and acquitted, at Chichester, after staying at Felpham near Bognor.

Brontë, Emily Born at Thornton in West Riding of Yorkshire. When she was 2, her family moved to Haworth Parsonage, where she spent the rest of her short life, except for a brief period when she worked as a teacher near Halifax and later in Brussels.

Carroll, Lewis Born at Daresbury, near Warrington, Cheshire, where his father was curate. Moved to Croft, near Darlington, Yorkshire, where his father became Rector. He was educated for a year at Richmond Grammar School (Yorkshire), then later at Rugby.

Chaucer, Geoffrey We don't know where he was born or even when exactly, but it is known that he lived over the Aldgate in London Wall as an excise officer. He also had a house in the country — in Kent — probably on the south bank of the Thames in what would be Greenwich, or Lewisham or perhaps Dartford today. His last official position was deputy forester in the King's Forest at Petherton in Somerset (1391–8) and he might have lived there for some time.

Clare, John Born Helpston, Northamptonshire (between Stamford and Peterborough) where he worked as a hedge-setter and day labourer. He went to school at Glinton. He was married at Great Casterton Church and shortly after moved to Northborough, 4 miles from his native village. He was later committed to an asylum in High Beech, Epping, whence he escaped. He was then admitted to Northampton General Asylum for the Insane where he spent the last 23 years of his life.

Coleridge, Samuel Taylor Born Ottery St Mary, South Devon, went to school in London. 'To the Nightingale' was written while he was at Bristol, Leigh Woods being noted for nightingales. Settled at Nether Stowey, Somerset, after his marriage where he wrote 'This Lime Tree Bower My Prison'. He stayed at Keswick in the Lake District to be near his friend, Wordsworth.

Farjeon, Eleanor Born Buckingham Street, off the Strand, London. For the rest of her life she lived in a succession of addresses in South Hampstead — 13 Adelaide Road; 196 Adelaide Road; 17 Lancaster Road; 137 Fellows Road; and finally 20 Church Walk, Hampstead village. During the First World War she spent two years in Houghton, Sussex, near Arundel. She loved Sussex as much as Hampstead and often stayed with friends at Billinghurst. Eventually she bought a cottage outside the village of Loughton, East Sussex. It is noteworthy that her *Nursery Rhymes of London Town* play upon the names of districts or monuments in London. Other verses, like 'All the Way to Alfriston', mention places she knew outside London.

Fuller, Roy Born at Failsworth, Lancashire.

Sir Gawain and the Green Knight In the dialect of the North-west Midlands as spoken in the Middle Ages.

Hardy, Thomas Born Higher Bockhampton, Dorset, very close to the village of Tolpuddle, whose Martyrs were deported to Australia. He was articled to an architect at Dorchester to which he returned in later life. He spent his twenties in London — Westbourne Park Villas and in Trinity Road, Tooting. The moving poem 'Beyond the Last Lamp' is about a distressed couple Hardy saw in a lane near Tooting Common. He met his first wife in North Cornwall. There are many poems, written much later, about this Cornish period of his life, for example, 'Near Lanivet 1872', 'At Castle Boterel' (Boscastle), 'Beeny Cliff', etc. After their marriage they lived for a while at Sturminster Newton; later they moved back to Dorchester.

Ingelow, Jean   Born Boston, Lincolnshire. At 14 she moved to Ipswich. She later moved to London, 6 Holland Villas Road, Kensington.

Keats, John   Born at a livery stable in Finsbury Pavement, London. At 9 or 10 he went to live at Church Street, Edmonton. His schooldays were passed at Enfield. He was apprenticed to a surgeon at Edmonton and then studied at St Thomas's and Guy's Hospitals. At this time he lodged at 8 Dean Street, Borough, also in St Thomas's Street and at 76 Cheapside in the City of London. He gave up medicine and went to the Isle of Wight where he wrote the sonnet, 'On the Sea'. Then later he lodged at Well Walk, Hampstead. 'Meg Merrilies' was written during a stay at Dumfries.

Kipling, Rudyard   Born Bombay, where he stayed till the age of 6. From 6 to 12 he lived at Southsea, Hampshire. From 12 he was at school at Westward Ho, near Bideford, North Devon, then he went back to India. From 1902 till his death in 1936 he lived at Burwash in Sussex.

Lear, Edward   Born Highgate Village, London. He lived for 4 years on Earl of Derby's estate, Knowsley Hall, near Liverpool.

Lee, Laurie   Born in Slad, near Stroud, Gloucestershire.

de la Mare, Walter   Born Charlton, S.E. London, educated at St Paul's Cathedral School. He worked in City of London offices of Anglo-American Oil Co.

Masefield, John   Born Ledbury, Herefordshire, educated at King's School, Warwick. At 13, he joined Merchant Navy Training Ship then situated in the Mersey.

Morris, William   Born in what was then Essex but is now London at Elm House, Walthamstow, at the edge of Epping Forest. When he was 6, his family moved to Woodford, Essex; he was educated at Marlborough. He lived in London at 17 Red Lion Square, and after his marriage at 41 Great Ormond Street. He had the Red House built for him at Bexley Heath, Kent. He set up a factory at Merton Abbey on the River Wandle at Wandsworth. He lived at Kelmscott Manor on the Thames at Lechlade.

Reeves, James   Born Harrow, Middlesex.

Rossetti, Christina   Born in London of a Neapolitan father and an English mother. One of Christina's two aunts acted as governess to the Marquis of Bath's children at Longleat, and Christina may have visited her there. Her mother's father lived in a country cottage in Buckinghamshire, which she visited.

Scannell, Vernon   As a baby he lived in Beeston, Nottingham (see his poem 'Auto-biographical Note'); his family moved to County Roscommon, Eire, for a couple of years, returning to live in Eccles, Lancashire. He finally spent the rest of his boyhood in Aylesbury, Buckinghamshire. His adult life has been lived in London, Dorset and West Yorkshire, where he now lives.

Service, Robert   Born Preston, Lancashire, studied at Glasgow University. He lived for some years in the Yukon.

Shakespeare, William   Born Stratford-upon-Avon, Warwickshire; attended the grammar school at Stratford. We know very few details of Shakespeare's life. His brother, Edmund, was buried in Southwark Cathedral, called in Shakespeare's day, St Mary Overy, on the south bank of the Thames near the Globe Theatre.

Stevenson, R. L.   Born at 8 Howard Place, Edinburgh. At 6 he moved with his family to Heriot Row. He often visited Colinton, just outside Edinburgh, where his grandfather was the minister. As a young man he was most adventurous, despite his ill-health, and travelled in Germany, France and Belgium, and eventually across America. The last years of his life were spent in Samoa.

Thomas, Edward   Born in Lambeth, South London. He was educated at local State schools and briefly at St Paul's School. He lived with his parents in Shelgate Road, Battersea, between Clapham and Wandsworth Commons. He married young and lived afterwards in rural Kent and Hampshire.

Tennyson, Alfred   Born at Somersby Rectory, Lincolnshire. After leaving Cambridge University, he lived in a succession of places — at High Beech in Epping Forest, at Tunbridge Wells and, after his marriage, at Warninglid, Sussex, Twickenham, Middlesex, and Farringford on the Isle of Wight. See Edward Thomas's *A Literary Pilgrim* for precise details, of the many places mentioned in or associated with his poems.

Wordsworth, William   Born at Cockermouth, Cumbria; went to school in Hawkshead. Lived at Grasmere (Dove Cottage) and later at Rydal Water. In early adult years lived near Coleridge in Somerset at Alfoxden and Racedown in Dorset. His poetry is naturally full of the people and landscapes of his native Cumbria.

References and Bibliography

BOOKS OF PEDAGOGICAL INTEREST

Bennett, J. and Chambers, A. (1984) *Poetry for Children: a Signal Bookguide*, Thimble Press, Stroud. **20, 22, 24, 25, 48, 134**

Benton, M. (1978) 'Poetry for children: a neglected art', *Children's Literature in Education*, Vol. 9, no. 3. **5**

Benton, M. and Fox, G. (1987) *Teaching Literature: Nine to Fourteen*, Oxford University Press. **13, 16, 17, 35, 44, 50, 52, 59, 61, 65, 136**

Blackburn, T. (ed.) (1966) *Presenting Poetry: A Handbook for English Teachers*, Methuen, London. **17, 55, 108, 136**

Bolt, S. and Gard, R. (1970) *Teaching Fiction in Schools*, Hutchinson Educational, London. **60, 64**

Brierley, J. (1976) *The Growing Brain*, NFER, Windsor. **10, 108**

Brierley, J. (1987) *Give Me a Child Till He Is Seven*, Falmer Press, Lewes. **10, 11**

Brierley, J. (1988) 'Putting the Heart Back into School', *The Sunday Times*, 28 February. **108**

Bryant, P. and Bradley, L. (1985) *Children's Reading Problems*, Basil Blackwell, Oxford. **11**

Calthrop, K. and Ede, J. (eds.) (1984) *Not Daffodils Again: Teaching Poetry 9–13*, Longman, York. **1, 4, 110, 136**

Carpenter, H. and Pritchard, M. (1984) *The Oxford Companion to Children's Literature*, Oxford University Press. **138**

Cass, J. (1967) *Literature and the Young Child*, Longman, London. **26, 27**

Causley, C. (1966) 'Poetry and the younger child' in T. Blackburn (ed.) *Presenting Poetry: A Handbook for English Teachers*, Methuen, London, pp. 89–98.

Chukovsky, K. (1971) *From Two to Five*, translated and edited by Miriam Morton, University of California Press, Berkeley, Calif. **17, 24, 86, 87, 90**

Clark, L. (1966) 'Poetry and young children' in T. Blackburn (ed.) *Presenting Poetry: A Handbook for English Teachers* Methuen, London, pp. 54–65. **17, 55, 108**

Clark, L. (1978a) 'Poetry and children', *Children's Literature in Education*, Vol. 9, no. 3.

The numbers in bold type after each entry indicate the page(s) in this book where the work is cited.

Clark, L. (1978b) 'A time and place for verse', *The Times Educational Supplement*, 3 November. **116**

Cook, E. (1976) *The Ordinary and the Fabulous*, Cambridge University Press. **16, 34, 35, 41**

Danby, J. F. (1967) *Approach to Poetry*, Heinemann, London. **48, 80, 81–84**

DES (1963) *Half our Future, A Report of the Central Advisory Council for Education — England*, HMSO, London. **1**

DES (1975) *A Language for Life* (The Bullock Report), HMSO, London. **1, 2, 5, 9, 33, 39, 43, 51, 57, 58, 128**

DES (1978) *Primary Education in England*, HMSO, London. **2, 12**

DES (1982a) *Bullock Revisited: a discussion paper by HMI*, HMSO, London. **7, 57**

DES (1982b) *Education 5–9: an illustrative survey of 80 first schools in England*, HMSO, London. **2, 12**

DES (1983) *9–13 Middle Schools*, HMSO, London. **2**

DES (1984) *English from 5 to 16 (Curriculum Matters 1)*, HMSO, London. **8**

DES (1985a) *Education 8–12 in Combined and Middle Schools*, HMSO, London. **2**

DES (1985b) *The Curriculum from 5 to 16: (Curriculum Matters 2)*, HMSO, London. **15**

DES (1987) *Teaching Poetry in the Secondary School: An HMI View*, HMSO, London. **1, 3, 5, 9, 10, 50, 51, 53, 59, 138**

Doyle, B. (1968) *The Who's Who of Children's Literature*, Hugh Evelyn, London. **138**

Eliot, T. S. (1933) *The Use of Poetry and the Use of Criticism*, Harvard University Press, Cambridge, Mass. **17**

Fox, G. (1976) *Writers, Critics and Children*, Heinemann Educational, London. **112**

Harrison, J. (1984) 'Discovering a new world', *The Use of English*, Vol. 35, no. 2, Spring, pp. 51–7. **62**

Hughes, T. (1967) *Poetry in the Making*, Faber & Faber, London. **9, 13, 31, 123, 136**

Morris, H. (1985) *The New Where's That Poem?*, Basil Blackwell, Oxford. **135**

Newton, E. and Handley, G. (1971) *A Guide to Teaching Poetry*, University of London Press. **90**

O'Malley, R. (1969) 'Poetry', in D. Thompson (ed.) *Directions in the Teaching of English*, Cambridge University Press, pp. 79–94. **35**

Opie, I. and Opie, P. (1962) *Dictionary of Nursery Rhymes*, Oxford University Press. **26**

Reeves, J. (1958) *Teaching Poetry*, Heinemann, London. **25, 27, 28, 53, 60, 71, 76, 81, 108, 109, 135**

Reeves, J. (1967) *Understanding Poetry*, Pan, London. **13, 136**

Reeves, J. (1971) *How to Write Poems for Children*, Heinemann, London. **136**

Sansom, C. (1978) *Speech and Communication in the Primary School*, A. & C. Black, London. **56, 63, 72, 75, 77, 79–80, 81**

Scannell, V. (1987) *How to Enjoy Poetry*, Piatkus, London. **13, 14, 44, 116, 136**

Smith, S. (1966) 'At school', in T. Blackburn (ed.) *Presenting Poetry: A Handbook for English Teachers*, Methuen, London, pp. 159–164. **108**

da Sola Pinto, V. (ed.) (1946) *The Teaching of English in Schools*, Macmillan, London. **55, 73**

Strong, L. A. G. (1946) 'Poetry in the school', in V. da Sola Pinto (ed.) *The Teaching of English in Schools*, Macmillan, London, pp. 1–16. **55, 73**

Thomas, E. (1985) *A Literary Pilgrim in England*, with an introduction by Michael Justin Davis, Webb & Bower, Exeter. **138**

Thompson, D. (ed.) (1969) *Directions in the Teaching of English*, Cambridge University Press. **35**

Thompson, D. (1978) *The Uses of Poetry*, Cambridge University Press.

Townsend, J. R. (1983) *Written for Children*, Penguin, Harmondsworth. **23**

Trelease, J. (1984) *The Read Aloud Handbook*, Penguin, Harmondsworth.

Webb, K. (1977) *I Like This Poem*, Puffin, Harmondsworth. **20, 21, 29, 102, 103**
Whitehead, F. *et al.* (1977) *Children and their Books*, Macmillan Education for the Schools Council, Basingstoke. **96**

BOOKS OF POETRY: ANTHOLOGIES AND SINGLE-AUTHOR COLLECTIONS

Aardema, V. (1981) *Bringing the Rain to Kapiti Plain*, Macmillan, London. **30**
Ahlberg, J. and Ahlberg, A. (1978) *Each Peach, Pear, Plum*, Kestrel, London. **28**
Ahlberg, J. and Ahlberg, A. (1983) *Peepo*, Puffin, Harmondsworth. **28**
Ahlberg, A. (1983) *Please Mrs Butler*, Kestrel, London. **31, 46**
Allen, R. (1975) *The First Night Gilbert and Sullivan*, Chappell, London. **45, 46**
Bashō (1966) *The Narrow Road to the Deep North and other Travel Sketches*, Penguin Classics, Harmondsworth. **125**
Belloc, H. (1977) *Cautionary Tales, and a Bad Child's Book of Beasts*, illustrated by N. Bentley, Duckworth, London. **46**
Benton, M. and Benton, P. (1979) *Watchwords*, Bk 1, Hodder & Stoughton, Sevenoaks. **135**
Benton, M. and Benton, P. (1981) *Watchwords*, Bk 2, Hodder & Stoughton, Sevenoaks. **135**
Benton, M. and Benton, P. (1982) *Watchwords*, Bk 3, Hodder & Stoughton, Sevenoaks. **135**
Black, E. L. and Davies, D. S. (eds.) (1980) *Passport to Poetry* (Bks 1–4), Cassell, London. **33, 47, 57, 76, 92, 93, 103**
Blake, Q. (1980) *Mister Magnolia*, Cape, London. **30**
Blakely, P. (ed.) (1978) *Nonsense Rhymes*, A. & C. Black, London. **135**
Blishen, E. (1985) *Oxford Book of Poetry for Children*, Oxford University Press. **135**
Briggs, R. (1983) *Mother Goose Treasury*, Puffin, Harmondsworth. **25**
Britton, J. (1960) *The Oxford Book of Verse for Juniors, 1–4*, Oxford University Press.
Cadbury's Third Book of Children's Poetry (1985) Beaver, London. **122**
Carroll, L. (1968) *Jabberwocky and other poems*, with pictures by Gerald Rose, Faber & Faber, London. **17, 30, 32, 45**
Carroll, L. (1974) *The Walrus and the Carpenter*, with illustrations by Tony Cattaneo. Warner, London. **30**
Causley, C. (1976) *The Tail of the Trinosaur*, Beaver, London. **47**
Causley, C. (1978) *The Puffin Book of Salt Sea Verse*, Puffin, Harmondsworth. **135**
Causley, C. (1983) *Figgie Hobbin*, Puffin, Harmondsworth. **18, 24, 46, 48, 50, 53, 105**
Chaucer, G. (1966) *The Canterbury Tales*, translated into modern rhyming verse by Nevill Coghill, Penguin, Harmondsworth. **35, 109**
Clare, J. (1966) *The Wood Is Sweet*, poems for younger readers chosen by D. Powell, Bodley Head, London. **13, 61**
Clark, L. (1972) *Secret as Toads*, Chatto & Windus, London. **50**
Clark, L. (1975) *Collected Poems and Verses for Children*, Dobson, London. **54**
Clark, L. (1979) *Stranger than Unicorns*, Dobson, London.
Coleridge, S. T. (1978) *The Rime of the Ancient Mariner*, illustrated by Mervyn Peake, Chatto & Windus, London. **22, 47, 61, 98, 114**
Crossley Holland, K. (1968) *Beowulf*, Macmillan, London. **35**
de la Mare, W. (1953) *Come Hither*, Constable, London (1978, Kestrel, London). **57–59, 68, 135**
de la Mare, W. (1970) *Collected Rhymes and Verses*, Faber & Faber, London. **21, 24, 31, 49, 62**

de la Mare, W. (1972) *Secret Laughter*, poems chosen by Eleanor Graham, Puffin, Harmondsworth. **61, 63, 77, 79, 95, 121**

Dickinson, E. (1970) *A Choice of Emily Dickinson's Verse*, selected by Ted Hughes, Faber & Faber, London. **10**

The Earliest English Poems, translated from the Anglo-Saxon by M. Alexander, Penguin Classics, Harmondsworth. **35, 61**

Eliot, T. S. (1964) *Old Possum's Book of Practical Cats*, Faber & Faber, London. **24, 32, 54**

Eliot, T. S. (1986) *Growltiger's Last Stand*, illustrated by Errol le Cain, Faber & Faber, London. **30**

Farjeon, E. (1973) *Nursery Rhymes of London Town*, illustrated by Macdonald Gill, Duckworth, London. **26**

Farjeon, E. (1976) *The Children's Bells*, Oxford University Press. **24, 26, 30–32, 49, 62, 76, 94, 100**

Flanders, M. and Swann, D. (1977) *The Songs of Michael Flanders and Donald Swann*, Elm Tree Books, London. **32, 46**

Foster, J. (ed.) (1984) *A Very First Poetry Book*, Oxford University Press. **135**

Foster, J. (ed.) (1985) *A Second Poetry Book*, Oxford University Press. **135**

Frost, R. (1964) *You Come Too*, favourite poems for young readers from his own work and edited by Robert Frost, Bodley Head, London. **21, 43, 70**

Fuller, R. (1977) *Poor Roy*, Deutsch, London. **21, 139**

Graham, E. (1967) *A Puffin Quartet of Poets*, Penguin, Harmondsworth. **32, 46**

Grigson, G. (1982) *The Penguin Book of Ballads*, Penguin, Harmondsworth.

Grisenthwaite, N. (1961) *Poetry and Life*, Bks 1–4 Schofield & Sims, Huddersfield.

Hardy, T. (1983) *Selected Poems of Thomas Hardy*, selected and introduced by James Reeves and Robert Gittings, Pan, London. **23, 70, 81, 95, 103**

Holbrook, D. (1961) *Iron, Honey, Gold*, Vols. 1 & 2, Cambridge University Press. **32, 56**

Hughes, T. (1977) *Meet My Folks*, Puffin, Harmondsworth. **17, 24, 46**

Hutchins, P. (1978) *The Wind Blew*, Puffin, Harmondsworth. **28**

Ireson, B. (ed.) (1970) *The Young Puffin Book of Verse*, Puffin, Harmondsworth. **135**

Ireson, B. (1983) *Rhyme Time*, Beaver, London.

Lear, E. (1977) *The Complete Nonsense Of Edward Lear,* edited by H. Jackson, Faber, London. **17, 44, 62**

Lear, E. (1982) *The Owl and the Pussy Cat*, illustrated by Gwen Fulton, Piccolo, London. **30, 32**

Lee, L. (1970) *Pergamon Poets No. 10, Charles Causley and Laurie Lee*, selected by Evan Owen, Pergamon, Oxford. **31, 42, 52**

Lloyd, J. Vernon (1972) *The Giant Jam Sandwich*, Cape, London. **29, 30**

Longfellow, H. W. (1986) *Hiawatha's Childhood*, Puffin, Harmondsworth. **29**

Macbeth, G. (1986) *Daniel*, Lutterworth Press, Cambridge. **29, 30**

Matterson, E. (1985) *This Little Puffin . . . Finger Plays and Nursery Games*, Puffin, Harmondsworth. **27**

McGough, R. (ed.) (1982) *Strictly Private*, Puffin, Harmondsworth. **135**

McGough, R. (ed.) (1986) *Noah's Ark*, illustrated by Ljiljana Rylands, Dinosaur, London. **29, 30**

McGough, R. and Rosen, M. (1979) *You Tell Me*, Kestrel, London. **44**

Miles, B. (1976) *Favourite Tales from Shakespeare*, with illustrations by V. Ambrus, Hamlyn, London. **132**

Milligan, S. (1975) *Silly Verse for Kids*, Dobson, London. **21, 44, 54, 97, 99**

Milne, A. A. (1983) *When We Were Very Young*, Methuen, London. **21, 22, 29, 61, 62**

Milne, A. A. (1987) *Now We Are Six*, Methuen, London. **29**

Moore, C. C. (1981) *The Night Before Christmas*, illustrated by Tomie de Paola, Oxford University Press. **22**

Nash, O. (1962) *Parents Keep Out*, illustrated by Martin Wells, Dent, London. **46**

Noyes, A. (1981) *The Highwayman*, illustrated by Charles Keeping, Oxford University Press. **21, 30, 103**

Opie, I. and Opie, P. (eds.) (1973) *The Oxford Book of Children's Verse*, Oxford University Press. **23**

Opie, I. and Opie, P. (eds.) (1977) *The Puffin Book of Nursery Rhymes*, Puffin, Harmondsworth. **25, 88**

Parker, E. W. (ed.) (1955) *Discovering Poetry, no. 1, The Journey Begins*, Longman, London.

Paterson, S. C. (ed.) (1967) *Narrative Verse*, Longman, London. **47, 104**

Plath, S. (1976) *The Bed Book*, Faber & Faber, London. **24, 29**

Provensen, A. and Provensen, M. (1982) *The Mother Goose Book*, Beaver, London. **25**

Reeves, J. (1973) *Complete Poems for Children*, Heinemann, London. **21, 31, 32, 46, 50, 57, 100, 121**

Reeves, J. (1976) *Prefabulous Animiles*, Heinemann, London. **32, 46, 109**

Rosen, M. (1981) *You Can't Catch Me*, illustrated by Q. Blake, Deutsch, London. **21, 30**

Ross, D. (ed.) (1972) *The Illustrated Treasury of Children's Poetry*, Collins, London. **135**

Rossetti, C. (1969) *Doves and Pomegranates*, Bodley Head, London. **24, 26, 48, 93, 122**

Sansom, C. (1974a) *Counting Rhymes*, A. & C. Black, London. **27, 72**

Sansom, C. (1974b) *Speech Rhymes*, A. & C. Black, London. **27, 72**

Sansom, C. (1975a) *Acting Rhymes*, A. & C. Black, London. **27, 72**

Sansom, C. (1975b) *An English Year*, Chatto & Windus, London. **50**

Sansom, R. (1964) *Rhythm Rhymes*, A. & C. Black, London. **27, 72**

Scannell, V. (1974) *The Apple Raid, and Other Poems*, Chatto & Windus, London. **50**

Serraillier, I. (1954) *Beowulf the Warrior*, Oxford University Press. **35–36**

Serraillier, I. (1966) *The Challenge of the Green Knight*, Oxford University Press. **35, 114**

Seuss, Dr (1958) *The Cat in the Hat*, Collins, London. **29**

Seuss, Dr (1962) *Green Eggs and Ham*, Collins, London. **30**

Seuss, Dr (1969) *The Foot Book*, Collins, London. **29**

Silcock, A. (1971) *The Faber Book of Verse and Worse*, Faber & Faber, London. **98**

Smyth, W. M. (ed.) (1959) *Further Poems of Spirit and Action*, Edward Arnold, London.

Spier, P. (1968) *London Bridge is Falling Down*, World's Work, Tadworth. **28**

Spier, P. (1969) *Hurrah, We're Outward Bound*, World's Work, Tadworth. **28**

Spier, P. (1971) *The Erie Canal*, World's Work, Tadworth. **28**

Spier, P. (1981) *The Fox Went out on a Chilly Night*, Puffin, Harmondsworth. **28**

Stevenson, R. L. (1985) *A Child's Garden of Verses*, illustrated by M. Foreman, Gollancz, London. **21, 22, 30, 49, 54, 61, 77, 94**

Stones, R. and Mann, A. (1980) *Mother Goose Comes to Cable Street*, Puffin, Harmondsworth. **25**

Swann, M. (1951) *Trippingly on the Tongue*, Macmillan, London. **72, 73, 93**

Thomas, R. S. (1972) *Young and Old*, Chatto & Windus, London. **50**

Ward, Kingdom, W. (1954) *A Book of Rhymes and Jingles*, A. & C. Black, London. **72**

Wilson, R. (ed.) (1987) *Out and About*, Kestrel, London. **135**

Wordsworth, W. (1970) *A Solitary Song*, chosen, and with an introduction by Edmund Blunden, Bodley Head, London. **42, 53, 54, 61**

Name Index

Subject Index